S0-AKZ-698

This Book Comes With a Website

Nolo's award-winning website has a page dedicated just to this book, where you can:

KEEP UP TO DATE – When there are important changes to the information in this book, we'll post updates

READ BLOGS – Get the latest info from Nolo authors' blogs

LISTEN TO PODCASTS – Listen to authors discuss timely issues on topics that interest you

WATCH VIDEOS – Get a quick introduction to a legal topic with our short videos

You'll find the link in the introduction.

And that's not all.
Nolo.com contains thousands of articles on everyday legal and business issues, plus a plain-English law dictionary, all written by Nolo experts and available for free. You'll also find more useful **books, software, online services,** and **downloadable forms.**

 **NOLO**
LAW for ALL

Get updates and more at
www.nolo.com

 **NOLO** # The Trusted Name
(but don't take our word for it)

"In Nolo you can trust."
THE NEW YORK TIMES

"Nolo is always there in a jam as the nation's premier publisher of do-it-yourself legal books."
NEWSWEEK

"Nolo publications . . . guide people simply through the how, when, where and why of the law."
THE WASHINGTON POST

"[Nolo's] . . . material is developed by experienced attorneys who have a knack for making complicated material accessible."
LIBRARY JOURNAL

"When it comes to self-help legal stuff, nobody does a better job than Nolo . . ."
USA TODAY

"The most prominent U.S. publisher of self-help legal aids."
TIME MAGAZINE

"Nolo is a pioneer in both consumer and business self-help books and software."
LOS ANGELES TIMES

4th Edition

The Foreclosure Survival Guide

Keep Your House or Walk Away
With Money in Your Pocket

Attorney Stephen Elias

Updated by Attorneys Amy Loftsgordon and Leon Bayer

FOURTH EDITION	SEPTEMBER 2013
Editor	KATHLEEN MICHON
Cover Design	JALEH DOANE
Book Design	TERRI HEARSH
Proofreading	SUSAN CARLSON GREENE
Index	ELLEN SHERRON
Printing	BANG PRINTING

Elias, Stephen.
  The foreclosure survival guide : keep your house or walk away with money in your pocket / Stephen Elias, Amy Loftsgordon, Leon Bayer. -- Fourth edition.
       pages cm
  Summary: "If you're one of the 2 million Americans who are having trouble making your mortgage payments or are already in jeopardy of foreclosure, this guide will give you the practical information you need, including: the ins and outs of foreclosure procedures, with state-by-state information on how to decide whether or not you should try to keep your house using bankruptcy to buy time or save your home and how to avoid "rescue" scams"-- Provided by publisher.
  ISBN 978-1-4133-1950-7 (pbk.) -- ISBN 978-1-4133-1951-4 (epub ebook)
  1. Foreclosure--United States--Popular works. I. Loftsgordon, Amy. II. Bayer, Leon D. III. Title.
  KF697.F6E43 2013
  346.7304'364--dc23
                                                                    2013013597

Please note

We believe accurate, plain-English legal information should help you solve many of your own legal problems. But this text is not a substitute for personalized advice from a knowledgeable lawyer. If you want the help of a trained professional—and we'll always point out situations in which we think that's a good idea—consult an attorney licensed to practice in your state.

Acknowledgments

I am fortunate that Mary Randolph was able to squeeze some time out of her duties as Nolo vicepresident in order to help me with this book. Having Mary Randolph as an editor is a joy all writers should experience at least once in their life. I thought I was taking on an impossible task— getting a credible book about foreclosures out in just a few months. Instead, with Mary's guidance, encouragement, and editorial assistance, I found the experience most enjoyable, and I'm immensely pleased with the end result.

Many thanks also to Terri Hearsh, Nolo's production wizard (and so very much more), who laid out the book in exactly the way I had hoped; and to Helena Brantley, Nolo's marketing director, who worked so tirelessly to get the book "out there" through a blizzard of media appearances.

I'm grateful to La Jolla, California, real estate lawyer William Simmons and bankruptcy guru Alan Rosenthal of the Bankruptcy Law Center of John D. Raymond in San Francisco, both of whom were kind enough to read the manuscript and provide detailed suggestions that made the book a whole lot better. Thanks also to Jim Turner, who was nice enough to provide a cover quote extolling my authorial virtues.

And last, but certainly not least, thanks to my wife, Catherine, and our son, Rubin, who were incredibly supportive of my participation in this project and who cheerfully picked up the slack caused by my temporary absence from our daily routine.

—Stephen Elias

About the Author and Updaters

Stephen R. Elias, the original author of this book, was an important and beloved part of the Nolo family for more than 30 years. His passing in late 2011 was a great loss to Nolo and to the communities and movements to which Steve gave so much.

Steve began his practice of law in 1970, first serving as a legal aid lawyer and a public defender before becoming an expert in bankruptcy and foreclosure law. Over the years, he provided low-cost, high-quality legal help to thousands of clients. He also wrote and edited more than 30 books for Nolo, many of which are best-sellers, including *How to File for Chapter 7 Bankruptcy* and *The New Bankruptcy.*

Amy Loftsgordon (Chapters 1–4 and 7–10) has worked in the area of foreclosure for over ten years, on the sides of both borrowers and lenders. She has also worked on legal process outsourcing initiatives, developed customized foreclosure-related training programs, and audited completed foreclosures to determine if they were processed in accordance with applicable laws. She received a B.A. from the University of Southern California and a law degree from the University of Denver Sturm College of Law. She is licensed to practice law in Colorado. Amy has authored numerous foreclosure articles on Nolo.com.

Leon Bayer (Chapters 5 and 6) has been practicing bankruptcy law in the Los Angeles area since 1979. His primary focus is on representing individuals and small businesses. He is a founding partner in the law firm of Bayer, Wishman & Leotta and is a Certified Specialist in Bankruptcy Law. In addition to maintaining his own bankruptcy blog, Leon authors the "Ask Leon" series on Nolo's "Bankruptcy, Debt & Foreclosure" blog. You can reach him at his firm's website: www.bayerwishmanbankruptcylaw.com.

Table of Contents

5 How Chapter 13 Bankruptcy Can Delay or Stop Foreclosure

6 How Chapter 7 Bankruptcy Can Delay or Stop Foreclosure

7 Fighting Foreclosure in Court

Your Foreclosure Companion

No word strikes greater fear in a homeowner's heart than "foreclosure." This book deals with how to think about foreclosure and provides a number of pathways and options that you can choose according to your individual circumstances and where you live.

If you want to keep your home, your best option is to work something out with your mortgage lender in a way that will satisfy both of you. If, on the other hand, you are ready and willing to leave your home, there are ways to follow that path that will leave you relatively flush rather than destitute.

Many people want to stay in their homes but need to change some aspects of their mortgages—the amount of principal, the interest rate, the monthly payment. Many home mortgage modifications happen under the federal government's Home Affordable Modification Program called HAMP, which assists borrowers by lowering their first-lien mortgage payments. Another program, 2MP (the Second Lien Modification Program), helps borrowers by modifying existing second mortgages. But lenders are also free to follow their own procedures for settling mortgage issues by offering in-house modifications, forbearance agreements, or repayment plans. (This is important since HAMP and 2MP are currently scheduled to end on December 31, 2015.) Chapter 4 of this book explains the different ways to make this happen.

For other homeowners, the best strategy is to walk away from their homes rather than pour money into what may be a hopeless cause (this approach is often called "strategic default"). If you take this approach, it often makes sense to stay in your home throughout the foreclosure process—the longer you can live in your home without making mortgage payments, the better off you'll be financially. However, if you are contemplating a strategic default, you should be aware of the consequences (such as a possible deficiency judgment) and take them into consideration as part of your decision-making process. A short sale or deed in lieu of foreclosure might work better in your circumstances, by allowing you to transfer title to the property without going through a foreclosure.

The goal of this book is to help you choose and implement the best strategy for your particular situation.

Changes in the Fourth Edition

In 2008, when the first edition of this book was published, home values were in free-fall and foreclosures were becoming all too common. Now, five years later, home values are starting to recover, though many homeowners continue to face foreclosure. Between then and now, a deep recession has stripped many homeowners of their employment. The percentage of homeowners who are underwater on their mortgages has risen to unprecedented levels, now exceeding 25%. And the degree to which these homeowners are underwater also has increased to alarming levels—often approaching 60% in the most impacted areas.

As the overall housing situation grew worse these past few years, the federal government tried to address the situation with the Making Home Affordable program, which includes HAMP and associated programs. Although the programs initially met with limited success, in 2011 and 2012, the government tweaked the programs so that more borrowers could qualify. The government extended deadlines, introduced HAMP Tier 2, and overhauled the HARP program, among other things. This edition outlines those changes. You are now more likely than ever to qualify for a loan modification, a refinance, or another type of relief under the program.

Additionally, certain states have enacted various homeowner protection laws, as well as foreclosure avoidance mediation programs, providing borrowers with more time and assistance prior to foreclosure. Sometimes the new laws changed the landscape of foreclosure in those states. For example, in Oregon and Hawaii newly implemented mediation laws pushed most lenders to begin filing judicial foreclosures whereas in the past most foreclosures were nonjudicial.

As robo-signing and other mortgage servicing misconduct have come to light, scrutiny on the practices employed by the mortgage servicing industry has grown even more intense. State and federal investigations led to a national lawsuit resulting in the national mortgage settlement and the independent foreclosure review. Both the national mortgage settlement and independent foreclosure review (as well as the subsequent independent foreclosure review settlement that essentially scuttled the program) are discussed in this edition.

In the past, short sale deals fell apart because of the amount of time required to obtain approvals from the lenders, often weeks or months. Now, many lenders and mortgage servicers have increased their personnel and streamlined the process to better keep up with increased requests for short sales. In mid-2012, the Federal Housing Finance Agency announced guidelines that establish strict short sale timelines for homeowners with Fannie Mae or Freddie Mac mortgages so that a homeowner can be more quickly and easily approved for a short sale. New guidelines have also been introduced regarding deeds in lieu of foreclosure and a streamlined modification initiative for Fannie Mae and Freddie Mac loans is being rolled out mid-2013.

And, of course, foreclosure scammers have also responded to changes in the industry by coming up with new and inventive ways to take advantage of distressed homeowners. This edition covers the latest scams that have emerged since the last edition and includes information about the federal MARS rule, which regulates mortgage assistance relief services.

What You'll Find in This Book

In addition to explaining HAMP and the changes that have occurred in the past several years, this book explains:

- the ins and outs of foreclosure procedures, with state-by-state information
- how to decide whether or not you should try to keep your house
- how you can get free help negotiating a mortgage modification
- how filing for bankruptcy can help you keep your house, and
- how to avoid foreclosure "rescue" scams.

The book also explains ways to make the most of your situation if your income and mortgage payments preclude keeping your house, such as:

- how long you'll likely be able to stay in your house—and save up money—if the foreclosure goes ahead
- how to do a short sale or deed in lieu of foreclosure if either strategy would be useful in your situation
- how to use bankruptcy to put a temporary wrench in the foreclosure gears, and
- how bankruptcy can eliminate debts and tax liabilities typically associated with foreclosure.

For many people who feel swamped with debt and are considering filing for bankruptcy, it makes absolutely no sense to keep pouring money into houses they are destined to lose. For others, it's completely sensible to do everything they can to keep ownership. Sometimes the reasons for these decisions are personal; sometimes they are economic.

In the end, you must make this decision for yourself—this book provides some useful guidance in helping you decide, and then helps you succeed in whichever strategy you choose to follow. If it's not in the cards for you to keep your house, the book shows you how to derive the greatest possible benefit from the situation—how to make really good lemonade from the lemons life has handed you, if you will.

The book also tries to provide some perspective on home ownership. To sum it up, your house is not your home. (I was reminded of that fact by someone who'd been raised as an "army brat" who talked about her mother's ability to recreate their home in whatever new quarters they occupied every couple of years.)

Owning the house where you live may feel like the American dream, and losing it might seem like the end of that dream. Believe me when I say that it's not. If you are eventually forced to give up the house you are living in, painful as it may be, it's a loss that you will recover from over time, both emotionally and financially.

But in the meantime, there is a lot you can do to restore your financial health and take control of the situation. Good luck!

Get Legal Updates and More at Nolo.com

You can find the online companion page to this book at:

www.nolo.com/back-of-book/FIFO.html

There you will find important updates to the law (federal and state foreclosure laws are changing rapidly), podcasts, links to online articles on foreclosure (including many articles on state-specific foreclosure procedures, state mediation programs, and other foreclosure articles tailored to the law in your state), links to helpful calculators regarding mortgage refinancing and loans, and more.

Foreclosure: The Big Picture

F oreclosure doesn't usually come as a big surprise to homeowners. You'll probably know, well before it happens, that you're going to have trouble making your mortgage payments. Maybe you've become unemployed or face unexpected medical bills, or maybe that adjustable-rate mortgage you took out a few of years ago is scheduled to reset at a much higher rate, making payments out of reach.

Once you do fall behind, you'll probably have a few months before your lender even starts the foreclosure process. The fact that foreclosure is a process—sometimes a long one—is good news for you. You don't need to panic. You'll have time to plan, negotiate, and evaluate your options—*if* you act as soon as you smell trouble coming. The more time you have, the better.

If your only problem is a few missed payments, your lender will probably be willing to let you get current over time or even add the missed payments to the end of the loan. If you've missed four or five payments, your lender may not be flexible—but you still may be able to work something out.

Indecisiveness May Cost You Big Time

If you're likely to lose your house sooner or later, your failure to immediately face this reality may cost you thousands of dollars. Here's why: Any mortgage payments you make now will do you no good if you end up losing your house in foreclosure. Assume your mortgage payment is $2,000 a month and you scrape together enough money each month to pay your mortgage because you don't want to lose your house. If $2,000 is way more than you can afford even in the short term, it's inevitable that you'll start missing payments. If you start missing payments six months down the road and you end up in foreclosure, the payments you scraped together during that six-month period will have been for naught unless you somehow find a way to get current on your mortgage payments or you file and complete a Chapter 13 bankruptcy. On the other hand, if you stopped paying your mortgage six months ago when you first realized that holding on to your house was a lost cause, you would now be $12,000 in the black.

CAUTION

Check for updates. Federal and state foreclosure laws are changing rapidly. Check this book's companion page on www.nolo.com for recent changes in the law. (See Your Foreclosure Companion for the link.)

Don't wait for the lender to contact you. As soon as you realize you're going to have trouble making your mortgage payments, you should start working on the problem. This chapter will show you how.

You're Not Alone

Even these days, houses are expensive—that's why most homeowners pay for them over 30 years, one monthly payment at a time. And it's not uncommon for people to find they just can't afford to keep making the payments. If you lose your job, get divorced, or face unexpected medical bills, keeping current on your house payments may be next to impossible.

Life events like these aren't the only reason for foreclosures. Many homeowners—about 34 million U.S. households, or roughly one-third of the nation—took money out of their homes in 2004 through 2007 by refinancing or borrowing against their equity, thereby increasing their debt loads. Many people who bought when prices were high got nontraditional mortgages (interest-only payments or adjustable rates with ultra-low teaser rates at the start), expecting to refinance or sell at a profit later. Others were encouraged by mortgage brokers (with a wink and a nod) to overstate their incomes, also with the expectation that rising prices would make the misstatements irrelevant. But because lenders have tightened credit, it's no longer easy to refinance a mortgage, even with a good credit history.

Meanwhile, the interest rates on many adjustable rate mortgages may move higher, making monthly payments soar beyond the ability of many homeowners to make them. And, selling their homes might not be an option for these homeowners because of the slump in residential market values.

CAUTION

Don't panic—and don't get scammed. Foreclosure rescue scams have popped up all over the country in response to the soaring foreclosure rate and the new government programs that offer various types of mortgage modifications. Almost without exception, you will be worse off with these scams than if you let the foreclosure go through. To find out how scammers work and what to look for, see Don't Get Scammed by a Foreclosure "Rescue" Company, below.

What to Expect

What happens next depends on whether you are trying to stay in your home or are resigned to moving on. (More about that choice later.)

If you want to keep your home. Your first move is to find a HUD-approved housing counselor to help you figure out what options are best for you, whether it be a modification, a refinance, or another mortgage solution. These folks are there to help you stay in your home and won't charge you a penny for their help. Go to www.makinghomeaffordable. gov and click "Get Started" then "Speak with a Housing Expert" or call 888-995-HOPE and ask for a HUD-approved counselor in your area.

Your HUD-approved housing counselor will help you determine which option is best for you, explain what documents you will need to provide to your mortgage company, and may be able to contact the mortgage company on your behalf. The counselor can also explain available programs under the Making Home Affordable program, like HAMP. See Ch. 4 and www.makinghomeaffordable.gov for eligibility details.

If a modification or refinance is not in the cards, and depending on the procedure required by your state, you'll receive some sort of notice (usually a formal written notice) that foreclosure is coming unless you make things right. Foreclosure procedures differ greatly depending on where you live and the nature of the loan. (Ch. 2 explains these procedures and highlights the variables you'll want to know about when planning your strategy.)

Unless you use one of the remedies explained briefly below (and in detail in later chapters), the foreclosure will end, usually after a few months, with the sale of the property, typically at a public auction. The foreclosure process is explained in detail in Ch. 2.

Your Options: An Overview

Here's a look at your main alternatives when you think foreclosure is on the horizon. We'll talk about these scenarios in detail later. For now, just try to get an idea of what you're dealing with.

Your Options If You Are Facing Foreclosure

- Check your eligibility for assistance under one of the government programs by visiting www.makinghomeaffordable.gov.
- Reinstate the existing loan by making up the missed payments, plus costs and interest.
- Negotiate a workout (such as a loan modification, forbearance, or repayment plan) with the lender with the help of a free HUD-approved housing counselor.
- Refinance the entire loan under the federal Home Affordable Refinance Program (HARP).
- Arrange a short sale or deed in lieu of foreclosure.
- Arrange a reverse mortgage, if you qualify.
- Delay the foreclosure sale by filing for Chapter 7 or Chapter 13 bankruptcy.
- Fight the foreclosure in court and either stop or delay it.
- Give up your house.

Reinstate Your Mortgage

If you have enough cash (or access to another loan), you can "reinstate" your mortgage by making up all the missed payments plus fees and interest the lender charges you. Your state's law will probably give you a certain amount of time to get this done, after the lender gives you notice that the foreclosure is beginning. (You can check your state's rule in the appendix.)

For example, in California you have the right to reinstate your loan for a period of three months after the lender mails you a "notice of default," or NOD. After that period ends, if you haven't negotiated a workout, the lender can and usually does accelerate the loan (notify you that it is declaring the entire amount due immediately) and send you a notice of trustee's sale, telling you that the house will be put up for sale in 20 days. California state law provides a further right to reinstate the loan up to five days before the foreclosure sale.

In some other states, the lender may accelerate the loan as soon as you fall behind in your payments, and the law does not give you an opportunity to reinstate (though the mortgage contract may provide that right). But more and more lenders are not eager to accelerate the loan and push ahead with foreclosure; they would prefer to work something out with you.

If you have enough resources to consider reinstatement, you can probably also work something out with the lender.

Negotiate a Workout

As mentioned, you should start with a HUD-approved housing counselor and a visit to www.makinghomeaffordable.gov. (See Ch. 4 for more on these resources.) With this assistance, you may be able to get:

- temporary relief from having to make your monthly payments or reduced monthly payments (forbearance)
- a plan to make up your missed payments (at the end of your mortgage or on top of your current payments within a specified period of time)
- a lower interest rate—and as a result, lower monthly payments, or
- a reduction in your principal loan balance.

The Home Affordable Modification Program (HAMP)

As mentioned in the opening pages of this book, HAMP has been both the nation's biggest hope and biggest disappointment in its efforts to bail out troubled homeowners. Nonetheless, over a million homeowners have obtained significant mortgage modifications under HAMP. So don't assume you won't gain anything through HAMP; find out whether you qualify and if so, what HAMP will do for you. HAMP is discussed in more detail in Chapter 4. Also discussed in Chapter 4 are a number of other government programs designed to address additional issues troubled homeowners face, such as what to do about second mortgages and how unemployed homeowners can get temporary relief from their mortgage obligations.

> **CAUTION**
> HAMP and most of the other government programs designed to help homeowners keep their homes are currently due to expire on December 31, 2015. While the Obama administration may extend these programs, by the time you read this book, the window of opportunity for these programs may well be very limited. You can check for updates on this book's companion page on www.nolo.com. (See Your Foreclosure Companion for the link.)

HUD-Approved Housing Counselors May Be Overwhelmed

As the number of people facing foreclosure continues to grow, the workload of HUD-approved counselors grows apace. Providing effective counseling in the foreclosure arena is a labor-intensive activity, which means that using a counselor may require patience and persistence on your part. If you are in the midst of a foreclosure, you may not be able to put up with the delays and inevitable glitches that seem to accompany the mortgage modification process, especially under HAMP. If you find yourself not getting the service you need from your HUD-approved counselor, you'll be tempted to pay someone to get the job done for you. Because scams abound, it's best to hire a lawyer. It's not that a lawyer will necessarily do a better job than a nonlawyer, but in most states you will have some type of recourse if the lawyer turns out to be just another scam artist.

Refinance

If you can refinance at a better rate and pay off your old loan, you can start fresh. Unfortunately, refinancing is tough these days unless you have equity in your house and the home value curve in your community is trending up rather than down. Of course, if your mortgage is owned or controlled (through securitization) by Fannie Mae or Freddie Mac and you qualify for a refinance under the Home Affordable Refinance Program (HARP), your refinancing worries may be over—the program is designed to help those who are unable to get traditional refinancing because the value of their homes has declined. (HARP is discussed in Ch. 4.)

File for Chapter 13 Bankruptcy

In this kind of bankruptcy, you come up with a plan for making your regular monthly payments and paying off the arrears. If the bankruptcy court approves your plan, you'll have three to five years to make the payments. Chapter 13 bankruptcy also reduces or eliminates your total debt load, making your mortgage more affordable in terms of your overall budget. In some situations (and depending on where you file the bankruptcy), you can get rid of a second or third mortgage entirely, reduce a first mortgage on a vacation or rental home to the market value of the house, and even reduce the interest rate on your first mortgage to 1.5 points above prime rate. If you live in one of the nonjudicial foreclosure states—where foreclosures regularly take place without the review of a judge or the benefits of a court hearing—Chapter 13 bankruptcy probably provides the best opportunity to challenge the legality of your mortgage and any threatened foreclosure. (See the appendix to find out whether your state is a nonjudicial foreclosure state.) Chapter 13 bankruptcy is discussed in Ch. 5.

File for Chapter 7 Bankruptcy

If you are current on your mortgage (or can get current in a hurry) but have no room in your budget to continue making your payments, filing for Chapter 7 bankruptcy can make your mortgage more affordable by reducing your total debt load—and so help to prevent foreclosure in the long run. Chapter 7 bankruptcy is quick (it takes about three months). It's also inexpensive if you represent yourself, which many people do. Chapter 7 bankruptcy typically will wipe out your unsecured debt— for example, credit card debt, personal loans, medical debts, and most money judgments. This will free up whatever income you were using to pay down those debts so you can put it toward your mortgage payments.

Even if you have decided to leave your house, bankruptcy can be of great assistance in keeping you in your home for a few extra months free of charge, as well as giving you a fresh start by wiping out liabilities arising from your mortgage or the foreclosure itself.

Despite these benefits, Chapter 7 bankruptcy may not be appropriate for you. For example, you may have more equity in your house than you can protect (exempt) in your bankruptcy, which means the bankruptcy would trigger an involuntary sale of your home. Also, unlike Chapter 13 bankruptcy, Chapter 7 bankruptcy provides little opportunity to mount a legal challenge to the validity of your mortgage or foreclosure proceedings. (Chapter 7 bankruptcy is discussed in Ch. 6.)

Take Out a Reverse Mortgage

A reverse mortgage is a way to tap into the equity of your home without selling the house. You get money from a lender and generally don't need to pay it back as long as you live in the house. The loan must be repaid if you sell your house, or permanently move out, or if the house is sold after your death.

Chapter 7 or Chapter 13 Bankruptcy: A Quick Comparison		
	Chapter 7	**Chapter 13**
Who qualifies	Anyone whose household income is below the state median OR who passes a "means test"	Anyone who has enough income to propose a reasonable repayment plan
Effect on foreclosure	Delayed two to three months	Delayed; possibly avoided
What happens to your property	You keep everything that is legally exempt; the rest is sold to repay your creditors.	You keep your property, but you must pay your unsecured creditors the value of your nonexempt property.
What happens to your mortgage	The amount you owe is discharged, but the lien created by the mortgage remains, and you must make payments to avoid foreclosure.	Your first mortgage will probably remain intact; second and third mortgages can be eliminated if they are not at least partially secured by the house's value.
What happens to your debts	Most debts are wiped out (discharged); some (such as child support and back taxes) survive.	You repay a percentage of debt over three to five years, under a repayment plan you propose to the court; if you finish the plan, the rest of the debt is wiped out.
How long it takes	Three to four months	Three to five years
Will you need a lawyer?	Probably not	Almost always

You'll be able to get a reverse mortgage (also called a home equity conversion mortgage) if you have substantial equity and are over age 62. These mortgages are heavily regulated by the Federal Trade Commission and can provide a safe approach to preventing foreclosure and preserving your equity for your own needs.

A reverse mortgage, because it takes part or all of your equity, leaves less value for you to pass on to your heirs at your death. Also, it may be harder to obtain a reverse mortgage in a time of rapidly decreasing property values because the reverse mortgage lender, like everyone else, will be uncertain about the amount of equity you have in the property.

Finally, even though you don't have to make payments on the reverse mortgage, you are responsible for paying the property taxes and insurance. This means that people on fixed incomes may be at risk of losing their homes if they don't keep up with the taxes and insurance.

RESOURCE
More information about reverse mortgages. Learn more at www.ftc.gov/bcp/edu/pubs/consumer/homes/rea13.shtm.

Fight the Foreclosure in Court

If you can show that the foreclosing party violated your state's procedural rules for foreclosures or the terms of your mortgage agreement, you might be able to derail the foreclosure, at least temporarily. An increasing number of bankruptcy courts are requiring foreclosing parties to present documentary evidence of ownership and authority for bringing the foreclosure action before letting the foreclosure proceed.

Because of the way mortgages were sold and resold during the real estate bubble, documentary evidence of ownership is often either missing or not available when the court reviews the foreclosure. Foreclosure defense attorneys also recently uncovered instances of lenders violating laws governing the recording, notarization, and assignment of mortgages. In some cases, major mortgage lenders temporarily ceased foreclosure activities pending internal investigations of their foreclosure practices. Violations of federal fair lending rules and other federal and state laws regarding consumer transactions may also provide protection against foreclosure. (Fighting foreclosures in court is discussed in Ch. 7.)

> **TIP**
>
> **Extra protections for service members.** If you are on active duty in the military, or have been on active duty within the previous year, you can delay the foreclosure lawsuit—and get other help as well. See Ch. 4.

Give Up Your House

For some people, it makes good economic sense to give up their houses and move on. If you arrive at this decision, there are several ways to say goodbye to your house. You'll want to choose the method that causes the least financial and emotional upset to you and your family. (There's much more about making this decision in Ch. 3.)

Walk Away

Although this book covers several basic approaches to giving up your home, frequently the best approach is to simply stop all further mortgage payments. When you walk away, you will almost certainly lose your house in foreclosure. However, while the foreclosure process chugs along, which can take months, you don't have to make mortgage payments to anyone but yourself. This can result in a sizeable nest egg, which you can then use when searching for new shelter. The subject of "walking away" is discussed throughout this book, most specifically in Ch. 8. Here we give you a brief overview of the subject.

People walk away for two main reasons. The most common reason is that the mortgage has become unaffordable due to an increase in interest rates, the loss of employment, or some other unexpected occurrence. Even after a mortgage modification, circumstances may still render the mortgage unaffordable.

The second reason for walking away is that your home has turned into a lousy investment. Even if you can afford your mortgage payments, you may be better off walking away if your mortgage is deeply underwater and you bought the house as an investment rather than a place to live. While it's impossible to predict what will happen to home values in the future, no economist specializing in home values is predicting a rapid return to previous values. As an example, let's say your house is 40% underwater. Your home's value would have to increase by at least 40% before you would have any equity in the home. This could easily take ten years or more, assuming an increase in home values of 4% a year. Because values are continuing to decline as this edition is being written, even ten years to gain any equity in your home is a stretch.

Strategic Defaults

Walking away from a home when you can afford to pay the mortgage has been labeled a "strategic default." The default is strategic because the homeowner voluntarily chooses to default after completing a cost–benefit analysis. Regulations governing Fannie Mae and Freddie Mac penalize strategic defaulters by effectively denying them new mortgages for at least seven years after foreclosure. If you hope to become a homeowner again in the near future, you should do your best to pursue a mortgage modification, which would indicate your intent to stay put even if you aren't making any payments. Additionally, as of March 1, 2013, Fannie Mae and Freddie Mac will let some borrowers who are delinquent or current on their payments give up their underwater properties and cancel the debts under special deed in lieu of foreclosure programs, if the borrowers meet certain criteria. These programs could provide an alternative to strategic default for some borrowers. For more on this topic, see Ch. 8.

Aside from not being able to acquire a new home loan after a strategic default, walking away can lead to other negative consequences:

- Sooner or later you will lose ownership of your home through foreclosure—unless you are able to successfully challenge the legality of the mortgage in state court or in bankruptcy.

- In most states, you can be sued for the difference between the amount your house was sold for at foreclosure and the amount you owed at the time of the foreclosure sale. Your liability for this difference, called a "deficiency," can be discharged in bankruptcy, but if bankruptcy is not for you, for one reason or another, you may be stuck with a large debt.
- The mortgage lender may write off the deficiency as a loss. The amount of the deficiency would then turn into taxable income for you. This tax liability can be avoided in several ways—including declaring insolvency or bankruptcy—but if you don't qualify for one of the exceptions, you can be nicked for a lot of money. More information about the potential tax liabilities related to foreclosure is provided in Ch. 8

Arrange a "Short Sale" Without Foreclosure

You can negotiate with your lender to sell your house, without a foreclosure, for less than the amount you owe on your mortgage. This is called a short sale. If you live in a state that allows your lender to sue you for the deficiency (the difference between the amount you owe on the mortgage and the sale price of your home), a short sale can be a good idea but only if you get your lender to agree (in writing) to let you off the hook for the deficiency.

If you have a second or third mortgage, you'll also need to get those lenders to sign off on the short sale. This is usually difficult (if not impossible) to accomplish because, by definition, a short sale produces less than is owed on the first mortgage and the holder of the second or third mortgage stands to get little or nothing from the deal.

Another pitfall of short sales is that the buyer of your home will probably want you to leave immediately after the sale closes. This won't be a problem if you don't mind leaving, but you'll miss out on the opportunity to build a healthy nest egg by living in the house without paying your mortgage.

If you qualify for a short sale under the federal Home Affordable Foreclosure Alternatives (HAFA) program, you can't be sued for the deficiency. You may also receive $3,000 in federal funds to help with your relocation. The HAFA program is described in more detail in Ch. 8.

Hand Over the House Without Foreclosure

You may be able to get your lender to let you deed the property over so that no foreclosure is necessary; this is called signing a "deed in lieu of foreclosure." But before you go this route, you'll want to have an agreement (in writing) that the lender won't go after you for any deficiency that remains after the house is sold. And once again, this remedy probably won't be available if there are second or third mortgages. As with short sales, some believe that a deed in lieu of foreclosure will be better for your credit than a foreclosure or bankruptcy.

How Will Your Choice Affect Your Credit?

Which of these options will leave you in the best shape when it's time to rebuild your credit score? The conventional wisdom is that a short sale or deed in lieu of foreclosure won't hurt your credit as much as a foreclosure or bankruptcy will.

Until recently, credit practices were fairly standard, and it was possible to more or less predict what impact a particular action would have on a person's credit. However, it's now virtually impossible to predict the availability (or cost) of consumer credit after a foreclosure, short sale, deed in lieu of foreclosure, or bankruptcy. Currently, subprime real estate loans are very hard to come by. Whether this tight credit will spread to credit cards and car loans remains to be seen. Your best up-to-date resource for matters involving credit is *Credit Repair* by Margaret Reiter and Robin Leonard (Nolo).

How You Can Stay in Your House Payment Free

The basic concept of foreclosure is that when a house is sold at an auction, the lender will recover the amount of the mortgage, and the new owner will move in and live happily ever after. Or maybe an investor will buy the home, rent it out for a while (maybe to you), benefit from some tax write-offs, and then sell it when it has gone up in value.

The thing is, that's not how it works these days. Unfortunately for the banks and investment communities, neither of these scenarios reflects reality for one simple reason: Prospective buyers are unwilling to offer the minimum bid—typically the amount necessary to pay off the first mortgage. And so the lender is stuck with property it doesn't want. Lenders aren't landlords; few have divisions that can rent the property out, manage it, and resell it when the time is right.

Primarily for this reason, many lenders are putting off foreclosure proceedings as long as possible, in the hopes of working something out with the homeowners to keep them in their houses—and keep at least some mortgage payments flowing in. Also, foreclosure proceedings are put on hold pending assessment by the mortgage servicer as to whether you qualify for a payment reduction under the government's Home Affordable Modification Program. See Ch. 4.

If, early on, you decide that you don't want to keep the house and will ultimately be moving on, you may be able to skip payments for many months before the foreclosure process finally begins. And even after the foreclosure sale, chances are great that you can keep living in the house for a while longer free of charge. In all but a few states, you can stay in your house until the new owner gives you a formal written notice demanding that you leave, and a court orders you out after you receive notice and a hearing is held. (See the information for your state in the appendix.)

Having payment-free shelter for many months—both before the foreclosure action is brought and after the sale—gives you a golden opportunity to save some money. And that will grease the skids when you do have to find a new place to live. (See Ch. 9 for more on how to come out of foreclosure with some cash in your pocket.)

Why Foreclosure Doesn't Have to Be So Bad

Okay, I may have already lost you on this one. But stay with me for a moment, because I'm convinced that home ownership can be overrated.

Americans take for granted that owning a home is superior to renting one, especially if you have a family. We accept the phrase "American dream" without question when applied to home ownership. And politicians are wringing their hands over the prospect of the American dream being lost for the millions of homeowners who face foreclosure.

From my own experience, having owned and rented in several different parts of the country, and having worked with clients throughout my career, I know that ownership is not an automatic key to happiness. (I go into this in more detail in Ch. 3.) For now, just try to open your mind to the possibility that renting rather than owning is not always a bad way to go, and that your particular dream need not include home ownership.

Don't Get Scammed by a Foreclosure "Rescue" Company

A large "foreclosure rescue" industry, much of which is a scam, has mushroomed right along with the number of foreclosures. If you are close to losing your home to foreclosure, you may receive an offer of help from a foreclosure rescue company. Companies scour public records and call homeowners who've received foreclosure notices.

The con artists who run these companies will tell you that they have resources that are unavailable to HUD-approved housing counselors and that they care about you and will find a way to save your "American dream." But unlike HUD-approved housing counselors, these companies aren't really trying keep you in your house. They're trying to make money. If you have equity in your house, they go after it. And if you've got only money in the bank, they'll go after that, instead.

How to Protect Yourself

- Never rely on an oral promise, such as, "Don't worry; you'll get the deed back in no time." Get everything in writing.
- Never sign an agreement unless you understand every word and phrase in it, even if you've had help from a HUD-approved housing counseling agency.
- Never sign anything that has blank lines or spaces. Representations and information you had no knowledge of can be inserted and appear to be part of the signed agreement.
- Never transfer ownership of your property to the "rescuer" or a proposed third-party lender.
- Never accept a loan that you can't afford or that must be paid back quickly at a high interest rate as a condition of staying in your house.

Scams That Target Home Equity

If you still have significant equity in your home, you are a prime target for the mortgage rescue scams aimed at getting ownership of your house away from you.

One common trick sounds especially good because the mortgage gets quickly reinstated, at least temporarily.

What you'll hear: "We'll buy your house right now—just temporarily, of course. We'll make the mortgage payments. You can stay right where you are, lease the house from us, and buy the house back when the loan is paid off."

What really happens: The foreclosure rescue company is confident that you won't be able to buy the house back, especially if it involves a big balloon payment, which is common. Ultimately, you lose your home and are quickly evicted. Eviction comes quickly because you have only the status of a tenant under the lease or rental agreement that was supposed to be temporary. By contrast, if the house had gone through foreclosure, you would have been able to stay there for months payment free as the foreclosure process wore on.

Another scam involves wresting ownership away from the homeowner without the homeowner's knowledge.

What you'll hear: "We'll get a workout with the lender. We'll handle everything—just send your mortgage payments to us and we'll pass them on to the lender."

What really happens: The papers you sign actually transfer ownership to the company. (This can easily be accomplished because people expect legal documents to be full of gibberish they don't understand or don't notice that the documents they sign have blank lines that can be filled in later with terms they never agreed to.) Instead of sending your mortgage payments to the lender, the scammer uses them to refinance the property. Then it sells the house to an innocent third party and disappears, leaving you without equity or a workout.

If You Don't Have Much Equity

If you have little or no equity in your home, you probably won't be approached by anyone who wants title; what would be the point? But if you are close to a foreclosure sale, there are plenty of other snake-oil peddlers out there.

For a stiff up-front fee—often in the thousands of dollars—they offer to help you fight your foreclosure by finding affordable loans or by negotiating with your lender for a mortgage modification, an interest rate freeze, or an arrangement in which your missed payments get added to the end of your loan. But not only will you not get results, there's a good chance that these people will disappear once your money is in their hands.

When the Home Affordable Modification Program was announced in March 2009, hundreds of brand-new "modification specialists" hit the street, many "certified" by schools set up to train former mortgage brokers for this new bonanza. These people are taking money for services that can be obtained for free from HUD-approved housing counselors or the Making Home Affordable website at www.makinghomeaffordable.gov.

> **EXAMPLE:** Frieda and Ted are in foreclosure. They are trying to negotiate a workout with their servicer but are continually told to be patient and that their proposal is moving through the process. Their home is due to be sold in three weeks and they are beginning to panic. They wake up one morning to find a flyer on their doorstep advertising the Compassionate Care Foreclosure Rescue Service, which seems tailor-made for their difficulties. The flyer asks, "Is your home about to be sold at a foreclosure sale? Are you having trouble negotiating with your mortgage servicing company? Want to refinance your mortgage at a low interest rate? We can help!"
>
> They call the number on the flyer and are referred to a "foreclosure rescue specialist," Nick, who tells them in a soothing voice that Compassionate Care has helped "thousands of people just like you" work out their mortgage difficulties and stay in their homes. After Frieda and Ted give him information about their plight, Nick tells them that he can negotiate with the servicer on their behalf and get an extension of the foreclosure sale date so they'll have more time to work something out. The fee: $1,500— up front.
>
> Frieda and Ted borrow the $1,500 from Frieda's son and send a cashier's check to Nick at a post office box, along with a signed power of attorney form that Nick says he needs so he can negotiate with the servicer. A few days later Nick tells them that he has gotten the foreclosure sale postponed. Two weeks later, after the date the home was to sold at the foreclosure auction, Frieda and Ted get a call from someone they've never heard of telling them that he bought their home at the foreclosure sale and wants to make arrangements for them to move out. Frieda and Ted call Nick in a panic. The number has been disconnected. Frieda and Ted have lost their home—and paid $1,500 for the privilege.

Mass Joinder Lawsuit Scams

In a mass joinder scam, a group claiming to be a law firm (often they're not a law firm at all or they use unqualified attorneys) sends out unsolicited mailings inviting distressed homeowners to participate in a lawsuit. The mailing informs you that you can join together with other homeowners to sue your lender and force it into providing loan modifications or stopping foreclosure. You then call the number listed on the mailing and talk to a sales representative who provides false information or makes misleading claims about the success of such a suit. To join in the mass joinder lawsuit, you must pay up-front legal fees that can range from $5,000 to over $10,000. Typically, once the scammers have taken your money, they either do nothing (and disappear with the funds) or file the lawsuits and neglect them, leading to dismissals.

Forensic Loan Audit Scams

In a forensic loan audit scam, you pay a company an up-front fee of several hundred dollars for a so-called forensic loan auditor to review your mortgage loan documents to determine if your lender complied with mortgage lending laws. Companies offering this type of service often claim that the audits find lender violations 90% of the time. They further claim that, if a forensic loan audit finds violations of the law, you can use the results to stop a foreclosure, force the lender to give you a loan modification, or rescind (cancel) your loan.

In fact, there's no evidence that forensic loan audits are effective in accomplishing any of these things. First of all, the "audit" is typically completed by a processor who simply plugs information from your loan origination documentation into loan compliance software, which then supposedly identifies violations and compiles them into an automated report. Secondly, often only minor violations are found. Even if the audit does find fraud, predatory lending, or other significant violations of state or federal law, you would need to file a lawsuit (either as an answer to the lender's judicial foreclosure complaint or as your own lawsuit in a nonjudicial foreclosure) against the lender to stop a foreclosure. Sending a copy of the audit report to the lender or telling it that you had a forensic loan audit done will have no effect on your foreclosure.

Profile of a Scammer: What to Look For

The people who prey upon homeowners in foreclosure use many tactics to gain your trust. Be wary of anyone who:

- contacts you by phone or mail or knocks on your door (legitimate foreclosure consultants don't seek you out; you must go to them)
- provides little or no information about the foreclosure process
- claims government affiliation
- uses "affinity marketing"—Spanish speakers marketing to Spanish speakers, Christians to Christians, senior citizens to senior citizens, and so on
- offers "testimonials" from other customers
- claims the process will be quick and easy (dealing with foreclosure is never quick and easy) and uses messages such as "Stop foreclosure with just one phone call" or "I'd like to $ buy $ your house" or "Do you need instant debt relief and CASH?" or
- tells you to cease all contact with the mortgage lender.

State and Federal Laws Governing Foreclosure Consultants

If a company approaches you using the above tactics, it very well may be breaking the law. Many states have laws governing the activity of foreclosure consultants. In addition, in 2010, the Federal Trade Commission (FTC) promulgated rules regulating "mortgage assistance relief services" (MARS) in an effort to protect homeowners from foreclosure consultant scams. Among other things, the MARS rule (now known as Regulation O) requires MARS providers to make certain disclosures about their services, prohibits advance fees, and bans certain misleading advertising claims. The FTC enforces the MARS regulation. To lodge a complaint with the FTC about a MARS company (in English or Spanish), call 1-877-FTC-HELP (1-877-382-4357). To learn more about the MARS regulation, go to www.ftc.gov/opa/2010/11/mars.shtm.

Foreclosure Nuts and Bolts

his chapter paints a general picture of how foreclosures work in your state. You might feel like skipping this information and getting on with deciding what to *do*—get right with your lender, fight the foreclosure, or walk away with the help of a short sale or the bankruptcy court. But you can't make smart decisions without some knowledge of how a foreclosure proceeds.

At the very least, you need to know what's coming if foreclosure looms. Here are the big issues:

- **How much time you'll have before your house is sold.** If you know that your house can be sold at auction in just 15 or 30 days after you first get notice of the foreclosure, you'll need to act differently than if you can count on three or four months in which to negotiate with the lender or try other strategies. Fortunately, even in short-notice states, you can pretty much count on learning about the intended sale in time to use one of the strategies explained in later chapters.

- **Whether or not your foreclosure will go through court.** In a little fewer than half the states, foreclosures are judicial, meaning they go through court; in the others, your house can be sold without a judge's approval in what is called a power of sale (nonjudicial) foreclosure. If you know that you won't lose your house unless a judge gives an official go-ahead, your strategy will likely be different than if your foreclosure will be proceeding without judicial oversight. This is because court foreclosures usually take longer than nonjudicial ones and it's easier to raise the common defenses to foreclosure when you automatically get face time with a judge.

- **Whether you'll be liable for a "deficiency judgment" if the foreclosure goes through.** If the house sells for less than you owe on it, in many states the lender can sue you for at least some of the difference. Homestead laws (state laws that protect your home equity from creditors) don't help you, because mortgage debt has priority over any homestead rights your state's law provides. One reason many people file for bankruptcy when faced with foreclosure is that bankruptcy eliminates liability for deficiencies.

Getting a Grip on Foreclosure Terminology

Here are a few terms you may run into. There are lots more definitions in the glossary. As with any system, getting the words right is half the battle.

Mortgages and deeds of trust. When you got a loan to buy your house, you agreed that the loan would be secured by the house. That meant that if you defaulted on your payments, the owner of the loan could foreclose—that is, take ownership of the house and evict you. Security agreements such as these are filed (recorded) in the local land records office. In some states, this security agreement is termed a mortgage, while in others it's called a deed of trust. With a few exceptions, mortgages can only be foreclosed in court, while deeds of trust can be foreclosed without going through court.

In this book, except when it makes a difference, I use the term mortgage to refer to either an actual mortgage or a deed of trust.

First, second, and third mortgages. The first loan you took out to buy your home is called the first mortgage. If you also borrowed a lesser amount for the down payment, or if you later took out a loan against your equity, this later loan is called a second mortgage. And finally, if you took out a third loan or arranged a line of credit to be secured by your home, you have a third mortgage.

Lenders and mortgage servicers. Chances are, the bank or other lender you got your mortgage from (the mortgage originator) quickly sold the mortgage to another entity, which in turn resold it, and so on. You are supposed to be notified of these transactions, but there is no requirement for plain English in these notices, and you may not know who really owns your mortgage or who is entitled to foreclose if you default.

Whether or not you know who your lender is, you've probably been dealing with a company termed a mortgage servicer. The servicer receives your payments and passes them on to whoever is entitled to receive them—perhaps an overseas bank or a trustee for a mortgage trust.

If you default on your payments but want to keep your house, your mortgage servicer will represent the lender in negotiations. If negotiations fail, the actual foreclosure proceeding will be started either by the lender itself or by a trustee authorized to foreclose.

TIP

Read the law. All of these foreclosure issues are discussed here, and the laws of each state are summarized in the appendix. You can also find state-specific summaries of foreclosure basics at www.foreclosure.com/foreclosure_laws.html. Nonetheless, you may be curious to find out for yourself what the statutes actually say, word for word. It is my firm belief that reading the law will give you a better understanding than I can give you in my necessarily brief summaries. So if you have access to a law library or the Internet and some patience, I suggest you use the citations on your state's page to look up the law for yourself. (Ch. 10 provides help on finding your state's laws online.) As I point out throughout this book, the actual amount of time for a foreclosure to go through may be considerably longer than state law requires. And banks frequently initiate widespread foreclosure moratoriums, some lasting months, for legal and economic reasons.

How Much Time You'll Have to Respond

If you are late on a mortgage payment or two, your lender will usually send a few letters reminding you to get caught up. Generally, after three or more missed payments, the mortgage servicer will send you a letter informing you that your loan is in default. (Most home mortgages and deeds of trust contain a clause that requires the lender to send a notice, typically called a breach letter or demand letter, that informs you that foreclosure proceedings will begin if you do not cure the default by a certain time, generally within 30 days. If you don't cure the default, the lender will officially start the foreclosure process.) Depending on your state and your circumstances, the foreclosure will be either judicial or nonjudicial. All states require that you get at least some notice before your house is sold because of foreclosure. See your state's page in the appendix for information on what kind of notice you can expect to receive.

If it's a judicial foreclosure (one that goes through court), you'll be given some time, typically between 15 and 30 days, to respond to the court complaint that starts the foreclosure lawsuit. In some states, the court, when it approves the foreclosure, orders the lender to publish a "notice of sale," which gives you even more time before you have to move.

You also get some presale notice for nonjudicial foreclosures. Most states require between 20 and 30 days, but it can be as little as 15 days before the sale (in Georgia, for example) or as much as four months (in Oregon and Utah). In some states, including California, you get two notices: one giving you a period of time to make up the missed payments (cure the default) and a second one (called a notice of sale) giving you the date of sale in the event you haven't caught up on the payments.

In most states, in addition to mailing you this notice by certified or first-class mail, the foreclosing entity must publish a notice in the "legal notices" section of a local newspaper of general circulation. (This is an admittedly weird concept that assumes you read the legal notices section.)

CAUTION

Scammers do read the legal notices. Once a formal notice of foreclosure is published, recorded at the local land records office, or filed in court, it's public knowledge that the homeowner is in financial trouble. Con artists may try to prey upon you, knowing that you're under stress. Don't fall for a foreclosure "rescue" scam. (How to spot risky deals and outright crooks is discussed in Ch. 1.)

It is also a common requirement that the foreclosing party post notices on the courthouse door and in other public places. In fact, in a few states, this is the only notice you may get. This is a little less weird than the legal notices publication, at least in small communities. One of your neighbors (if not you) may see a notice posted in a public place and let you know.

Many people facing foreclosure are like the proverbial deer in the headlights: stunned and unable to react quickly. Don't be one of them. This notice period gives you precious time to plan a strategy that is most advantageous to you.

If you or a family member is on active military duty, you have some extra protections, including the right to demand that a judge evaluate the merits of the foreclosure even if you are living in a state where nonjudicial foreclosures are the norm. (The Servicemembers Civil Relief Act is discussed in Ch. 4.)

Extra Protections If You Have a High-Cost Mortgage

The states listed below have special rules for foreclosures when you have a high-cost mortgage. Each state defines high-cost mortgages differently, but typically they are mortgages where interest and prepayment penalties are significantly higher than those being charged for standard mortgages.

Generally, these laws require lenders to give you more notice before foreclosure, and there may be more lenient reinstatement rules (discussed in Ch. 1). If you are in one of these states, check your state's page in the appendix. You'll find a brief summary of what constitutes a high-cost mortgage in your state, the protections you're entitled to, and a citation that will help you find the statute if you want to look it up.

Arkansas	Indiana	New Jersey
California	Kentucky	New Mexico
Florida	Massachusetts	New York
Georgia	Nevada	South Carolina
Illinois		

In or Out of Court?

Foreclosures take one of two major paths: judicial (in court) or non-judicial (out of court). If your home loan is secured by a mortgage, chances are excellent you'll have a judicial foreclosure. If your loan is secured by a deed of trust, you'll probably have a nonjudicial foreclosure. The real estate industry in a particular state—and the laws that industry's lobbyists have pushed through that states legislature—pretty much determine whether mortgages or deeds of trust are used there.

A judicial foreclosure often takes longer—a lot longer—than a nonjudicial one. A judicial foreclosure also gives you a ready-made opportunity to oppose the foreclosure and assures that your home won't be lost to foreclosure unless a judge signs off on it. Judicial oversight is an important protection against illegal tactics by the foreclosing party.

Foreclosure by Possession

In Massachusetts, New Hampshire, and Rhode Island, an arcane procedure called foreclosure by possession lets the lender take possession of a house by "peaceful entry." Because of legal uncertainties regarding title and what constitutes peaceful entry, these laws are not used very often, if ever. If you are late on a mortgage payment or two, your lender will usually send a few letters reminding you to get caught up. Generally, after three or more missed payments, the mortgage servicer will send you a letter informing you that your loan is in default. (Most home mortgages and deeds of trust contain a clause that requires the lender to send a notice, typically called a breach letter or demand letter, that informs you that foreclosure proceedings will begin if you do not cure the default by a certain time, generally within 30 days. If you don't cure the default, the lender will officially start the foreclosure process.) Depending on your state and your circumstances, the foreclosure will be either judicial or nonjudicial. If you live in one of these states, you should ask a HUD-approved housing counselor (see Ch. 4) whether this method of foreclosure is used in your area.

Do You Have a Mortgage or a Deed of Trust?

As you'll see, it isn't always clear what the foreclosure process will be. Even in a state that typically requires foreclosures to go through court, nonjudicial foreclosure may be permitted if the loan is secured by a deed of trust rather than by a mortgage and if allowed by state law. On the other hand, even if a first mortgage is foreclosed nonjudicially in a particular state, home equity lines of credit (HELOCs) and home equity loans typically must be foreclosed judicially (usually under the state's enforcement of judgments act). That's because these types of loans often aren't secured by a mortgage or deed of trust but rather by a consumer security agreement, legally a different sort of animal that can only be enforced in court.

Not sure which document was used to secure your home loan? You can find out by:

- reviewing your original paperwork (that pile of documents you got when you closed escrow on your house)
- calling your mortgage servicer (the company to whom you make your payments)
- asking a counselor at a local HUD-approved housing counseling agency (more about these great sources of help in Ch. 4) how foreclosures generally proceed where you live
- visiting your local land records office and pulling up the recorded document (under your name or address) on the public-access computer, or
- checking your local county clerk and recorder's website. Sometimes there is an online search tool you can use to find out which documents have been recorded (such as a mortgage or deed of trust) on your property.

In some states, the borrower has a right to request a judicial foreclosure even if a deed of trust authorizes a nonjudicial foreclosure. See your state's page in the appendix for more information on whether you've got this option.

Judicial Foreclosures

If you live in one of the states listed in the table below, and your home loan is secured by a mortgage, the foreclosure will probably take place in court.

In judicial foreclosures, your lender gets things started by filing a foreclosure lawsuit in the local court. You will receive official notice of the lawsuit when a sheriff or process server personally serves you with (or posts on your door, in some cases):

- a summons explaining your right to file a written response to the lawsuit and telling you how long you have to do so, and
- a copy of the document (called a petition or complaint) that requests the foreclosure and sets out the reasons the judge should issue a foreclosure order.

You can contest the foreclosure or let it proceed. If you do respond, the court will set a date for a hearing, at which you and the lender will present your evidence and arguments. After the hearing, the judge will either:

- order the foreclosure to go ahead (and in many states, set the sale date)
- postpone a final decision to give the lender more time to fill in a missing gap (proof of ownership, for example), or
- dismiss the case, sending the lender back to the drawing board.

In two states, Connecticut and Vermont, a judge who approves the foreclosure can order ownership (title) to be transferred then and there. This is called a strict foreclosure.

States Where Judicial Foreclosure Is Customary	
Arizona (sometimes)	New Jersey
Connecticut	New Mexico (sometimes)
Delaware	New York
Florida	North Dakota
Hawaii	Ohio
Illinois	Oklahoma (if the homeowner requests it)
Indiana	Oregon
Iowa	Pennsylvania
Kansas	South Carolina
Kentucky	South Dakota (if the homeowner requests it)
Louisiana	Vermont (sometimes)
Maine	West Virginia (sometimes)
Nebraska (sometimes)	Wisconsin

Shift Between Judicial and Nonjudicial Foreclosures in Oregon

In the past, most Oregon foreclosures were nonjudicial. In 2012, however, most lenders in Oregon filed judicial foreclosures. There were two main causes for this shift. In July 2012, the state implemented a Foreclosure Avoidance Mediation Program law, which only applied to nonjudicial foreclosures. In order to avoid the mediation program, many lenders proceeded judicially instead.

Also in 2012, an Oregon appellate court ruled that lenders must record loan ownership changes (when the lender or servicer transfers your mortgage to another company) with the county before starting a nonjudicial foreclosure. *Niday v. GMAC Mortgage LLC*, 251 Or. App. 278 (2012). This ruling meant that foreclosure cases involving Mortgage Electronic Registration Systems (MERS) had to go through the courts. (For more on MERS, see Ch. 7.)

This changed again mid-2013. The Oregon Supreme Court overruled the appellate court in *Niday*, so that MERS cases no longer have to go through court. And the Oregon legislature expanded the foreclosure mediation program to include judicial foreclosures. Because of these changes, it is likely that lenders will shift back to using the nonjudicial foreclosure process.

Judicial foreclosures are seldom if ever permanently derailed, but they can be significantly delayed. If you have grounds to fight the foreclosure, either because the foreclosing party can't prove its case or because you offer proof that casts doubt on the foreclosure's legality, such as evidence that the party seeking to foreclose doesn't own the loan, it can take many months before the case is resolved one way or the other.

Eventually, if the foreclosure is legally appropriate, the judge authorizes your house to be sold at auction or, in the strict foreclosure states, transferred directly to the lender.

Here's how a typical judicial foreclosure might proceed:

Peter and Mary bought their house two years ago at the then-reasonable price of $400,000. They made a 10% down payment and borrowed the other $360,000. The house now has a market value of just $325,000. Peter was laid off from his $60,000-a-year job and now earns $10 an hour. He and Mary can no longer afford their payments.

They live in Ohio, a judicial foreclosure state. Once they miss three payments, the lender sends them a written notice that foreclosure proceedings won't start for 30 days and that the proceedings can be avoided if they make up the missed payments plus costs and interest. Peter and Mary decide to let the foreclosure happen, given that they have no equity in the house, they won't be able to make the payments (even if modified downward), and the prospects for future appreciation of the property are bleak.

Two weeks later, Peter and Mary are served with a copy of a summons and foreclosure complaint that the lender has filed in the local court. They have 28 days to respond. They visit a lawyer, who tells them they may be able to put off the foreclosure sale by filing a response contesting the allegations in the complaint and demanding a trial. Unfortunately, the lawyer wants too much money. Peter and Mary could do some research into possible defenses and represent themselves, but they decide they really can't afford the house any longer and will have to move anyway. They let the 28 days go by without responding.

The court issues a default judgment (that's what happens when you don't respond to a suit filed against you) that authorizes sale of the property. After the judgment, the property is appraised (because it can't be sold for less than two-thirds of its appraised value at the foreclosure sale) and then notice of the date, time, and place of sale is published for three consecutive weeks in a newspaper of general circulation in the county where the property is located. The lender files the notice of sale with the court at least seven days prior to the sale and sends a copy to Peter and Mary, as well as to the other parties that have appeared in the case. Then, on the specified date, the property is put up for sale at auction. But because no buyer comes forward to pay the asking price, ownership goes to the lender.

The entire process, from the time Peter and Mary got the first notice from the lender until the auction, takes about three and a half months.

Had Peter and Mary contested the foreclosure and made the foreclosing party prove it owned the loan (an increasingly common defense; see Ch. 7), the process might have dragged on for many more months.

Even though Peter and Mary lose ownership of their home, they don't have to move out right away. The lender may let the house sit, waiting for the market to improve. In the meantime, there is no law preventing Peter and Mary from remaining in the home payment free until they receive an official, written eviction notice from the sheriff requiring them to vacate the premises. In fact, they are doing their neighbors, and the lender, a favor by maintaining the property through their occupancy. (See Ch. 9.)

Nonjudicial Foreclosures

If your loan is secured by a deed of trust—as is the custom in the states listed below—the foreclosure will probably be nonjudicial. This means a court will not oversee the procedure (except in a few states, where a judge signs off on the foreclosure). If, however, your loan is secured by a mortgage, the foreclosure will likely be judicial. The foreclosure could be judicial for a variety of other reasons as well (for example, because of a title issue). See your state's page in the appendix for information about your possible right to choose a judicial foreclosure.

The deed of trust authorizes the entity named as trustee in the deed of trust to foreclose on the property if you ever default. The deed of trust typically allows the foreclosure to proceed outside of court.

Your state's law sets out the specifics of the foreclosure procedure, including how much notice you get, how the property will be sold (typically at a public auction), and what rights (if any) you have to reinstate the loan before the foreclosure date or recover title to the property after it's sold.

> ⚠ CAUTION
> **Time may be short.** You have to be on your toes when a fore-
> closure looms in a nonjudicial state. That's because you have very little notice of
> the foreclosure sale, and once it happens you may be permanently out of luck.

States Where Nonjudicial Foreclosure Is Customary	
Alabama	Nevada
Alaska	New Hampshire
Arizona (sometimes)	New Mexico (sometimes)
Arkansas	North Carolina
California	Oklahoma (unless homeowner requests judicial)
Colorado	Oregon
District of Columbia	Rhode Island
Georgia	South Dakota (unless homeowner requests judicial)
Idaho	Tennessee
Maryland	Texas
Massachusetts	Utah
Michigan	Vermont (sometimes)
Minnesota	Virginia
Mississippi	Washington
Missouri	West Virginia (sometimes)
Montana	Wyoming
Nebraska (sometimes)	

Here's how a typical nonjudicial foreclosure might proceed:

When Jason and Emilia bought their home for $400,000 two years ago, it seemed like a great deal—but now it's worth only about $350,000, less than they owe on their loan. Jason and Emilia live in California, where nonjudicial foreclosures are the norm. Like most

California homebuyers, they signed a promissory note and a deed of trust when they bought.

The deed of trust authorizes the trustee (a California title insurance company) to "accelerate" the entire loan (declare the whole enchilada due immediately) and sell the property at a public auction if Jason and Emilia default on their monthly payments or fail to maintain the insurance and pay property taxes. However, California law requires the lender to first give the homeowner some time to get current on the loan—this is called reinstating the loan by making up the missed payments plus costs and interest. (See Ch. 1.)

After they miss three payments, Jason and Emilia receive (by certified mail) a 30-day notice notifying them that if they do not catch up on all of the payments, a foreclosure will be initiated. They decide to punt and avoid responding. A short time later, they receive (also by certified mail) a notice of default. It gives them 90 days to reinstate the mortgage by making up the missed payments, plus interest and costs. (In most nonjudicial foreclosure states, the notice of default gives homeowners from 15 to 90 days; a few provide up to 120 days, and a few provide only notice by publication.) Jason and Emilia don't have the cash to make up the payments, and they are unable to work out a repayment plan with their lender. After the 90 days pass, they receive another document: a 20-day notice of intent to sell the property at an auction on the courthouse steps at a specific time.

At the auction, no one meets the minimum bid, and the property ends up with the lender. Because the lender doesn't take immediate action to have Jason and Emilia evicted, they continue living there payment free for another six months, until the house is sold to a new owner who wants to take possession. The new owner first tries to negotiate a move-out date with Jason and Emilia, but that doesn't work. So the owner follows the California eviction laws for taking possession from former homeowners, and serves Jason and Emilia with a three-day notice to quit.

Although Jason and Emilia are legally entitled to stay until the new owner goes to court and gets an eviction order (about a two-month process), they decide to move out to avoid having the eviction case on their credit record. Even so, Jason and Emilia have remained in their home for one year without making a payment, and have managed to save most of the money they would have paid for shelter during that period—which will make it easier for them to move out and find a new place to live. (See Ch. 9 for more on coming out of a foreclosure with some serious cash in your pocket.)

Deficiency Judgments: Will You Still Owe Money After the Foreclosure?

When deciding whether to fight a foreclosure, take steps to avoid it, or just walk away, you'll want to know whether you'll be stuck for the money that the lender loses because of your default. This is usually measured as the difference between what the lender ends up with at the end of the day and the amount of your loan. It's called a deficiency, and it can be many thousands of dollars.

> **EXAMPLE:** Jonas owes $350,000 on a house he bought for $400,000 but that is now worth $300,000, according to a recent appraisal. He is no longer able to earn overtime at his job and falls behind on his payments. The lender threatens foreclosure and Jonas doesn't qualify for a workout. Not wanting to fight the foreclosure or file for bankruptcy, Jonas hands the keys to the lender and walks away.
>
> The lender forecloses on the property and schedules it for auction at a minimum bid of $300,000. No bids are made, so the property reverts to the lender. In Jonas's state, the lender can sue for the difference between the property's value and the amount owed on the loan—in this case, $50,000. Unless Jonas files for bankruptcy to wipe out this debt, the lender (or more likely, a collection firm) will sue to obtain a judgment, then use the judgment to go after his paycheck and bank account.

You may not have to worry about a deficiency judgment. A few states prohibit lenders from suing for deficiencies stemming from mortgages on principal residences. (Loans that fit in this category are called non-recourse loans, because the lender has no recourse if you default.)

In almost every nonjudicial foreclosure state, the lender cannot recover a deficiency without bringing a separate lawsuit and getting a money judgment. Usually, the lender won't pursue the deficiency because of the expense. In a judicial foreclosure, on the other hand, most states allow the lender to seek a deficiency judgment as part of the underlying foreclosure lawsuit; a few states require a separate lawsuit.

Many states limit the amount of the deficiency to the difference between the loan and the property's fair market value. For instance, if the loan is for $400,000, the fair market value is $350,000, and the property is sold for $300,000, the deficiency judgment is limited to $50,000. This is so even though the lender technically lost $100,000— the difference between the loan amount and the sales price. Fair market value typically is determined by a fairly complex statutory appraisal process set out in state statutes.

You can wipe out a deficiency judgment by filing for Chapter 7 or Chapter 13 bankruptcy. Check the appendix to find your state's rules on deficiency judgments.

Taxes

Unsurprisingly, how you deal with foreclosures can have tax consequences.

Income Taxes

Essentially, if there's a deficiency in the course of a foreclosure or another type of sale, the amount is considered your taxable income, unless the deficiency arose from a loan used for the acquisition or improvement of your principal home. (This issue is discussed in more detail in Ch. 8.)

Capital Gains Tax

If your adjusted tax basis on your house is less than the sale price of the house, you may incur a capital gains tax. For example, if you bought your house for $200,000 and it sells for $300,000, you have a $100,000 capital gain, minus the cost of any improvements you added to the property. This gain will be taxed at the capital gains tax rate, subject to your one-time exclusion ($250,000 for one person, $500,000 for a married couple). Check with a tax expert to see whether you'll face a capital gains issue at the sale or foreclosure of your house. If you will, consult a bankruptcy lawyer for advice on how filing for bankruptcy might help.

Can You Keep Your House? Should You?

f foreclosure looms because you've missed some payments, or you think you will soon, it's time to face what's probably the toughest question of the whole process: whether or not you should try to hang on to your house.

Of course, you must take a good look at whether it's financially feasible to try to keep your house. But the decision isn't always a simple matter of finances and cash flow. You'll need to sort through emotional factors, too. Would the loss of your residence be so catastrophic that you would do anything to keep it, or might you be better off letting go and moving on? Could you accept it as an economic setback rather than a personal failing?

This chapter will help you figure these things out. Then you can move forward, either to take steps to keep your house or to start planning how to give it up in the most emotionally and economically advantageous way. The next chapters discuss how to take these next steps after you decide what direction you want to go in.

The Emotional Part of Foreclosure

It's important to acknowledge that the prospect of losing your house can be a psychological blow as well as a financial and practical one. You can't avoid these emotional realities—you're not a machine—but facing them can help you approach the situation in as calm and rational manner as possible.

Dealing With Fear

If you're like many homeowners, the thought of foreclosure triggers fears of ending up on the street. So let me reassure you: It just doesn't happen like that.

Foreclosure is an orderly process. You'll get notice before the process starts and before the house is eventually sold, if it comes to that (see Ch. 2). And these days you will most likely have at least several months after the foreclosure sale before you will actually have to move out. This is due to the fact that many lenders have a backlog of foreclosures, as do many court systems (in judicial foreclosure states). Plus, in many nonjudicial and judicial states, the lender will have to initiate a separate court action to evict you, which will take some time. (See Ch. 9 for a more detailed explanation of how this works.)

Even if the property ends up in the hands of a new owner at the foreclosure sale, in almost all states, the new owner will have to give you a formal written notice to leave. Typically, you'll have from three to 30 days. And if you don't leave at the end of that period, the new owner will have to go to court and get an eviction order. In other words, you'll almost certainly have enough time to make new housing arrangements.

Were You Nesting or Investing When You Bought Your House?

Much of this chapter—and the book, for that matter—assumes that you have an emotional attachment to your house. But maybe you don't, or at least not much of one. Maybe you bought your house primarily as a way to build some wealth. Some of my bankruptcy clients lived in rental apartments and rented out the houses they owned. Others, while living in their houses, were ready to move on, if necessary, in the same way any other small business owner would move on when the economics of the business dictate. The fact is that the residential housing boom presented a small business opportunity to many people.

If you bought your house primarily as an investment, your decision-making process should be based on the economics of your situation. If you are way upside down, get out the best way you can. If you are close to the line, decide whether or not to hang in there and hope things get better. If you are living in your house but aren't particularly attached to it, stay as long as legally possible without making a payment. (See Ch. 9.)

Grieving for Your Loss

You may not have thought of it in these terms, but you are likely to go through a grieving process when faced with the loss of your house. It's something like what you might experience if you were contemplating the loss of your marriage or career.

In her seminal book, *On Death and Dying*, psychiatrist Elisabeth Kubler-Ross identified five stages that patients commonly experience when given a terminal prognosis. To a lesser extent, people facing the possibility of foreclosure often go through similar stages, which are:

- denial (This isn't happening to me!)
- anger (Why is this happening to me?)
- bargaining (I promise I'll make every mortgage payment on time from now on!)
- depression (I don't *care* anymore.)
- acceptance (I'm ready to make lemonade out of lemons.)

Denial. People commonly ignore the first warning signs of impending foreclosure—the missed payment, the call from the lender, even the formal notice of default that is the prelude to a foreclosure sale. Envelopes are unopened, notices go unread, and phone messages are quickly erased. Homeowners know something bad is happening but cling to the hope that something—anything—will come along to bail them out or that they can ride out the current situation until the housing or job market rebounds.

Anger. When it finally dawns on them that they might actually lose their house, they become angry—with themselves, their spouse, the lender, or maybe the president of the United States. After all, it must be someone's fault that they signed a variable interest note that would reset much higher in a year or two, or that they bought a house they obviously couldn't afford in the hopes they could refinance their way to an affordable mortgage.

Bargaining. Anger gives way to negotiation. They tell themselves that if somehow they can avoid losing their home, they will make all their mortgage payments on time, hew to a strict budget, and even get a second job, if necessary.

Depression. As the foreclosure sale draws nearer and negotiations with their mortgage servicer drag on, the reality of the possible loss of their home sets in and they may become physically ill and unable to deal with the daily grind. Each day begins and ends in fear.

Acceptance. The state of depression turns into a state of acceptance that the foreclosure is coming and must be dealt with—which results in:
- a search for new quarters
- a plan to fight the foreclosure
- a visit to a bankruptcy attorney, or
- a resolve to remain in the home as long as possible, payment free.

Avoiding the "American Dream" Trap

Owning real estate—as opposed to leasing or renting it—is commonly equated with achieving the American dream. We take for granted that owning a home is superior to renting one, especially if you have a family. Indeed, politicians and community activists are wringing their hands over the prospect of the American dream being lost for the millions of homeowners who face foreclosure.

To a large extent, we have been sold on this idea by industries that stand to benefit from a robust housing market and governments that depend on property taxes. There are, however, many more important aspects to the American dream than owning a house. Democracy, freedom, public education, and equal economic opportunity come to mind.

Your House Is Not Your Home

You will likely have an easier time dealing with foreclosure if you understand (and remind yourself regularly) that your house and your home are not necessarily the same thing. A home is where you and your loved ones live. It's about your neighbors, your memories, and shelter from the storm. Your home is where you sit down to a family meal, entertain friends, and get in touch with your creative side by arranging furniture, hanging art and family portraits, or changing the wallpaper. A home is where you can relax after work or return after a trip.

In essence, home is a concept you can take with you whether you buy another house or end up renting. Sure, you would probably rather stay where you are, but the fact that you may have to move should be seen for what it is: a temporary interruption in your life from which you are certain to recover. In fact, finding a new place to live can lead you to new opportunities, new friends and neighbors, new community activities, and a different perspective on life.

You Are Not Your House

In the same way your house is not your home, you are not your house. It's deeply ingrained in our culture that the size and location of the house we live in indicate our value as human beings. For example, given the opportunity, most of us would prefer to live in a large house with a stunning view. It's not because we need a large house—average household size has gone down just as average house size has gone up. But for most of us, a large fancy house provides the status and self-esteem we crave.

Home Ownership Is Overrated

From my own experience, and having counseled thousands of bankruptcy clients, I believe home ownership is vastly overrated. As you may remember from your days as a tenant, renting has definite advantages. It offers freedom from the economic burdens and stress every homeowner feels when faced with the need to pay for rodent control, a new paint job, a new roof or furnace, an expensive city assessment for road improvements, increasing property tax, broken water pipes, and a variety of other problems that homeowners are naturally heir to. It can be a real luxury to be able to call the landlord when a big-ticket maintenance problem—for example the water heater—rears its ugly head.

If you need to relocate, get away from neighbors, or travel over long periods of time, renting gives you flexibility that you lack with home ownership. And if you want to stay put, a long-term lease is a good hedge against having to move before you are ready.

If you're putting an inordinate amount of money into your mortgage, you quite likely are making sacrifices in other important areas of your life, such as your family's health, your children's education, charitable contributions, or visits to far-flung relatives, to name but a few common expenses. Living in poverty-like conditions just to remain in your house doesn't make a whole lot of sense to me, especially if your house is worth a lot less than what you owe on it. You should think twice about holding on by your fingertips to a house that is not likely to appreciate in value any time soon and which is unlikely to ever produce much equity.

The Economics of Foreclosure: What You Need to Know

Apart from the emotional considerations that surface whenever a foreclosure is threatened, there are economic factors you just can't ignore. Before you can decide whether or not to try to keep your house, you need to answer a few questions about your financial situation— which has no doubt changed since you bought your house.

Do You Have Equity in Your House?

To a large degree, your options depend on whether or not you still have equity in your house. When you bought your house, presumably it was worth more than the amount you borrowed to buy it. If your house is still worth at least as much as you owe on it, it may make sense to oppose the foreclosure (see Chs. 5, 6, and 7) or sell it and get out from under the loan.

These days it's not so easy to know what your house is worth. Estimates of real estate values are traditionally based on the amounts that similar houses in the neighborhood have recently sold for. To find out that information, you can use www.zillow.com, www.housevalues. com, or similar websites (search for "home value calculators"). Local real estate brokers and agents can also give you an estimate by looking at similar sales in your neighborhood.

If there are other foreclosures going on in your community, a house similar to yours may have sold for far less than you could get for your house if you could afford to be patient. Also, buyers will pay substantially more for a well-kept home than for one that has been trashed, as many foreclosed homes are.

In truth, because prices plunged so much over the past few years, even professional appraisers have difficulty telling what a house is worth. Although prices fell 10% to 20% nationwide, many people in California reported home price decreases of 50% to 60%. Similar "hot spots" were reported in other areas of the country, such as Florida, Nevada, Arizona, Utah, and parts of Texas. The only real way to find out your house's market value is to put it up for sale and see what you can get.

That said, take the best estimate you can come up with and use the simple worksheet below to help you determine what, if any, equity you have in your house.

Homeowners' Equity Worksheet

1. Market value of your home $ _____

2. Costs of sale (if unsure, put 5% of market value) $ _____

3. Amount owed on all mortgages $ _____

4. Amount of all other liens on the property $ _____

5. Total of Lines 2, 3, and 4 $ _____

6. Your equity (Line 1 minus Line 5) $ _____

When Will Real Estate Values Start Going Back Up?

Judging by history, home prices will ultimately rise again. As Mark Twain is reputed to have advised a young man, "Buy land! God ain't making any more of it."

No formula can predict how soon this particular bust will be over. At the time of this writing, roughly five years since the start of the housing collapse, there are starting to be signs of recovery. However, factors that indicate it might go on for at least another year or two, include:

- Underwater homes remain prevalent in many parts of the country. Nationally, home prices have started to rise again, but the recovery is irregular and housing prices aren't going up everywhere. While prices in some of the cities that were hardest hit during the foreclosure crisis, including Phoenix and Las Vegas, are recovering, other cities (like Chicago) are not doing as well. (Nonjudicial foreclosure states, such as Arizona and Nevada, tend to clear out foreclosure inventory quicker so the most rapid appreciations are often in those areas.)

- Overall, foreclosures have been declining since 2010, but some states are still experiencing high volumes. In several judicial states, like Florida and New York, the courts remain severely overloaded and will probably even see an increase in foreclosures for the next few years.

- Credit markets remain tight.

- Continued high unemployment is likely.

- There is a lack of trust in the mortgage and real estate markets caused by unreliable information throughout the entire mortgage transaction chain (loan applications, appraisals, bond ratings, Wall Street offerings) that drove the housing finance industry in the boom years.

- Many consumers are tapped out and increasingly unable to make good on any of their debts, mortgages included.

There is, in fact, no guarantee that your house will ever recover its original value. As the old saw goes, you don't want to throw good money after bad. If the housing market doesn't rebound quickly, every sacrifice you make now to keep your house could be for naught if you ultimately lose it.

Can You Keep Making Your Monthly Payments?

There is no point in putting time and effort (not to mention emotional energy) into trying to hang on to your house if you really, truly can't afford it. If, for example, you were one of the many homebuyers in recent years who were counting on your house's value going up so you could refinance your way out of an unfavorable mortgage, you may have no choice but to move. People who have lost their jobs in the economic recession are in the same boat.

Many people are current on their mortgages but just about to go under. It's not uncommon for people to pay upwards of 50% of their gross (not take-home) income towards their overall mortgage debt. That leaves little or nothing left for food, utilities, transportation, out-of-pocket medical costs, and the like. Quite simply, their economic position is untenable.

Here's how to think about whether or not you can really afford your current loan.

Use the Standard Ratios

For decades, the conventional wisdom was that you shouldn't pay more than 25% of your gross income for shelter. Slowly that figure crept up as lenders relaxed their rules to underwrite ever-increasing numbers of mortgages. Under HAMP (Tier 1) of the Making Home Affordable program (see Ch. 4 for more on how this modification program works), this percentage has settled in at 31%. Under this thinking, if you are paying more than 31% of your gross income on your first mortgage, you are at serious risk of default. So, for example, if you are paying $3,100 a month on your first mortgage (including tax and insurance), your annual gross income should be in the neighborhood of $120,000. If your income is $75,000 a year, your first mortgage payment (including tax and insurance) shouldn't exceed about $1,937 a month. This is obviously a cookie-cutter approach—especially because second mortgages and home equity lines of credit aren't included in that 31%.

In terms of deciding whether your home is affordable as a factual matter, there may be times when the 31% figure can be thrown out the window. If, for example, you have a child with special needs or two kids in college, your mortgage payment might not be affordable even if it's below the 31% threshold. And if you have few other expenses (for example, you live simply, don't own a car, and grow some of your own food), you might be able to afford a mortgage payment that is a higher percentage of your income.

How Much of Your Income Should Go to Your Mortgage?		
	Maximum Mortgage Payment	
Annual Gross Income	25% of monthly income	31% of monthly income
$50,000	$1,042	$1,292
$75,000	$1,562	$1,938
$100,000	$2,083	$2,583
$125,000	$2,604	$3,229

Use an Online Calculator

The Internet is chock full of calculators that purport to tell you how much house you can afford. They're very easy to use, but they make some assumptions that might not quite work for you.

My favorite is the Nolo mortgage affordability calculator. To use it, go to www.nolo.com/legal-calculators/index, then click "How much mortgage might I qualify for?" Another one of my favorites, at the CNN Money website, assumes a loan is affordable if your:

- mortgage payment is no more than 33% of your income (or 28%, if you want to be conservative), and
- total nonmortgage debt payments (credit cards, student loans, and the like) aren't more than 36% of your gross income.

You can find the CNN Money calculator at http://cgi.money.cnn.com/tools/houseafford/houseafford.html. For other calculators, do an online search for "home affordability calculators."

As I said, these formulas tell you how much you can borrow, according to the general opinion of the housing finance industry. They may be somewhat dated given the current chaos of the mortgage and credit markets.

Do a Budget

You can take a no-nonsense look at your income and expenses and see whether there is room in your budget for your current or projected mortgage payments. If the numbers don't add up the first time around, see what expenses you can trim.

Don't know where to start? You're not alone. (Once upon a time we all had to learn about budgeting before we could graduate from high school. No more. Most of us are clueless.) As you might guess, lots of websites offer budgeting software and spreadsheets. One that offers a combination of free and low-cost services is www.debtsteps.com/budget-calculators.html. Or just search for "online budget planning" to come up with a list.

Ask a Budget-Counseling Agency

Everyone who files for bankruptcy must, by law, take a budgeting class in order to receive a discharge of their debts. To meet this demand, hundreds of companies, for-profit and nonprofit alike, have set up shop to deliver debtor education classes. These organizations can also help you with budgeting, even if you're not planning to file for bankruptcy.

The courses are taught online or by telephone and mail. The fee averages about $50.

For a list of agencies that have been approved by the Department of Justice for bankruptcy purposes—although you don't have to file for bankruptcy to use them—go to www.justice.gov/ust/eo/bapcpa/ccde/de_approved.htm. Because budgeting is pretty much the same everywhere, and because you don't need to show up in person, you can use a service even if it's far from where you live.

Last but certainly not least, HUD-approved housing counselors can also provide budgeting help to people trying to save their homes from foreclosure. (See Ch. 4.)

Could You Reduce Your Debt Load?

If you don't have enough cash each month to keep making your existing mortgage payments, there are a few ways that you might be able to make them affordable. Basically, you need to either get the mortgage payments reduced or get your hands on more cash.

Here are the main ways to go about this (all of which are discussed elsewhere in the book):

- **Modify your mortgage.** Use the mortgage modification (Home Affordable Modification Program, or HAMP) part of the federal Making Home Affordable program to lower the payment on your first mortgage (including taxes and insurance). Under regular HAMP (Tier 1), a participating mortgage servicer must consider a sequence of modification steps until your monthly payment, including taxes and insurance, is reduced to 31% of your verified monthly gross income. To reach the 31% target, your payment would first be lowered by decreasing the interest rate on your mortgage to as low as 2%. If that doesn't bring it down to 31%, the next step would increase your loan period to as long as 40 years. If that still doesn't work, your servicer would allow you to go short on your current payments and make them up at the end of your mortgage term in the form of a balloon payment.

  If you don't qualify for a modification under Tier 1, you might qualify under Tier 2. Borrowers who may be eligible under HAMP Tier 2 include those who have been previously found not eligible for a regular HAMP modification, borrowers who defaulted on a HAMP trial payment plan, and borrowers who lost good standing under a permanent modification. Also, rental properties are eligible for modification under Tier 2 under certain circumstances.

  Under Tier 2, your mortgage servicer may lower the monthly mortgage payment by capitalizing the arrears, reducing the interest rate (to a permanent, fixed rate), extending the term of the loan to 480 months, and principal forbearance. Following modification, your debt-to-income ratio must fall between 25% and 42%.

Ch. 4 provides a more detailed look at this program.

If you aren't eligible for HAMP, you can still negotiate with your lender for lower payments using this same basic approach because you might qualify for a loan modification through its in-house procedures.

- **File for Chapter 13 bankruptcy** and come up with a repayment plan that will let you reduce the amount of your monthly payments on your other debts and get rid of them altogether in three to five years.
- **File for Chapter 7 bankruptcy** to get rid of your unsecured debts, such as those from credit cards, medical services, or signature (personal, unsecured) loans, so you'll have a greater share of your income to devote to your mortgage.

When It Makes Sense to Keep Your House

Your answers to the questions discussed above, about your equity and your budget, will largely determine whether or not you should try to keep your house.

You Have at Least Some Equity in Your House

If you have equity in your house and are facing foreclosure because of missed payments or a rapid increase in your mortgage interest rate, it may make sense to hold on to the house if for no other reason than to protect your equity. Needless to say, the more equity you have, the stronger this reasoning.

You Can Afford Future Monthly Loan Payments

If you have some equity in your house and think you can afford future monthly mortgage payments, it's probably worth it to try to hang on to your house.

If you don't think you can afford your monthly payments, see Could You Reduce Your Debt Load? above for ideas on how to free up more of your income or change the payments themselves.

When Equity Doesn't Help You Pay the Mortgage

It's not uncommon for people with fixed or limited incomes (disability or retirement income, or low-paying jobs) to own homes with affordable mortgage payments and with substantial equity ($50,000 or more). But they can't borrow against this equity because their income level won't support repayment of the loan, so the only way to benefit from the equity is to sell the house. However, because they would still need affordable shelter, selling may not be an option, especially in this market.

Even people with higher incomes may not be able to borrow against their equity, either because credit has dried up, they have bad credit, or because other debts and their lifestyle won't support repayment of a new loan.

If you are 62 or older, you might benefit from taking out a reverse mortgage. With a reverse mortgage, a homeowner can tap into the equity in his or her home to provide cash to help meet expenses. A reverse mortgage is different from a traditional mortgage in that it does not require you to make monthly payments to the lender to repay the loan. Instead, loan proceeds are paid out to you according to a plan, which consists of a monthly payment, a line of credit, a lump sum, or a combination of these options. The reverse mortgage loan becomes due and payable when you:

- sell the property
- permanently move out (for example, to a nursing home)
- do not meet the obligations of the mortgage (such as paying taxes and insurance), or
- die.

Because reverse mortgages are premised on stable real estate values, you are unlikely to qualify for one unless you have a lot of equity in your house— at least enough to convince the lender that it'll recoup its investment even if values continue to drop.

When It Makes Sense to Give up Your House

It's never an easy decision, but if you are behind on house payments and find yourself significantly upside-down on your mortgage, there's not much point, from an economic perspective, in trying to keep the house unless you can get your mortgage payment reduced under HAMP or by working something out with your lender (and many lenders do want to keep you in your house; see Ch. 4).

It probably makes sense to give up your house if it is now worth at least 25% less than you paid for it. That's because your house's value would have to appreciate by as much as it dropped for you to come out even, and that will likely take several years at a minimum.

What if you recently bought your house with no down payment (or almost none) or took out an interest-only loan? In that case, you had no equity to begin with—so right now you could give up the house without losing much, financially, right? It's true that you wouldn't lose any equity by walking away from your mortgage, but you could end up liable for some or all of your mortgage or home equity loan debt if you don't file for bankruptcy. You might (especially with a home equity loan) be taxed on the amount of the mortgage debt lost by the lender (although there are several ways to avoid this tax liability). (See Ch. 8.)

If you decide that the smartest course is to give up the house, you have more decisions to make—important ones. How you choose to proceed can make a very big difference to your financial future.

Your options (all of which are discussed later in the book) include:
- a short sale—that is, getting the lender's permission to sell the house for less than you owe
- a deed in lieu of foreclosure (getting your lender to accept the deed back in exchange for an agreement to call off the foreclosure)
- letting the foreclosure happen, staying in your house payment free for months until you get a notice to leave, and building up your cash reserves, or
- filing for Chapter 13 or Chapter 7 bankruptcy to eliminate foreclosure-related liabilities and delay the foreclosure sale for at least several months, thereby extending the time you can remain in the house payment free.

Although for many it's painful to give up a house, try to keep in mind that doing so may make things much easier for you and your family in the long run. You will probably be able to stay in the house for months without making any more mortgage payments—giving you time to save some money, which will make moving easier. And if it's any consolation, remember that you are among literally millions of Americans who find themselves in the same boat during these tough times.

Negotiating a Workout

W hen you are at risk of defaulting on your mortgage, or have already fallen behind on your payments, you may have a number of options for keeping your house.

Refinance your mortgage under the federal Home Affordable Refinance Program. Usually, refinancing is available only if you have equity in your home—something that is increasingly rare in many parts of the country. However, under the government-sponsored refinance program known as the Home Affordable Refinance Program (HARP), you may be able to refinance your current mortgage into a 15- or 30-year fixed-rate mortgage. This may not reduce your payment much in the short term, but it will help avoid nasty interest rate resets that might be in your future under your current mortgage. HARP is discussed later in this chapter.

Lower your monthly mortgage payment under the Home Affordable Modification Program, or HAMP. HAMP provides a way to lower the monthly payment on your first mortgage and your second mortgage, in some cases, under the Second Lien Modification Program (2MP). These programs are also discussed later in this chapter.

Negotiate for a modification of your mortgage or payment terms outside of HAMP. It's clear that HAMP is the main attraction. However, for various reasons, you may not qualify for its benefits. Even then, it still may be possible to negotiate a modification with your mortgage lender if, like many, it would rather have you stay in your house than foreclose on it. You would do well to use a HUD-approved housing counselor to help you head off the foreclosure. The counselor can explain your options, negotiate with your lender, and do a lot for your peace of mind. See Using a HUD-Approved Housing Counselor, below.

File for bankruptcy. If you can't work out an agreement that will let you stay in your house under certain conditions—and you don't have the wherewithal to reinstate your mortgage under your state's law (see Ch. 2)—your next step is to explore filing for Chapter 13 or Chapter 7 bankruptcy. Chapter 13 can give you time to make up your missed payments and might lower your other secured debt payments (your car note or a short-term home equity loan, for example). Chapter 7 bankruptcy can quickly do away with credit card and other unsecured debt and free up income to use toward your mortgage payments, thereby allowing you to keep your home.

Challenge the foreclosure in court. Finally, you may be able to successfully challenge the foreclosure in court because of irregularities in the paperwork or the procedures followed by the foreclosing party. Courts throughout the country have disapproved of foreclosures in circumstances where the record of mortgage ownership is incomplete or where court documents have been fraudulently prepared. You will likely take this route only if your negotiations with the lender have failed.

This chapter concentrates on the various ways you can change the terms of your mortgage or the amount of your monthly payment as a strategy to keep your home. Later chapters cover filing for bankruptcy and fighting foreclosure in court.

How Bankruptcy Can Help

Filing for bankruptcy can be a marvelous way either to save your house or at least to stay in it payment free for longer than you would otherwise.

It's important to understand that Chapter 7 bankruptcy will keep you in your home long-term only if you file while you are still current on your mortgage. It will help you by wiping out (discharging) your other debts, freeing up your income to make your house payments. Chapter 13 bankruptcy, however, can keep you in your home long-term even if you are behind on your payments. (See Chs. 5 and 6.)

Do You Have Enough Time to Negotiate?

It can take a while to work things out with your lender (typically through its representative, a mortgage servicing company). If you're not sure how much time you've got left before your house is sold in foreclosure, find the page for your state in the appendix and see how much notice you're entitled to. Your failure to keep track of time constraints can sink your attempt to keep your house.

In the past it was common for homeowners to negotiate with their servicers right up to the moment when the foreclosure sale was scheduled to occur. Then, when the negotiations fell through—as they frequently did—there wasn't enough time to stop the sale from going through. While this scenario (called "dual tracking") can still happen, it is less likely if you are working with your servicer to sign up for one of the government foreclosure prevention programs.

Additionally, certain laws restrict dual tracking (proceeding with foreclosure while simultaneously working with the borrower on a loan modification). For example, California's new Homeowner Bill of Rights (effective January 1, 2013) prohibits dual tracking, among other things. Under this law, mortgage servicers must make a decision to grant or deny a first lien loan modification application before starting or continuing the foreclosure process on a California property. Even if the lender denies the loan modification, it still cannot foreclose until any applicable appeals period has expired (generally 30 days from the date of the written denial). Go to the California Attorney General's website at http://oag.ca.gov/hbor for more information.

Also, the $25 billion national mortgage settlement in 2012 restricts the nation's five largest mortgage servicers (Bank of America, Citi, JPMorgan Chase, Wells Fargo, and Ally/GMAC) from dual tracking. (See "The National Mortgage Settlement," below.)

Pursuant to the Dodd-Frank Wall Street Reform and Consumer Protection Act, the Consumer Financial Protection Bureau has issued new mortgage servicing rules effective as of January 10, 2014. Once these rules go into effect, mortgage servicers cannot start a foreclosure until 120 days after a borrower falls delinquent (which provides a reasonable amount of time to submit a loan modification application) and cannot begin the foreclosure process if a loss mitigation application is pending. Also, mortgage servicers cannot move for a foreclosure judgment or order of sale, or conduct a foreclosure sale, if a borrower submits a complete loss mitigation application after foreclosure has been initiated (so long as it is more than 37 days before a scheduled foreclosure sale), while that application is still pending, subject to a few exceptions. More information about the new rules can be found at www.consumerfinance.gov/regulations/2013-real-estate-settlement-procedures-act-regulation-x-and-truth-in-lending-act-regulation-z-mortgage-servicing-final-rules/.

Still, as mentioned, you should be aware of when a foreclosure sale might happen and know the date before which you should take other steps to prevent the foreclosure sale—such as filing for bankruptcy or suing to stop the foreclosure in nonjudicial foreclosure states.

The lessons are obvious: Get started as soon as you can, and be assertive if you don't get a timely response.

Your negotiations with your mortgage servicer will probably take much longer than you think. Although it may feel like the servicer is dragging its feet, it is likely not doing it intentionally. In many cases, the servicer can't tell you about the status of your negotiations until it gets word from the mortgage owner—which will likely not be your original lender but rather the trustee of a mortgage trust or an investor who bought the rights to your mortgage.

Because of the number of defaults flooding the system, there is often no way most servicers can process your modification on time in many states unless either of the following is true:

- You begin the process when you first realize you can't make your payments.
- The lender agrees in writing to—or is required to under the law—put off the foreclosure sale while you are negotiating.

If a foreclosure sale looms in the near future—two weeks should have the alarm bells ringing—consult a bankruptcy lawyer immediately. Filing for bankruptcy is the only sure way to stop an imminent sale unless the lender voluntarily agrees in writing to pull back. (See Chs. 5 and 6 for more on bankruptcy.)

CAUTION

Avoid foreclosure rescue scams. Companies that offer to rescue you from foreclosure on the eve of a foreclosure sale are all too often con artists. (See Don't Get Scammed by a Foreclosure "Rescue" Company in Ch. 1.)

Why Lenders Delay Foreclosing

Just because a lender can foreclose doesn't mean it will foreclose. Lenders delay foreclosing for a number of reasons.

Delay is frequently due to abrupt policy changes on the part of the major banks, whether they are servicers, investors, or lenders. Whenever word leaks out about an irregular practice engaged in by one major lender, both that lender and other major lenders will announce a moratorium on foreclosures until they investigate the matter further.

Take, for example, the "robo-signing" scandal, which was uncovered in a deposition in a Chapter 13 bankruptcy. In the deposition, a bank official admitted to signing thousands of documents every week, falsely stating under oath that he had personal knowledge of the information in those documents. It turned out that this practice, known as robo-signing, was used by a broad spectrum of mortgage servicers and entities seeking foreclosures in judicial foreclosure states. Once word of the robo-signing scandal spread, virtually all the major servicers and lenders announced temporary holds on foreclosures, at least in judicial foreclosure states where signed affidavits typically are required. This delay lasted for several months.

Delay is also frequently caused by changes in federal or state law or federal regulations that require banks to take additional steps prior to initiating foreclosure. For example, the Consumer Financial Protection Bureau recently issued new mortgage servicing rules effective as of January 10, 2014, which could potentially hold up foreclosures. Foreclosure delays generally tend to occur whenever new regulations go into effect since lenders and servicers often back off from foreclosing until they are confident they have appropriate procedures in place to be in compliance with the latest requirements.

Finally, some large lenders have been deliberately holding back on foreclosures, fearing that excessive numbers of foreclosures will exacerbate the decline in home values.

Using a HUD-Approved Housing Counselor

As a general rule, the sooner you hook up with a HUD-approved housing counselor, the better. These counselors work for free (they are paid through government grants and in some cases grants from major mortgage lenders who really do want to avoid foreclosures if at all possible) and are well trained in the various foreclosure-prevention programs and techniques of negotiation. You can have no better advocate if you are trying to avoid a foreclosure or negotiate a mortgage modification.

Finding a HUD-Approved Counselor

The federal Department of Housing and Urban Development (HUD) has a list of approved counselors. You can find a counselor at www.hud.gov/offices/hsg/sfh/hcc/hcs.cfm or by calling 800-569-4287.

You can also find a counselor by visiting The Homeownership Preservation Foundation at www.995hope.org or by calling 888-995-HOPE. Counselors can also be accessed through the Making Home Affordable website at www.makinghomeaffordable.gov.

For general information about HUD-approved housing counselors, including their training, their funding, and why they want to help you stay in your home, visit www.hud.gov/offices/hsg/sfh/hcc/hcc_home.cfm.

As the number of foreclosures continues to rise, many counselors are finding themselves swamped with work. You may not get your calls returned promptly—or returned at all, in some cases. Be patient. But if you do run out of patience at some point and decide to handle your own negotiations, first get a good understanding of the different types of loss mitigation options available, such as loan modifications, repayment plans, forbearance agreements, short sales, and deeds in lieu of foreclosure. (Loan modifications, repayment plans, and forbearance agreements are discussed later in this chapter, while short sales and deeds in lieu of foreclosure are covered in Ch. 8.)

Once you call your servicer or contact a HUD-approved housing counselor, your servicer will send you a "workout package" of forms, along with some information about your options. After you fill out and return the forms, you and your servicer can start talking about possible arrangements.

The servicer will have some discretion to make deals, but will have to contact the lender for anything out of the ordinary. For example, say you are three months behind on your mortgage because you were laid off, but you are now back at work and can make up the missed payments over six months in addition to meeting your current obligation. Most mortgage servicers have authority to sign off on this kind of short-term arrangement. But if you need two years to make up the missed payments, the servicer might have to get permission to make a deal.

If your servicer is not responsive to your attempts to work things out, contact your lender directly. If you don't know who your lender is—which is quite common due to the rapid changes in the marketplace—you can find out from your servicer. The servicer is required by law to give you that information—and you can sue if it doesn't.

Which Servicers are Participating in HAMP?

As we mention throughout this book, the Making Home Affordable foreclosure and modification rules are voluntary for the banks—unless the bank is operating with bailout money from the federal Troubled Asset Relief Program (TARP) or holding loans owned or serviced by Fannie Mae or Freddy Mac. For the rest of the servicers, the Treasury Department has offered incentives to sign up. Currently, over 100 servicers have agreed to participate in the Home Affordable Modification Program. You can find a list of these servicers at the Making Home Affordable website at www.makinghomeaffordable.gov (click "Get Started" then "Contact Your Mortgage Company").

Can a HUD-Approved Housing Counselor Always Help You?

Housing counselors can do a lot, but they are limited by mortgage servicer and lender policies regarding what are termed loss mitigation measures.

If you've missed a payment or two but haven't received a notice of intent to foreclose (or something similar), you have a decent chance of working something out with the help of a counselor or with the servicer directly. You may be able to keep your house and perhaps get a more affordable mortgage payment for the future.

If you are way behind on your payments (four or more months) and have already received a notice of default (in states that require them) or even a notice of sale, your chances of working something out aren't as good. At this point, the servicer is unlikely to consider you a good candidate for keeping current in the future, whatever your payments may be.

What Happens When You Contact a HUD-Approved Counselor

When you call a HUD-approved counselor, you will be scheduled for an interview (by phone or in person) that will probably take between 60 and 90 minutes. The counselor will want to get a handle on your income, your debts, your property, your mortgage, the value of your home, and what kind of arrangement you think you can live with. You likely will need to do some homework before your appointment.

From the information you provide, the counselor will categorize your situation as easy to resolve, needing some serious negotiations to keep you in your house, or something that can't be solved with the servicer.

Information to Gather Before You Call

- Information about your first mortgage loan (have your monthly mortgage statement handy)
- Recent pay stubs
- Benefit statements from Social Security, disability, unemployment, retirement, or public assistance
- Your last tax return
- If you're self-employed, an up-to-date profit and loss statement
- Monthly household expenses
- Information about any second mortgage or home equity line of credit on the home
- Account balances and monthly payments due on all of your credit cards, student loans, car loans, and so on
- Information about your savings and other assets

If Your Case Is Easy to Resolve

You have missed only two or three payments because of a temporary economic setback through no fault of your own, and you can show that you'll be able to make your payments in the future.

The counselor will call a dedicated loss mitigation hotline made available by your mortgage servicer and get an okay to a workout on the spot. Typically, you'll get an agreement that lets you make up the missed payments over a period of between three months and a year, depending on your situation. Or the agreement may add the missed payments to the end of your mortgage.

It's hard to generalize about how long it takes to get an agreement in your hand if your case looks like an easy one to the counselor. It all depends on the volume of cases being negotiated by your counselor and lender, and the priority assigned to your case. It's not uncommon for this process to go on for months.

If You Need Serious Negotiating Help to Keep the House

You have missed three or four payments and are on the verge of receiving a notice of intent to foreclose or even a notice of intended sale. If you're going to be able to make future payments, you need some type of modification of your mortgage principal or interest payment, and you need a way to deal with the missed payments.

You will work with the counselor to come up with a proposal you can live with. It may involve an agreement on your part to give up some expenses (for instance, eliminating satellite TV, pulling your children out of private school, or suspending contributions or repayments to a retirement plan) in exchange for the lender's agreement to make the changes in your mortgage that will make it possible to stay in your house.

The foreclosure counselor will communicate your proposed workout to the mortgage servicer, and the servicer will pass it on to a special analyst (employed by the servicer) to see whether or not the lender will accept it. There will probably be some negotiation, with your counselor advocating for your position or something close to it. Depending on whether the servicer's right hand knows what its left hand is doing, you may receive a notice of default or a notice of intent to begin foreclosure proceedings even while negotiations are still going on.

As the time of a threatened foreclosure draws near, you may start to panic at the lack of movement in your talks. As mentioned, if you get within a couple of weeks of a scheduled sale without finalizing an agreement, you should talk to a bankruptcy lawyer to see whether bankruptcy would be an appropriate way for you to stop the foreclosure sale and give you more time to work something out with your lender.

Servicers Must Appoint Relationship Managers

Making Home Affordable guidelines require the 20 largest servicers to appoint what they call a "relationship manager" (RM) to serve as the homeowner's single point of contact when being evaluated for a potential HAMP modification, the Home Affordable Unemployment Program (UP), or Home Affordable Foreclosure Alternatives (HAFA). (The UP program is discussed later in this chapter, while HAFA is covered in

Ch. 8.) The relationship manager is responsible for communicating and working with the borrower through the entire process.

A relationship manager is expected to be knowledgeable about the borrower's situation and current status in the loss mitigation process and to be able to suggest options to help the borrower remain in his or her home. Additionally, the RM is supposed to be aware of Making Home Affordable rules and timelines and must coordinate with the borrower and in-house and third-party servicer personnel to promote compliance with these requirements. If the loan is later referred for foreclosure, the RM must be available to respond to borrower inquiries regarding the status of the foreclosure

While these rules apply only to the largest servicers, the U.S. Treasury encouraged all participating mortgage servicers to adopt the new guidance for providing borrowers with a single point of contact, and most have agreed to do so (though just how this is done is left up to the servicers).

Additionally, the California Homeowner Bill of Rights (discussed above) and the national mortgage settlement (discussed below) require servicers to provide borrowers with a single point of contact during the loss mitigation process.

If the Only Way to Avoid Foreclosure Is to Sell or File for Bankruptcy

You have received a notice of intent to foreclose and either you are unlikely to have enough income to stay current on your payments (even if they are reduced, and even if you could reduce your overall debt load by filing for Chapter 7 bankruptcy) or you have a poor credit score.

Your counselor will probably tell you that a satisfactory workout isn't going to happen and that you should do whatever you must to avoid foreclosure, which would likely put a heavy hit on your credit score. The counselor will likely suggest unloading your house in a short sale (which usually means selling it for less than you owe on it) or offering a deed in lieu of foreclosure to the lender (giving the house to the lender in exchange for a promise not to sue you for what you still owe on the mortgage).

Some counselors might suggest that you consult a lawyer about the possibility of filing for bankruptcy. Many, however, avoid the "B" word if at all possible, because the lenders (or in many cases, their funders) don't like it. I don't think foreclosures are always a bad thing, and I *do* think that bankruptcy is sometimes the most appropriate response. For example, a short sale might be marginally better for your credit record in the future (no one really knows these days), but you most likely would have to leave your house much sooner than you would if you let the foreclosure continue. That means you would give up the opportunity to save money by staying in your house for months—perhaps many months—without making payments. Finally, in a short sale you may be liable for the deficiency or, if your lender forgives you for the deficiency, the income tax on that forgiven debt, whereas bankruptcy would help you avoid these liabilities. Keep in mind that a counselor who attempts to sell you on a short sale or talk you out of bankruptcy may be passing on the lenders' and servicers' views, which may not best serve your economic interests.

If you still want to keep your home even if your counselor tells you a workout is not in the cards, it's time to think about bankruptcy. Filing for Chapter 13 bankruptcy might allow you to keep your house. (See Ch. 5.) At this stage, filing for Chapter 7 bankruptcy won't keep you in your house in the long run, but it can help you stay there payment free for an extra couple of months. (See Ch. 6.)

The Making Home Affordable Program

In 2009, the federal government initiated a series of programs that were intended to help homeowners avoid foreclosure. The first two programs were called the Home Affordable Refinance Program (HARP) and the Home Affordable Modification Program (HAMP). A number of additional and supplementary programs were subsequently promulgated by the Treasury Department. Together, these Making Home Affordable programs are the main game in town when it comes to trying to save your house by refinancing or modifying your mortgage to make your monthly payments more affordable. Many of the Making Home

Affordable programs (including HAMP and HARP) are scheduled to end on December 31, 2015. These programs are briefly described below. More detailed information is available through the Making Home Affordable website at www.makinghomeaffordable.gov.

I especially want to direct your attention to the material under the "About MHA" tab on the Making Home Affordable home page. Between the questions and answers provided in the "Frequently Asked Questions" Section and the material in this book, you should have a pretty good idea of how the various Making Home Affordable programs work.

The Refinancing Programs

Before the housing crash, many homeowners periodically refinanced their mortgages. The two primary reasons were to either reduce the mortgage payment or extract equity from the house. Borrowers assumed that housing values would continue to go up and that debt accumulated through refinancing (and through additional mortgages, such as home equity lines of credit, or HELOCs) would ultimately be absorbed by the increase. When the great housing crash grew into full bloom near the end of 2008, virtually all refinancing activity ground to a halt. Homeowners unable to refinance were left holding the bag. When the government stepped in to address the burgeoning foreclosure crisis, it naturally turned to refinancing as one of the primary remedies.

The government started with the Home Affordable Refinance Program (HARP) and subsequently initiated several additional, more targeted refinance programs—none of which has been very successful in terms of the number of homeowners who have been helped. HARP is set to expire on December 31, 2015. The expiration date has been extended before and may be extended again. To find out whether HARP is still in effect at the time you are reading this book, visit the Making Home Affordable website at www.makinghomeaffordable.gov and do a search for "HARP."

CAUTION

Check the MHA website. Below, I provide a brief overview of HARP and the other refinance programs on the chance that they will still be available if and when you need them. Check the Making Home Affordable website for the latest news about HARP and associated programs.

The Home Affordable Refinance Program (HARP)

HARP was intended to stimulate a return to refinancing as a means for borrowers to reduce mortgage payments and to move into stable mortgages, such as 15- or 30-year fixed mortgages. The program was originally designed to help millions of underwater or almost-underwater homeowners refinance, but had very limited success when first introduced. Consequently, in the fall of 2011, President Obama announced an overhaul to the HARP program, which changed it in several ways. The most significant change was the removal of the limit on the amount that homeowners could be underwater. (The original version of HARP only permitted refinances for mortgages that were up to 125% of the current value of a home.) Now, to be eligible for HARP, you must meet all of the following requirements:

- Your loan is owned or guaranteed by Fannie Mae or Freddie Mac. (If you're not sure whether Fannie Mae or Freddie Mac owns your mortgage, use the look-up tools at www.fanniemae.com/loanlookup and www.freddiemac.com/mymortgage.)
- Your loan was sold to Fannie Mae or Freddie Mac on or before May 31, 2009.
- You did not previously refinance your mortgage under HARP, unless you have a Fannie Mae loan and refinanced under HARP between March and May 2009.
- Your current loan-to-value ratio is 80% or greater.
- You are current on your mortgage payments.
- You have not had a late payment in the past six months and no more than one late payment within the last year.

As of January 2013, there have been 2.2 million refinances through HARP since the inception of the program. Though the program has fallen short of its goals, recent data from the Federal Housing Finance Agency shows a significant uptick in refinancing activity among underwater borrowers following changes to the program.

FHA Short Refinance

Recognizing that many homeowners aren't eligible for HARP, the Treasury Department rolled out another refinancing program known as the FHA Short Refinance. The program is not mandatory for mortgage servicers. If your mortgage servicer chooses to participate, the program provides guidelines for the servicer to follow.

If you are current on your mortgage but owe more than your home is worth, and your mortgage servicer volunteers to participate in the FHA Short Refinance program, the servicer is required to reduce the amount you owe on your first mortgage to no more than 97.75% of your home's current value. For example, if your home's value is $125,000, the servicer would have to reduce your mortgage to an amount no greater than $122,188, despite the amount of your current mortgage. So, even if you currently owe $250,000, your mortgage after the refinance would not be greater than $122,188. Clearly, most servicers—and the owners of the mortgages being serviced—are unlikely to participate in this program if homeowners' mortgages are severely underwater.

To be eligible for an FHA Short Refinance, you must meet all of the following requirements:

- Your mortgage is not owned or guaranteed by Fannie Mae, Freddie Mac, the FHA, the VA, or the USDA.
- You owe more than your home is worth.
- You are current on your mortgage payments.
- You occupy the house as your primary residence.
- You meet the standard FHA underwriting requirements.
- Your total debt does not exceed 55% of your monthly gross income.
- You have not been convicted within the last ten years of felony larceny, theft, fraud or forgery, money laundering, or tax evasion in connection with a mortgage or real estate transaction.

Treasury/FHA Second Lien Program (FHA2LP)

If you have a second mortgage on your home and the servicer of your first mortgage agrees to participate in the FHA Short Refinance program (discussed just above), you may qualify to have your second mortgage reduced or eliminated through the Treasury/FHA Second Lien Program (FHA2LP). Under FHA2LP, the total amount of your mortgage debt after the refinance cannot exceed 115% of your home's current value. This means that if your first mortgage is reduced to 97.75% of your home's current value under the FHA Short Refinance program, your second mortgage would be reduced to no more than 17.25% of your home's current value under FHA2LP. For example, if your home is worth $125,000 and your first mortgage is reduced to $122,188, your second mortgage would have to be reduced to $21,563 or less.

To be eligible for FHA2LP, you must be eligible for an FHA Short Refinance and you must have obtained your mortgage on or before January 1, 2009. Like the FHA Short Refinance program, participation in FHA2LP by mortgage servicers is completely voluntary. Most mortgage servicers will be unlikely to participate in FHA2LP so long as borrowers are severely underwater on their mortgages. According to the Making Home Affordable website, only a handful of mortgage servicers (about a dozen) have agreed to consider homeowner applications for relief under FHA2LP.

TIP

Contact the VA or FHA directly. The FHA-Home Affordable Modification Program (FHA-HAMP) provides assistance to borrowers in modifying FHA loans. To obtain further information, call FHA's National Servicing Center at 877-622-8525. The Veteran's Administration (VA) has issued guidance to mortgage servicers so borrowers can obtain HAMP-style modifications for loans guaranteed by the VA. Call the Veterans Affairs Regional Loan Center at 877-827-3702 to learn more about loss mitigation programs offered by the VA.

The Home Affordable Modification Program (HAMP)

If you are having a tough time making your mortgage payments and you qualify for HAMP, your monthly mortgage payment could be lowered. According to the January 2013 housing scorecard produced jointly by the U.S. Department of Housing and Urban Development and the U.S. Department of the Treasury, as of December 2012, more than 1.1 million homeowners have received permanent modifications through HAMP. On average, borrowers saved approximately $545 on their mortgage payments each month and 87% of homeowners who started HAMP in the previous 2½ years received permanent modifications.

You may be eligible for HAMP if you meet all of the following criteria:

- You obtained your mortgage on or before January 1, 2009.
- You don't owe more than $729,750 on your home or single unit rental property.
- You don't owe more than $934,200 on a two-unit rental property; $1,129,250 on a three-unit rental property; or $1,403,400 on a four-unit rental property.
- The property has not been condemned.
- You have a financial hardship and are either delinquent or in danger of falling behind (nonowner occupants must be delinquent in order to qualify).
- You have sufficient documented income to support the modified payment.
- You must not have been convicted within the last ten years of felony larceny, theft, fraud or forgery, money laundering, or tax evasion, in connection with a mortgage or real estate transaction.

See More About HAMP, below.

Second Lien Modification Program (2MP)

If your first mortgage is (or was) permanently modified under HAMP, and you have a second mortgage on the same property, you may be eligible for a modification or principal reduction on your second mortgage under 2MP. According to the Making Home Affordable website, "2MP is designed to work in tandem with HAMP to provide a comprehensive solution for homeowners with second mortgages to increase long-term affordability and sustainability." If the servicer for your second mortgage is participating in this program, it will automatically evaluate you for a second lien modification. Relatively few servicers have chosen to participate in 2MP, but they include the largest of the large lenders, such as Bank of America, Wells Fargo, Chase, Citi, and GMAC.

You may be eligible for "2MP" if you meet all of the following criteria:

- Your first mortgage was modified under HAMP.
- You must not have been convicted within the last ten years of felony larceny, theft, fraud or forgery, money laundering, or tax evasion in connection with a mortgage or real estate transaction.
- You have not missed three consecutive monthly payments on your HAMP modification.
- You owe more than $5,000 on your second mortgage.
- Your monthly second mortgage payment is more than $100.

Like HAMP, 2MP is set to expire on December 31, 2015.

Principal Reduction Alternative (PRA)

The PRA program was designed to help borrowers whose homes are worth significantly less than they owe by encouraging servicers and investors to reduce the amounts owed on their homes. While this program may sound like the answer to your prayers, your servicer ultimately has complete discretion as to whether it will actually reduce your principal.

You may be eligible for PRA if you meet all of the following requirements:

- Your mortgage is not owned or guaranteed by Fannie Mae or Freddie Mac.
- You owe more than your home is worth.
- You live in the home that carries the mortgage you want to modify.
- You obtained your mortgage on or before January 1, 2009.

- Your mortgage payment is more than 31% of your gross (pre-tax) monthly income.
- You owe up to $729,750 on your first mortgage.
- You have a financial hardship and are either delinquent or in danger of falling behind.
- You have sufficient documented income to support the modified payment.
- You must not have been convicted within the last ten years of felony larceny, theft, fraud or forgery, money laundering, or tax evasion in connection with a mortgage or real estate transaction.

Most mortgage servicers are required to come up with written standards for evaluating a homeowner for a possible reduction in mortgage principal. However, since they are not required to offer a principal reduction, it is not surprising that the number of principal reductions completed under the PRA program is still relatively small as of this writing.

To encourage investors to consider and expand the use of PRA, the U.S. Department of Treasury issued program guidance in early 2012, which tripled financial incentives for investors who agree to reduce principal for underwater homeowners under the program. The largest servicers participating in this program include Bank of America, Citi, Chase, and Wells Fargo. It is also worth noting that the terms of the $25 billion national mortgage settlement has caused these same servicers to increase their use of non-PRA principal reductions. As part of the settlement, the servicers were required to allocate $17 billion to reduce the principal balance of home loans for borrowers who are in default or at risk of default on their loan payments. (See "The National Mortgage Settlement," below.)

Home Affordable Unemployment Program (UP)

If you are unemployed and having a tough time making your mortgage payments, you may be eligible for UP. UP provides a temporary reduction or suspension of mortgage payments for 12 months or more while you look for a new job. This type of temporary relief is more commonly known as forbearance.

You may be eligible for UP if you meet all of the following requirements:

- You are unemployed and eligible for unemployment benefits.
- You occupy the house as your primary residence or it is a rental property.
- You obtained your mortgage on or before January 1, 2009.
- You owe up to $729,750 on your home.
- You are delinquent on payments or default is imminent.

Loans that were previously modified under HAMP are not eligible for a UP forbearance plan if they are in good standing. However, homeowners who were previously determined ineligible for HAMP, who become unemployed during a HAMP trial period plan, or who lost good standing under a permanent modification may be considered for UP.

Information to Provide When You Apply for Mortgage Modification

- Information about the monthly gross (before tax) income of your household, including recent pay stubs if you receive them or documentation of income you receive from other sources
- Your most recent income tax return
- Information about your savings and other assets
- Information about your first mortgage, such as your monthly mortgage statement
- Information about any second mortgage or home equity line of credit on the house
- Account balances and minimum monthly payments due on all of your credit cards
- Account balances and monthly payments on all your other debts, such as student loans and car loan
- A letter describing any circumstances that caused your income to be reduced or expenses to be increased (job loss, divorce, illness, etc.) if applicable

During a UP forbearance, you may be required to make a partial payment of no more than 31% of your monthly gross (pretax) income including unemployment benefits. At the end of your UP forbearance, you will be evaluated for a HAMP modification.

UP is not currently available to homeowners with mortgages held by Fannie Mae and Freddie Mac. However, both entities have their own forbearance programs for unemployed homeowners; contact your mortgage servicer to find out the eligibility requirements. Over a hundred servicers have signed up to participate in UP, including Bank of America, Citi, Chase, and Wells Fargo. The program is set to expire on December 31, 2015.

More About HAMP

HAMP consists of a two-tier system. Once your servicer determines your initial eligibility for HAMP (Tier 1), it is required to perform a "net present value" (NPV) analysis. A loan's NPV is what it would cost (in cash flow) to modify your mortgage payments compared to the cost of taking the property through foreclosure and selling it. If the NPV analysis shows that it would cost the lender more to foreclose than to modify your loan, your mortgage servicer is required to notify you, enter into modification discussions, and modify the mortgage terms under the program's guidelines. If the NPV analysis shows that the lender would not save money by agreeing to a modification rather than foreclosing, the lender still has the option of offering you a loan modification under the program's guidelines. If your request for a HAMP modification is rejected, you can do your own NPV analysis at a website offered by the Making Home Affordable program. Visit https://checkmynpv.com.

The modification program's ultimate goal is to adjust the interest rate and possibly the duration of your mortgage so that your debt-to-income ratio will be no higher than 31%. In other words, your payment on your first mortgage, including taxes and insurance, will be no more than 31% of your gross income. Your debt-to-income ratio won't include payments on a second mortgage on your house, installment payments on a car or other secured property, or mortgages on other houses you happen to own. You can find an easy-to-use calculator on www.makinghomeaffordable.com

that will help you determine your debt-to-income ratio (click "Tools," then "Payment Reduction Estimator").

To get to the 31% debt-to-income goal, your servicer will first reduce the interest rate to as low as 2% (typically for five years), and, if necessary, extend the term of the loan to a maximum of 40 years from its inception. Using this process, the servicer will reduce your payment to a 38% debt-to-income ratio (assuming your debt-to-income ratio is higher than that). After that point, the federal government will share equally in the cost of the rest of the reduction down to 31%.

> **EXAMPLE:** Your gross income is $8,000 per month, and your mortgage payment (including interest and insurance) is $3,400. That means you're spending about 42.5% of your income on housing. Reducing your interest rate by a couple of points would get your mortgage payment down to $3,000, giving you a debt-to-income of about 38%. Up to this point, the entire cost of the modification would fall on your lender. However, to get the payment down to 31% of your gross income, the government and the lender would share equally in the cost. To bring your debt-to-income ratio down to 31%, or a mortgage payment of approximately $2,500, the lender would continue to decrease your interest rate until it reached 2%, and if that still left you above 31%, it would lengthen your mortgage term. Mission accomplished.

Servicers can also modify a mortgage loan by reducing its principal or delaying payment on part of the principal until the end of the loan (forbearance). It's more likely, though, that the servicer will adjust the interest rate and the length of the loan, rather than forgive or forbear any principal.

As of June 2012, borrowers who are ineligible for regular HAMP (Tier 1) may quality for HAMP Tier 2. Homeowners that may be eligible for a loan modification under Tier 2 include:

- Homeowners who did not qualify for HAMP (Tier 1) because their debt-to-income ratio was 31% or lower.

- Homeowners who previously received a HAMP trial period plan, but defaulted in their trial payments.
- Homeowners who previously received a HAMP permanent modification, but defaulted in their payments, and therefore lost good standing.

Additionally, Tier 2 expanded HAMP to include rental properties.

Tier 2 allows for a final debt-to-income ratio of between 25% and 45%, which is achieved by capitalization of arrears, interest rate reduction, reamortization, and principal forbearance.

Under HAMP, foreclosure proceedings are supposed to be suspended while you are engaged in the modification process. If you don't make your payments on the new mortgage during the three-month trial period, the foreclosure can proceed again.

For a general discussion of this program and calculators to help you arrive at key ratios and likely payments if your mortgage is modified, visit www.makinghomeaffordable.com (click "Tools," then "Payment Reduction Estimator").

Incentives for Lenders and Mortgage Servicers

Participating in the mortgage modification program is voluntary for mortgage servicers, though if a mortgage servicer accepted any federal bailout money, its participation is mandatory. Most of the big ones have already indicated their willingness to play along (see the list set out earlier). One reason: The program provides monetary incentives to servicers for keeping people in their homes and to lenders for agreeing to modify mortgages. (The incentives make it less likely that a servicer would make more money by foreclosing than it would by modifying a mortgage to the 31% debt-to-income level.)

The program also includes incentives for mortgage servicers who are able to extinguish second liens (second mortgages, for example) on the property. Getting rid of second liens will make mortgages more affordable, improve loan performance, and help prevent foreclosures. To this end, the government is also offering financial incentives to second mortgage holders to go along with the Making Home Affordable programs.

Starting the Modification Process

Your mortgage servicer is supposed to contact you if you appear to be eligible for the program, though there is no guarantee this will happen. Before contacting your servicer, it's a good idea to talk to a HUD-approved housing counselor about your options. (See "Finding a HUD-Approved Counselor," above.) To request a modification, follow the steps on www.makinghomeaffordable.gov (click "Get Started," then "Request a Modification").

TIP
Don't pay for modification assistance. Under no circumstances should you pay anyone to help you modify your mortgage. According to promotional materials, a bevy of mortgage brokers are being retrained to negotiate mortgage modifications, charging $1,000 and up for the same services you can get for free from a HUD-approved housing counselor. Because some states prohibit people from taking money up front to help rescue people from foreclosures, some modification companies use lawyers—who can accept up-front payments in most states (but with restrictions in California and a few other states)—to pitch their services. Lawyers can be helpful in certain situations—for instance, to challenge a foreclosure in court or to help you file for bankruptcy—but they have no magic keys to the kingdom of mortgage modifications. You and your wallet will be better off with a free HUD-approved housing counselor.

Digging Deeper Into the Making Home Affordable Guidelines

The Making Home Affordable website is designed for homeowners and is therefore written in plain English. However, the government has also prepared a handbook for mortgage servicers that lays out all of the requirements for participation in the various refinancing and modification programs. While this material is harder to read than you might wish, it provides a wealth of detailed information that, if mastered, will help you understand what's going on with your Making Home Affordable refinance or modification and give you a way to monitor whether your servicer is getting it right. To access this handbook, go to www.hmpadmin.com, click "Programs," then "Program Guidance." Make sure you are looking at the most recent release (Version 4.1 at the time of this writing).

Weigh Your Options

Before signing off on any new mortgage terms, ask yourself whether you would be better off holding on to your house or walking away. If you can get a lower payment under the new laws, you may be more inclined to keep your house. But the decision may depend on just how big a reduction you can get and whether your negative equity is so large that it makes more sense to use the foreclosure process as a means to put away some money. In other words, even if you can get your monthly payments reduced by several hundred dollars, you might be better off allowing your house to be foreclosed on—by not paying your mortgage, you could save thousands of dollars during what is often a very slow foreclosure process.

If you decide that it's in your best interest to walk away from your mortgage, but you want to stay in the house as long as possible payment free, the only effect the new laws are likely to have is to lengthen the time you can stay before you have to leave. That's because mortgage lenders must suspend foreclosure proceedings during the processing period (and because they will be busy negotiating modification terms with other homeowners, making them less efficient in bringing foreclosure actions).

Basic Workout Options

If you aren't eligible to benefit from one of the government programs, you still may be able to work something out with your servicer.

Repayment Plan: Keeping Current and Catching Up

With a repayment plan, you arrange to make up missed payments over time and stay current on your ongoing payments. This approach is usually the most feasible and easiest to negotiate with your servicer. For it to work, your income will have to be able to cover both current and makeup payments.

For example, say you are four months behind on your payments of $2,000 a month, for a total of $8,000. Paying an extra $800 a month over the next 11 months would bring you current. Why 11 months, when you could pay back the $8,000 in ten? The eleventh month would account for 10% interest you'd likely be charged on the arrears. The actual numbers might be a little different, but you get the idea.

If you could pay only $2,400 a month (the $2,000 payment plus $400 to make up the arrears), your plan would be for 20 months, plus additional time to pay the interest. You might even get your servicer (or lender) to sign off on an agreement that gives you three or four years to get current.

The longer it will take you to catch up, the likelier it is that your servicer will have to get permission from the lender. If the lender will have to sign off on your proposed plan, and you are running up against your foreclosure sale date, you should definitely ask—in writing—for an extension that the servicer thinks will be sufficient to either work out an arrangement or give you time to fight the foreclosure. Some servicers will tell you right up front whether a proposed plan will work or is off the table. Other servicers will string you along. You'll just have to make sure that you aren't forgoing other possible solutions (such as bankruptcy, a court action challenging the foreclosure, a statutory reinstatement, or redemption of the mortgage), just because the servicer tells you the solution is "in the pipeline."

Be Aware of Deferred Junior Mortgages

If your servicer agrees to a reduction of your mortgage principal and then the value of the house goes back up, the lender will want to be able to get some of its original principal back. To do this, the mortgage industry has come up with a device for recapturing some mortgage principal, called "deferred junior mortgages." These devices commit you to pay them off when you sell or refinance the house. They can't, however, be enforced by foreclosure or a lawsuit.

> **EXAMPLE:** Aura was recently laid off from a job paying $36 an hour and has found a new job paying $28 an hour. In the meantime, the house she bought for $240,000 two years ago has fallen in value to $180,000. To keep her house, Aura will need a substantial reduction in her payments. Because she has a good payment history and a decent credit score, the lender agrees to reduce the principal due on her mortgage to the house's market value ($180,000), which results in the reduced payments Aura needs to stay in the house.
>
> In exchange, Aura agrees to a deferred junior mortgage for $60,000 at 6% interest. Under the terms of this deferred junior mortgage, Aura will not face foreclosure or a lawsuit for failure to pay off the mortgage, but will have to pay it off if she refinances the principal mortgage or sells the house.
>
> Three years later, Aura would like to sell the house. However, a sale will not generate enough cash to cover both the principal mortgage and the deferred junior mortgage, so Aura is stuck with the house until times get better or she gets rid of the deferred junior mortgage by filing for Chapter 7.

Don't Forget: Statutory Reinstatement or Redemption

Many states give you, by law, the right to reinstate your mortgage (make it current) or redeem the loan (refinance the entire loan). (See Ch. 1.) Your state's page in the appendix lists the time limits for the exercise of these procedures if they're available in your state. Typically, you must exercise them before the foreclosure sale date, although some states give you a period of time after the sales date to redeem the mortgage by paying it off in full (plus interest and costs).

If you think either of these options might work for you, pay attention to the deadlines. For example, if your state gives you only 30 days after you receive the notice of default to reinstate the mortgage, don't let negotiations drag on past that date, unless reinstatement is clearly not in the cards.

If you do have the financial ability to reinstate the mortgage, you surely can work something out with the servicer in regard to your missed payments, given enough time. If you need a reduced monthly payment, as well as a means to make up missed payments, reinstatement won't work; instead, you'll need to redeem the mortgage by refinancing it at a lower interest rate.

Forbearance: Getting a Break From Payments

Under a forbearance agreement, the servicer (or lender) agrees to reduce or suspend your mortgage payments for a period of time. In exchange, you promise to start making your full payment at the end of the forbearance period, plus an extra amount to pay down the missed payments. Forbearance is most common when someone is laid off or called to active military duty for a relatively short period of time and cannot make any payments now but will likely be able to catch up soon.

In forbearance, unlike a repayment plan, the lender agrees in advance for you to miss or reduce payments for a period of time. But both forbearance and repayment plans require extra payments down the line to bring the loan current. Forbearance for three to six months is typical; forbearance for longer periods is less so.

Modification: Lowering Your Payments

Unlike repayment plans and forbearance, mortgage modifications are designed to lower your monthly payments over the long term. You might be able to get a modification, but even if your lender is willing to make modifications in the right circumstances, don't be too surprised if your attempt doesn't yield much.

Many homeowners can't come close to making their current payments now or in the future. There are many reasons, including:

- Their income streams were disrupted by layoff or injury and new jobs at the same pay are just not available.
- They were in over their heads from the beginning, because of predatory loan practices or their own misstatements about their income and debt loads.
- Their interest-only loans caused principals to reach preset caps, which in turn dramatically pushed their monthly payments upwards to unaffordable levels.
- Their interest rates reset higher (currently not as big a problem as was originally feared, due to continued low short-term interest rates engineered by the Federal Reserve).
- Something happened in their lives that required them to reprioritize their budgets—for instance, a medical emergency or a child in trouble.

If you can't afford your mortgage payment now or won't be able to in the near future, mortgage modification is the best approach to remaining in your house.

The National Mortgage Settlement

Historically, mortgage servicers have made grievous errors when it comes to managing homeowners' accounts, as well as engaged in harmful loan servicing practices. In fact, over the past few years, state and federal investigations into foreclosure activities have uncovered extensive mortgage servicing misdeeds, including:

- robo-signing (where foreclosure documents were signed by people who had no knowledge about whether the information contained in the documents was correct)
- inaccurately notarized documents
- improper foreclosure procedures, and
- deceptive practices in the loan modification process (such as telling borrowers that a loan modification was imminent while simultaneously foreclosing).

As a result of these investigations, in February 2012, 49 state attorneys general and the federal government reached a historic settlement with five of the nation's largest banks. The settlement holds them accountable for the servicing violations that contributed to the mortgage crisis in this country and provides up to $25 billion in relief to current and former homeowners. It also sets new national standards for loan servicing that are designed to correct the types of conduct that harmed consumers during recent years.

The settlement provides benefits to borrowers whose loans are owned or serviced by the following five major mortgage servicers:

- Ally/GMAC
- Bank of America
- Citi
- JPMorgan Chase, and
- Wells Fargo.

If your loan is serviced by one of the servicers above, but owned by Fannie Mae or Freddie Mac, you are not eligible for benefits under the settlement. Also, borrowers in Oklahoma are not covered since that state elected not to join the settlement.

The National Mortgage Settlement, cont'd.

Here are some of the remedies that you might be entitled to under the settlement:

- Loan modification, for first and second lien loans
- Refinancing. If you are current on payments you're your home is underwater, you are eligible for relief, as long as your current interest rate is above 5.25%, and the refinanced rate would reduce your monthly payment by at least $100 or the interest rate by 0.25%. (The banks are supposed to notify borrowers who qualify for loan modifications and refinancing, but if your loan is serviced by one of the five settling banks, you are encouraged to contact your mortgage servicer directly to find out if you are eligible.)
- Cash payouts for borrowers who lost their homes. Homeowners who lost their homes because they were not properly offered loss mitigation options or were otherwise improperly foreclosed on between January 1, 2008 and December 31, 2011 were eligible to make a claim for a cash payout from a $1.5 billion fund, though the deadline to make a claim passed on January 18, 2013. The exact amount of the payment to be made to each eligible claimant (expected to be mailed mid-year in 2013) is not yet known but, according to the national mortgage settlement website, it will exceed $840.

To learn more about the national mortgage settlement, go to www. nationalmortgagesettlement.com or contact your mortgage servicer.

Here are some of the ways your servicer might modify a mortgage to reduce your payments and perhaps to reduce the outstanding balance of your loan to the value of your home:

- Reduce your mortgage's interest rate to the current market rate, if it's lower than what you're supposed to be paying now.
- Convert from a variable-rate to a fixed-rate mortgage, which could bring the payment down if the interest on the variable-rate mortgage has already reset, and will prevent a jump in payments if the reset looms in the near future.

- Extend the loan's repayment period—for instance, from 30 years to 40. This will bring down the monthly payment but delay for many years the time when you can begin to build equity.
- Reamortize the loan. This involves adding the amount of the missed payments to the principal balance and issuing a new loan at a new interest rate for a new period of time. Reamortization can result in an increased payment (for example, if the interest rate stays the same or increases) or a reduced one (for example, if the interest rate is reduced and the loan period is increased).

Workouts for Government-Backed Mortgages

Special workout options are available to you if your mortgage is:

- owned or guaranteed by the Federal National Mortgage Association (Fannie Mae) or the Federal Home Loan Mortgage Association (Freddie Mac)
- insured by the Federal Housing Administration (FHA), which operates under regulations and guidelines issued by the federal Department of Housing and Urban Development (HUD)
- guaranteed by the Veterans Administration (VA), or
- financed by a direct loan from the Rural Housing Service (RHS).

You should know if one of these agencies has purchased, insured, or guaranteed your mortgage, because you will have been informed in writing. But if you don't remember and don't want to tear your house upside down looking for the paperwork, ask your housing counselor, mortgage servicer, or lender.

If you are working with a HUD-approved housing counselor. You have all the usual workout options plus some additional ones, giving you a much better chance of working something out that the lender will approve of. You can get help and information about these different options from the counselor.

If you are working directly with your mortgage servicer. Your mortgage servicer should give you information about the special options available for your particular type of mortgage, and even distribute any explanatory materials produced by the governmental entity for its customers.

Freddie Mac. If you run into problems with your mortgage servicer when trying to arrange a workout on a mortgage owned or guaranteed by Freddie Mac, call 800-FREDDIE and ask to speak to someone in the loss mitigation department. These are the people who can assess your situation and either explain the rules for servicers of Freddie Mac mortgages or help you arrange a workout.

Fannie Mae. If you encounter problems with your mortgage servicer when trying to arrange a workout on a mortgage owned or guaranteed by Fannie Mae, call the appropriate regional office, listed below.

Fannie Mae Regional Offices		
Midwestern	Illinois, Indiana, Iowa, Michigan, Minnesota, Nebraska, North Dakota, Ohio, South Dakota, Wisconsin	312-368-6200
Northeastern	Connecticut, Delaware, Maine, Massachusetts, New Hampshire, New Jersey, New York, Pennsylvania, Puerto Rico, Rhode Island, Vermont	215-575-1400
Southeastern	Alabama, District of Columbia, Florida, Georgia, Kentucky, Maryland, Mississippi, North Carolina, South Carolina, Tennessee, Virginia, West Virginia	404-398-6000
Southwestern	Arizona, Arkansas, Colorado, Kansas, Louisiana, Missouri, New Mexico, Oklahoma, Texas, Utah	972-773-HOME (4663)
Western	Alaska, California, Guam, Hawaii, Idaho, Montana, Nevada, Oregon, Washington, Wyoming	626-396-5100

FHA-insured loans. If you have an FHA-insured loan, your lender must send you a copy of HUD Publication PA-426, *How to Avoid Foreclosure,* no later than the end of the second month of delinquency on your mortgage payments. This document will outline all of your workout options for loans insured by the FHA.

Rural Housing Service (RHS) loans. If your loan is guaranteed by the RHS, you can call the Centralized Servicing Center (CSC) toll-free phone number at 800-414-1226 or go to www.rurdev.usda.gov, click "Contact Us," then "Housing Programs/Centralized Servicing Center" to learn about workout options.

Fannie Mae and Freddie Mac's Streamlined Modification Initiative

Beginning July 1, 2013, Fannie Mae and Freddie Mac will offer a new, simplified loan modification process (the "Streamlined Modification Initiative") to help troubled borrowers avoid foreclosure and stay in their homes. The key feature of this program is that borrowers do not have to document their hardship or financial situation to receive the streamlined modification, which is different from HAMP and other loan modification programs. Borrowers simply must demonstrate a willingness and ability to pay by making three on-time trial payments, after which the mortgage will be permanently modified.

Under the Streamlined Modification Initiative, mortgage servicers are required to send you a letter offering you a modification if you meet all of the following criteria:

- Your loan is owned or guaranteed by Fannie Mae or Freddie Mac.
- You are 90 days to 24 months delinquent on your mortgage.
- You have a first-lien mortgage that is at least 12 months old.
- Your loan-to-value ratio is equal to or greater than 80%.

Loans that have been previously modified two or more times are ineligible for the program. Second homes and investment properties are eligible to participate.

Although servicers are required to evaluate borrowers for eligibility for this program, you should call your mortgage servicer as early as possible if you are struggling to make your payments so you can be evaluated for the most appropriate alternative to foreclosure. The program is scheduled to end on August 1, 2015.

Foreclosure Avoidance Mediation Programs

In the past few years, many states have implemented mediation programs to assist borrowers in finding ways to avoid foreclosure. Some states, such as Nevada and Connecticut, have instituted statewide foreclosure avoidance mediation programs, while in other states there are certain counties or municipalities that have implemented such programs. The programs vary, but most force the lender to at least discuss non-foreclosure options with you before it can complete the foreclosure. If you participate, you may have a better chance of achieving some type of workout. Or, by participating you may be able to delay the foreclosure.

Mediation, sometimes called a conciliation conference, consists of a meeting between you, your lender, and an impartial third party (the mediator). At the meeting, the parties discuss the borrower's financial situation and try to negotiate a way to keep the home or give up the property without going through a foreclosure. Generally, the foreclosure is postponed while the mediation talks are ongoing and, by working together, the parties are sometimes able to reach an agreement to avoid foreclosure by way of a:

- loan modification
- repayment agreement
- forbearance agreement
- short sale, or
- deed in lieu of foreclosure.

Visit the "Foreclosure" area on www.nolo.com, for articles on state foreclosure mediation programs. Or check *Foreclosures*, by John Rao, et al. (National Consumer Law Center), for more information on state foreclosure avoidance mediation programs.

Special Protections for Service Members on Active Duty

If you're on active military duty, and you took out a mortgage before you went on active duty, you are entitled to a raft of protections against foreclosure. The federal law that provides these benefits is called the Servicemembers Civil Relief Act (SCRA).

Judicial Foreclosure Is Required

Probably the most important protection for families in nonjudicial foreclosure states (see Ch. 2) is that the SCRA requires a court order before your house can be sold in foreclosure. If the lender forecloses without a court order while you are on active duty or within one year thereafter, the sale is invalid. (This protection period will be reduced to the time of active duty service plus 90 days beginning January 1, 2015, unless action is taken by Congress.) Even threats to foreclose without going to court are illegal. Because judicial foreclosures are much more expensive and typically take much longer than nonjudicial foreclosures, you may have a better chance of working something out with the lender.

You can delay (the legal term is "stay") a foreclosure procedure for a period of time, not less than 90 days, so long as you meet certain criteria and if you request it from the court in writing. A HUD-approved foreclosure counselor (or military legal services if you are deployed out of the country) can help you with a letter to the court.

Default Judgments Can Be Reopened

If the lender starts a foreclosure lawsuit and you don't respond to it, the court will order a default judgment against you. But you can reopen the judgment if it is entered while you're on active duty or within 60 days after your active duty ends. You must take action to reopen the judgment within 90 days after your release from active duty.

Interest Rates Must Be Reduced

The interest rate on a mortgage incurred before you entered active duty must be reduced to 6% while you're on active duty and one year thereafter. (The interest rate is also limited to 6% for all other types of obligations, such as car loans and credit cards, while you are on active duty.) Past payments of interest over 6% while you were on active duty must be forgiven (refunded), and the mortgage payment must be reduced to reflect the lower interest rate while it is in force.

To get the interest rate reduction, you must notify the creditor in writing of your duty status and include a copy of the military orders requiring active duty status. You must send this notice no later than 180 days after your active duty status ends. It can be retroactive to the day your active duty started.

> **EXAMPLE:** Susan is a National Guard member. She and her husband sign a mortgage to buy a house at a subprime interest rate of 9%. Their payments are $1,900 a month. Six months later, Susan is called to active duty and deployed to Iraq. Her husband continues paying the mortgage at the required rate while Susan serves in Iraq for 15 months. When she returns home and is released from active duty, she learns from a military counselor that she was entitled to have the mortgage payments reduced while she was on active duty.
>
> She promptly sends a notice to the lender of her entitlement to the 6% interest rate, with a copy of her Iraq deployment orders, and demands that retroactive adjustments be made. She receives a check for $6,000. That's 15 months times $400, the amount her payment would have been lowered had the interest rate reduction been made when she went on active duty.

Lenders can not negatively affect your credit rating for receiving the benefits you're entitled to under the SCRA.

More State Protections

In addition to the federal law, many states have their own statutes that provide additional protections for service members. Your state's page in the appendix lists the citations for your state's law.

How Chapter 13 Bankruptcy Can Delay or Stop Foreclosure

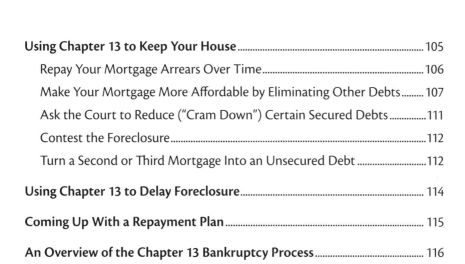

Chapter 13 bankruptcy can help you save your house in a number of different ways. How? It gives you time to make up your missed payments, can make your mortgage more affordable in the long term by reducing your overall debt load, and may allow you to eliminate a second mortgage. It also gives you a friendly forum for challenging the legality of your mortgage and any pending foreclosure. And even if you decide to give up your house, Chapter 13 can help you substantially delay your move-out date.

You get these crucial benefits by proposing to the court a feasible Chapter 13 debt repayment plan that satisfies all the legal requirements. In most cases, a plan will pass muster if it shows enough probable income to meet your regular and necessary living expenses (including your mortgage and payments towards any arrearage that has occurred) and to pay off certain debts, such as back taxes and child support. If you have any money left over, it would go to repaying your unsecured debt such as credit card bills and court judgments. Chapter 13 plan requirements are explained in more detail below.

It won't be easy to stick to a repayment plan for three to five years, but if you can, you'll be well rewarded. All of your remaining unsecured debt will be wiped out—and you won't lose your house.

The benefits of Chapter 13 bankruptcy start the minute you file. That's because filing for bankruptcy immediately stops a foreclosure in its tracks. As soon as you file, the federal bankruptcy court automatically issues what's known as an automatic stay. This is a court order that bars all of your creditors, including mortgage lenders, from making any attempt to collect a debt you owe unless they get court permission. And once the bankruptcy judge approves your repayment plan, you will be safe from foreclosure over the entire plan period, as long as you keep making the required plan payments and your loan payments.

RESOURCE

More information on Chapter 13 bankruptcy. This chapter gives only an overview, to help you determine whether or not Chapter 13 bankruptcy might help you save your house—or at least keep you living in it longer. To learn more about this powerful remedy, see:

- the bankruptcy and foreclosure areas of www.nolo.com
- *The New Bankruptcy: Will It Work for You?* (Nolo), which explains your bankruptcy options, and
- *Chapter 13 Bankruptcy: Keep Your Property & Repay Debts Over Time* (Nolo), a step-by-step guide to filing for Chapter 13 bankruptcy.

Using Chapter 13 to Keep Your House

In a typical Chapter 13 case, the court will protect your property from foreclosure provided that you resume paying your normal monthly mortgage payments and pay back your mortgage arrears within your plan period, which will be between three and five years. In this way, the Chapter 13 bankruptcy allows you to gradually bring your loan current, in small affordable steps. This is what makes your Chapter 13 plan such an important tool for saving your home—when the court approves your plan, the lender is ordered to go along with it.

If you stick to your Chapter 13 repayment plan, you can:

- repay missed mortgage payments (your mortgage arrears) over the life of the repayment plan, three to five years (this essentially forces your lender to accept a mortgage reinstatement plan)
- pay a fraction (or sometimes, nothing) of your unsecured debts during the plan period and probably eliminate these other debts entirely when you complete your plan, freeing up money for you to pay towards your mortgage
- ask the court to reduce ("cram down") certain secured debts to the value of the collateral (for instance, reduce your $20,000 car note to the actual value of the car, say $12,000, reducing your monthly payments)
- contest the legality of your mortgage or a proposed foreclosure, if appropriate
- contest any claims for costs and fees that are added to the missed payments you'll repay as part of your plan (these costs are commonly made erroneously)
- get rid of (strip off) liens on your home created by second and third mortgages, as long as they are wholly unsecured by your

home (that is, if your home were sold the proceeds would be insufficient to pay back any portion of the lien), and

- resume your regular monthly mortgage payments.

Repay Your Mortgage Arrears Over Time

In many ways, your Chapter 13 bankruptcy repayment plan is like a plan you might negotiate with the mortgage servicer. (See Ch. 4.) Either way, you have an opportunity to get your mortgage current over time. Of course, if the only reason you are filing Chapter 13 is to get time to get your mortgage current, and you could get a similar deal from the servicer, you'll be better off not filing for bankruptcy, at least as far as your credit score is concerned. On the other hand, if your mortgage servicer refuses to work with you, then Chapter 13 may be your best option for saving your home.

> **EXAMPLE:** Freddie owes $3,600 in missed mortgage payments. He receives a notice of default that gives him a month to pay up or lose his house. His mortgage servicer refuses to work with him because of a previous notice of default—the lender doesn't think he's a good credit risk.
>
> Freddie had fallen behind on his mortgage because he was laid off, but now he's working again. If he files for Chapter 13 bankruptcy and is able to reduce payments on unsecured debt (like credit cards), he'll be able to afford a repayment plan, under which he will resume normal payments on his mortgage and also make up the arrears over three years. He proposes to pay down the arrears at the rate of $110 a month: $100 for the debt plus $10 a month for the trustee's fee.

Part of the problem in workouts with a mortgage servicer is that servicers typically add on a wide variety of fees and costs, which make it difficult for the homeowner to reinstate the mortgage. In Chapter 13 bankruptcy, you can challenge the validity of these fees and costs on a variety of grounds. (See Ch. 7 for more on challenging claims submitted by mortgage servicers in and out of bankruptcy.)

It's important to understand that unless you challenge the legality of your mortgage in some way, you will be able to keep your house through Chapter 13 only if your plan will enable you to stay current on your mortgage as well as pay off an arrearage over the life of your plan. And you must propose a plan showing not only that you can make plan payments but also that you can keep current on all your other reasonable and necessary monthly expenses, such as utilities, transportation, car note, insurance, and the like. Further—and this is a deal breaker for some would-be Chapter 13 filers—you must pay some types of debts in full during the course of the plan. For example, if you owe recent back taxes, the court won't approve your repayment plan unless it shows that you can pay off the taxes in full while your plan is in effect.

Another issue in some Chapter 13 bankruptcies is that under your plan you must be able to pay your unsecured creditors at least as much as they would have received in a Chapter 7 bankruptcy from a partial liquidation of your property. See the discussion of Chapter 7 bankruptcy in Ch. 6. The good news is that this is not much of a factor for many Chapter 13 bankruptcy filers because they can frequently claim all or most of their property as exempt.

Finally, your plan must provide for a payment to the trustee of roughly 10% of the amount of all payments you make to creditors through the repayment plan.

Make Your Mortgage More Affordable by Eliminating Other Debts

Americans are up to their eyeballs in debt—an average of $43,874 in debt for every man, woman, and child in 2010, according to the Federal Reserve. It's not uncommon for me to see clients of moderate means who owe credit card debt exceeding $50,000. If you are looking to save your house, and Chapter 13 bankruptcy might get the job done, chances are great that you'll also greatly reduce, if not eliminate, your debt load. Chapter 13 gives you three to five years not only to work out your mortgage problems but also to deal with your unsecured debt (debt not secured by collateral) once and for all.

To eliminate credit card and other unsecured debt in Chapter 13 bankruptcy, you must be willing to commit all of your disposable income to repaying all or part of your debt (taking into account that you must also pay down other debts such as mortgage arrears or recent back taxes) over a three- to five-year period. Any unsecured debt that remains at the end of your plan is discharged (canceled), unless it is one of the types of debt that survives bankruptcy, such as child support or student loans.

Disposable income is computed in two entirely different ways, depending on whether your income is above or below your state's median income, and on which judge you end up with. The reason for this uncertainty is that the law regarding disposable income changed radically in October 2005, and the courts are still sorting it all out.

For the vast majority of Chapter 13 bankruptcy filers, disposable income is the income you have left over every month after taxes and other mandatory deductions are subtracted from your wages, you pay necessary living expenses, and you make payments on your car notes and mortgages.

> **EXAMPLE:** Terry's net income, after mandatory deductions such as taxes and insurance, is $4,000 a month. Out of this must come a mortgage payment of $1,500, a car payment of $500, and $1,800 for utilities, food, transportation, insurance, medical prescriptions, and other regular living expenses. The $200 that's left over each month is Terry's disposable income.

If your household income is higher than the median in your state for a household of your size, you must propose a five-year plan. Your household consists of all people who are living as one economic unit, regardless of relationships and age. Usually this means people who are living under one roof, but not always. Someone who is living apart but freely shares income with the rest of your household could still be a member of the household. For example, a person on active duty who isn't living with you except when on leave would be a member of your household.

Your household disposable income will be partially computed on the basis of IRS expense tables that may or may not match your actual expenses. Also, your disposable income will likely be based on what you earned the past six months, not necessarily on what you are earning now. In other words, the court may rule that you have disposable income even when, in fact, you don't. Weird? You bet, and many commentators, including bankruptcy judges, have said so. Nonetheless, this is the result Congress apparently intended in its landmark bankruptcy legislation of 2005.

In *Hamilton v. Lanning*, 130 S. Ct. 2464 (2010), the United States Supreme Court ruled that notwithstanding the relatively clear mandate from Congress, bankruptcy courts can take into consideration changes in income that are "known or virtually certain" to be in place in the future, even if the debtor's income over the previous six months would require higher or lower payments under the proposed Chapter 13 plan. The ramifications of the *Lanning* case are working their way through the lower courts. However, the basic idea is that if you have lost your job but had a good income over the past six months, you may base your proposed plan payments on your actual (and likely future) rather than prior income.

If your household's income is lower than the median income for a similarly sized household in your state, you are entitled to propose a three-year plan. However, you can request that the court approve a five-year plan if you need the extra time to meet your payment obligations. For example, say you must pay unsecured creditors $25,000 under your plan. If your plan lasts for three years, you would have to pay $692 a month (plus certain administrative expenses). With a five-year plan, you would pay only $411 a month.

To determine whether you are a high-income or low-income filer, you first compute the average monthly gross income you received from all sources, taxable or not (except for funds received under the Social Security Act) during the six months that immediately precede the month in which you will be filing for bankruptcy. You then multiply that figure by 12 and compare the result with your state's median income.

EXAMPLE: Justin plans to file for Chapter 13 bankruptcy in June. He lives in California and has four people in his household. He will have to compute his average gross income from all sources (except Social Security) for December of the previous year through May of the current one. It comes out to $6,000 a month. He multiplies this figure by 12 for an annual figure of $72,000. Because the median income for a California family of four is more than $76,000, he qualifies as a low-income filer.

RESOURCE

Get free help online. You can use www.legalconsumer.com to help you make these calculations and comparisons. The median income figures change at least once a year.

It's important to know that you can propose a Chapter 13 plan even if you have very little disposable income to pay down your unsecured debt, and even if you pay off only a small fraction of that debt.

EXAMPLE 1: Rubin owes $36,000 in unsecured debt, consisting of credit cards and personal loans. His income is below the median for his state, and he has $200 disposable income left over each month after paying all his living expenses and monthly contractual debt (a $1,000 mortgage and a $450 car loan). Rubin successfully proposes a plan that will pay his unsecured creditors $200 a month for 36 months. It comes to a total of $7,200, which is 20% of his unsecured debt. The rest will be discharged if he completes the plan.

EXAMPLE 2: Lynn also has $200 of disposable income each month. She has both unsecured debts and $3,000 in missed mortgage payments. In her Chapter 13 repayment plan, a portion of her disposable income will be used to make up some missed payments, and the rest will go to her unsecured debt. For example, if she has a three-year plan, $83 a month would go for the missed payments, and the other $117 would go to repay 12% of the unsecured debts.

Nothing in the bankruptcy law requires a minimum percentage of repayment; it's left up to the judge. Some bankruptcy judges will accept plans that pay even a smaller percentage of unsecured debt than shown in these examples. In fact, some plans have been approved that pay 1% or even less. But some judges won't approve a plan unless it provides for repaying a certain higher minimum percentage of debt.

Ask the Court to Reduce ("Cram Down") Certain Secured Debts

Chapter 13 bankruptcy judges can reduce (cram down) certain secured debts to the market value of the collateral that secures the debt. They can also reduce interest rates to the going rate in bankruptcy cases (roughly 1.5 points above the prime rate). If you can get the judge to reduce your payments on a secured debt, you will have more money to pay towards your mortgage—and a better shot at proposing a Chapter 13 plan that the court will confirm.

EXAMPLE: Allison bought a new car for $24,000, taking a seven-year note for $38,000 (including the principal and interest), with monthly payments of $475. Three years later, when Allison files for Chapter 13 bankruptcy, she still owes $24,000, even though the car's market value has fallen to $14,000.

As part of her Chapter 13 plan, Allison asks that the note be crammed down to $14,000 and that the interest rate on her loan be reduced to 4%, the approximate going rate in bankruptcy cases. The court approves this cramdown, and Allison's monthly car payment is cut roughly in half.

A cramdown is usually available only for:
- cars bought at least 30 months before you file for bankruptcy
- other personal property items (furniture, jewelry, computers) bought at least one year before filing
- rental or vacation homes (but not your primary residence)

- loans on mobile homes that your state classifies as personal property (not real estate), and
- loans secured by your home that you can pay off within five years.

Contest the Foreclosure

You may be able to fight a foreclosure in your state's courts whether or not you file for bankruptcy. But if you file for Chapter 13 bankruptcy, you can ask the bankruptcy court to decide whether the facts upon which a proposed foreclosure is based are erroneous.

For example, suppose you contest the foreclosure on the ground that your mortgage servicer failed to properly credit your payments. A bankruptcy court decision in your favor on this point would eliminate the basis for the foreclosure should you later drop your Chapter 13 case or convert it to a Chapter 7 bankruptcy. Unlike some state courts, the bankruptcy court is a comparatively friendly forum for homeowners challenging foreclosures. (See Ch. 7 for more on the grounds for contesting a foreclosure.)

Turn a Second or Third Mortgage Into an Unsecured Debt

If you're like many homeowners, your home is encumbered with a first mortgage, a second mortgage (often used for the down payment in an 80-20 financing arrangement), and even a third mortgage (maybe in the form of a home equity line of credit). Most likely, the holder of the first mortgage is pushing the foreclosure. But if you have fallen behind on your first mortgage, you are probably behind on your second and third mortgages as well. Would it help you keep your house if you no longer had to pay the second or third mortgage? You know the answer: Reducing your overall mortgage debt load could only help you meet your first mortgage obligation.

One of the great features of Chapter 13 bankruptcy is that in many (but not all) bankruptcy courts you can get rid of (strip off) all mortgages that aren't secured by your home's value. Let's say that you have a first mortgage of $300,000, a second mortgage of $75,000, and $50,000 out on a home equity line of credit. Presumably, the value of your home when you took on these debts was at least equal to the total value of the mortgages, or $425,000. But if the house is now worth less than $300,000, as a practical matter the house no longer secures the second and third mortgages. That is, if the house were sold, there would be nothing left for the second or third mortgage holders.

If your second and third mortgages were considered secured debts, your Chapter 13 plan would have to provide for you to keep current on them. However, when they are stripped off, they are reclassified as unsecured debts. This means you have to repay only a portion of them—just like your other unsecured debts. And as explained earlier, the amount of your disposable income, not the amount of the debt, determines how much of the unsecured debt you must repay.

> **EXAMPLE:** Sean files for Chapter 13 bankruptcy and proposes a three-year plan to make up his missed mortgage payments. He also owes $60,000 in credit card debt and has disposable income of $300 a month. His house's value is $250,000. He owes $275,000 on his first mortgage, $30,000 on the second, and $15,000 on a home equity loan.
>
> Because his house's value has fallen below what he owes on the first mortgage, there is no equity left to secure the second mortgage or home equity loan. So his Chapter 13 plan would classify these two formerly secured debts as unsecured. When they're added to the $60,000 in credit card debt, he's got a grand total of $105,000 unsecured debt. Because all he has is $300 per month in disposable income, his plan would repay a little more than 10% of his unsecured debt—including a little over 10% of his formerly secured second and third mortgage debt.

This also means that under your Chapter 13 plan you won't have to make up payments missed on your second or third mortgages. And because you're no longer making current payments on the second or third mortgage, the total amount you pay each month will be reduced by a considerable amount.

⚠ CAUTION

Find out whether your court will let you get rid of liens.
Although eliminating a lien when there is no equity to secure it is logical
and permitted by many courts, some courts refuse to allow it. They reason
that stripping a lien from a house is tantamount to modifying a residential
mortgage, something that is not allowed by the bankruptcy laws. At some
point, this issue is likely to be resolved by higher federal appellate courts. For
now, if this is a major reason you are considering Chapter 13 bankruptcy, you
need to know how your court would address it. Contact a local experienced
bankruptcy attorney to get that information.

Using Chapter 13 to Delay Foreclosure

Even if you can't realistically expect to keep your house, you don't
necessarily have to give it up right now. Filing for Chapter 13
bankruptcy can buy you more time—probably at least six months—
before the house is sold in foreclosure.

For starters, filing for Chapter 13 will usually bring foreclosure
proceedings to an immediate halt. (Under certain circumstances, if
you have filed for bankruptcy in the past, the stay may not apply.) Your
lender can still ask the court to let it proceed with the foreclosure, but
the judge probably won't consent if there is any chance at all you can
propose a plan to keep your house.

If you propose a feasible repayment plan, you can delay foreclosure
for a minimum of three months, and possibly longer if the judge
approves your plan or at least gives you a chance to amend it. If the
court ultimately refuses to confirm your plan, and you convert to
Chapter 7 bankruptcy, you'll likely have another two or three months
before the foreclosure sale will be allowed to proceed.

I see nothing wrong with filing under Chapter 13 if you are able to
propose a feasible plan, and by filing for bankruptcy you can stay in your
house a while longer. If real estate values come back up and your income
situation improves, you may be able to keep the house after all.

CAUTION
Don't file for bankruptcy unless you can do so in good faith.
Because Chapter 13 provides such an excellent opportunity for hanging up a foreclosure action, it has become a favorite means to that end. Some people file, keep the case alive as long as possible, file again as soon as it's dismissed, and so on. This can land you in big trouble down the line.

Merely filing a case puts the automatic stay into effect, without any review of your filing history by the judge, so it takes a while for the court to spot you as a bad-faith filer. But when it finally does, it can ban you from further filings—and refer you to the U.S. Attorney for a perjury prosecution if you made any significant misstatements in your paperwork.

Coming Up With a Repayment Plan

The heart of a Chapter 13 bankruptcy is your repayment plan. It shows how much income you have to repay your debts, how long the plan will last, and what debts (and what proportion of them) you propose to repay.

As mentioned, there is no set percentage of your debt that you must repay. It all depends on how much disposable income you have available for this purpose. Keep in mind that courts will consider income you receive from roommates, domestic partners, and other members of your household if they are chipping in to help you save your home.

A Chapter 13 repayment plan lasts several years: three if your income is below the median income for your state and five if it is over. (See Ch. 6 for how to determine whether your household income is above or below your state's median.)

Your plan must show that your income (plus proceeds from any property you plan to sell) will let you do all of the following:

- stay current on all your contractual obligations, such as a mortgage and car note (unless you plan to voluntarily give the house or car back to the lender)
- pay off any arrears you owe on these contractual obligations
- meet your normal monthly expenses

- pay off certain priority debts, such as back taxes and child support or alimony, in full over the life of your plan
- devote all of your disposable income to repayment of a percentage of your unsecured debt, such as credit card and personal loan debt
- pay your unsecured creditors at least as much as they would have gotten had you filed for Chapter 7 bankruptcy—that is, the value of your assets that would be sold in a Chapter 7 bankruptcy to pay your creditors (see Ch. 6), and
- pay the bankruptcy trustee (the official who collects the money you pay under your plan and distributes it to your creditors) a fee of about 10% of all payments you make under the plan (this amount can be large or small, depending on whether you pay your current mortgage payments directly to your lender or through the trustee).

Not everyone can propose a plan that the court will approve. For example, a plan must provide for paying priority debts in full. So if you owe $50,000 in back taxes, and your disposable income would pay only $25,000 of the taxes over the life of your plan, the judge will refuse to confirm the plan. (Many of these roadblocks to plan confirmation, however, can be overcome. Be sure to talk to a bankruptcy attorney before you scrap your plan to file for Chapter 13.)

RESOURCE

More information on repayment plans. See www.nolo.com for more on the requirements for Chapter 13 bankruptcy plans.

An Overview of the Chapter 13 Bankruptcy Process

When you file for Chapter 13 bankruptcy, your court papers must disclose what you own (real estate and personal property), your debts, and your financial transactions going back several years. You also will have to show that you've filed income tax returns for the previous four years. Your proposed repayment plan is due 14 days after you file your first papers.

But before you can even file for bankruptcy, you must complete some basic credit counseling. And you'll have to get some personal financial management counseling after you file but before you get your Chapter 13 discharge.

The Creditors' Meeting

About a month after you file for Chapter 13 bankruptcy, you are required to attend a creditors' meeting, conducted by the trustee assigned to your case by the court. At this meeting the trustee will go over your proposed plan and explain how the trustee thinks it should be changed. Your mortgage or auto lender may also send a representative to ask you questions about your plans for the property—and express any objections the lender has to your proposed plan. Plans seldom sail through the first time.

The Confirmation Hearing

About a month after the creditors' meeting, you may be required to attend a confirmation hearing in the bankruptcy court. The confirmation hearing is where the bankruptcy judge decides whether or not to approve your latest proposed plan. If there is a problem with your plan—for example, you don't show enough income to make the mandatory payments—the judge or trustee may shoot it down.

But unless the judge decides that you'll never be able to submit a feasible plan, you may have an opportunity to change it so that it will conform to the judge's view of the federal bankruptcy code requirements. If you are given the chance to amend, another confirmation hearing will be scheduled, usually about 30 days later.

If there are still problems with your case, the court may do one of the following: give you a second chance to fix your amendment; order your case to be dismissed; or allow you convert your case to Chapter 7 bankruptcy. If you do convert your case to Chapter 7 bankruptcy, you might have another two to three months in court even if the lender managed to get court permission to go ahead with the foreclosure before your Chapter 7 discharge. (See Ch. 6.)

The Typical Chapter 13 Timeline	
Day 1	Papers filed to start the bankruptcy
Day 14	Repayment plan must be filed
Day 31	First plan payment must be made
Day 46	Creditors' meeting held
Day 76	Confirmation hearing held
Day 106	Second confirmation hearing held, if necessary

Completing the Plan

It's tough to complete a Chapter 13 repayment plan. That's because a person who files for Chapter 13 bankruptcy is in a fragile economic condition to begin with. All it takes is a layoff, medical emergency, divorce, or simply fatigue at living within a strict budget for so long to cause someone to fall behind on plan payments. In fact, only about one-third of all Chapter 13 bankruptcies are successfully completed.

If your income does drop significantly during the course of your Chapter 13 bankruptcy, you may be able to modify your plan or get a hardship discharge. More likely, however, you will be given the choice of converting your case to a Chapter 7 bankruptcy or having it dismissed entirely. Most people faced with this choice opt to convert to Chapter 7 bankruptcy and discharge what's left of their debts. But you might choose dismissal instead if you have nonexempt property you would be forced to part with in a Chapter 7 bankruptcy (for example, your family grand piano, which the trustee could sell for $5,000).

Just because you might not complete your Chapter 13 bankruptcy doesn't mean you shouldn't start it. If and when you do default, you may be in a better situation to keep your house or at least sell it for a profit. See Using Chapter 13 to Delay Foreclosure, above.

If you do complete your plan and meet the other Chapter 13 requirements (such as giving the trustee an annual financial report and keeping current on your taxes and any child support obligations), you will receive a bankruptcy discharge. It usually cancels whatever nonpriority unsecured debt that has not been paid off in your plan, which not uncommonly is 75% or more of the unsecured debt you started with.

There are a few exceptions to a Chapter 13 discharge, the most common of which are:

- debts you didn't list in your bankruptcy papers
- civil judgments arising from willful or malicious acts
- debts for death or personal injuries arising from drunk driving
- back child support or alimony not paid off as part of your plan
- taxes first due less than three years prior to your bankruptcy filing date, for which a return was filed less than two years before your bankruptcy filing date, and which were assessed within 240 days of your bankruptcy filing date
- debts arising from your fraudulent acts (if proven by the creditor in bankruptcy court), and
- court-imposed fines and restitution.

Relief Under Chapter 13 After a Chapter 7 Discharge

The bankruptcy code prohibits you from receiving a Chapter 13 discharge if your case is filed within four years of the filing of a prior Chapter 7 case (in which a discharge was granted). However, according to most courts that have ruled on this issue, you are entitled to file a Chapter 13 bankruptcy at any time after a Chapter 7 even if you won't qualify for a discharge of your debt.

Why would you want to file a Chapter 13 bankruptcy if you can't discharge debt under it? Simply, many Chapter 7 debtors are left with liens and debts that survive the Chapter 7 bankruptcy, and Chapter 13 provides a structured way to deal with them. Because, by definition, your Chapter 7 bankruptcy has discharged all (or most) of your debt, you don't really need the Chapter 13 discharge. For instance, a number of homeowners who file Chapter 7 are left with second mortgage liens on their home—because liens aren't discharged in Chapter 7 bankruptcy. Chapter 13 would provide a way to pay off such a lien over the life of the plan, or in some instances get rid of it altogether. However, some courts will not allow lien stripping in a Chapter 13 bankruptcy if you are not eligible for a discharge. Check with a local bankruptcy attorney to determine the rule in your jurisdiction.

Another reason: Suppose you come out of Chapter 7 owing a lot of back child support (which is not discharged in Chapter 7). You can file a Chapter 13 and propose a repayment plan that would be considerably more affordable than what you are being offered by the child support enforcement agency. Again, you wouldn't be discharging the child support but rather obtaining protection from the court against unreasonable repayment demands, garnishments, and the like.

Will You Need a Lawyer?

It's hard to handle your own Chapter 13 bankruptcy; you most likely will need an attorney to represent you, especially if you are trying to save your house rather than just to postpone the foreclosure sale. This is because an involuntary dismissal (a greater possibility if you are representing yourself) would greatly set back your plans to keep your house. But if you're not really counting on keeping the house, a dismissal won't surprise or dismay you as much. In any event, you do have the right to represent yourself, and you may have to if you flat out can't afford to pay the stiff attorneys fees. (See Ch. 10 for information on finding, choosing, and working with a lawyer and other helpful resources.)

An Attorney May Be More Affordable Than You Think

If you currently are not paying anything on your mortgage but could afford to pay at least some of it, it might only take you a couple of months to save enough money to pay a lawyer to represent you in Chapter 13 bankruptcy and either challenge the mortgage or delay the foreclosure for many additional months. And the longer you delay the foreclosure, the more cost-effective it is to pay an attorney to help make it happen—because you'll have that many more months to build your savings by not making mortgage payments.

Why You Need a Lawyer in a Chapter 13 Case

- Chapter 13 bankruptcy often requires a lot of negotiating with creditors and the bankruptcy trustee to reach agreement on an acceptable repayment plan.
- Chapter 13 bankruptcy requires at least one appearance in court before the bankruptcy judge (the confirmation hearing) and often several more.
- Chapter 13 cases can have many variables, such as valuation of property, reducing liens to the value of the collateral, creating a plan that doesn't discriminate among debtors, and often, requests for plan modifications or hardship discharges.
- An experienced lawyer can help you understand the specifics of your case, including the types of debts you have and the amount or percentage you must repay.
- Local rules, court procedures, and how judges interpret the law vary by jurisdiction and court. A knowledgeable local bankruptcy attorney will know what's standard in your area.

RELATED TOPIC

How to find a good attorney. Chapter 10 provides tips on how to choose a lawyer.

How Chapter 7 Bankruptcy Can Delay or Stop Foreclosure

Chapter 7 bankruptcy will delay a foreclosure rather than block it permanently. You're more likely to be able to keep your house if you file for Chapter 13 bankruptcy (see Ch. 5). But even if you think you'll need to give up your house sooner or later, Chapter 7 bankruptcy can still be very valuable when you're facing foreclosure.

Filing for Chapter 7 bankruptcy offers different benefits, depending on your situation.

If you want to keep your house and are current on your first mortgage, you can get other debt canceled, freeing up money which may make it easier to pay your first mortgage. If the home's value is less than the first mortgage, then a Chapter 7 bankruptcy can have the practical effect of eliminating (at least temporarily) the need to make payments on a second or third mortgage after your bankruptcy. This is because your bankruptcy will eliminate the debt owed under the second or third mortgage (which means the owners of these debts can't sue you for money) and a foreclosure by the holder of the second or third mortgage will be off the table because, by definition, the proceeds of the foreclosure sale would all go to the first mortgage holder. Of course, if your home sufficiently appreciates in value to substantially exceed the amount you owe on the first mortgage, a second or third mortgage lien may then "come back" and have to be dealt with. See Eliminating Payments on a Second or Third Mortgage, below.

If you decide to give up your house, you may be able to:

- delay foreclosure proceedings for two to four months, and
- get all or most of your debts permanently canceled so that you can have a fresh start after foreclosure.

Bankruptcy is a wonderful way to deal with various debts. Simply put, with a few exceptions, the debts all go away. And that's not all, as they say in the late-night TV ads. Credit card debts, medical bills, and most money judgments arising from lawsuits over breach of contract or negligence go away as well. So if you are up to your neck in these types of debt, bankruptcy is something to seriously consider, whether you want to free up income to pay your mortgage (by eliminating payments on dischargeable debts), or whether you are headed towards a foreclosure and want to get a fresh start.

Of course, Chapter 7 bankruptcy is not for everyone. You have to qualify to file and there are the obvious psychological barriers. And if you have good credit, it will take a hit with bankruptcy. Of course, most people filing for bankruptcy already have bad credit, in which case filing for bankruptcy won't make a huge difference, credit wise.

CAUTION

If you're interested in modifying your mortgage, see a HUD-approved counselor before you file for bankruptcy. If you are seeking a modification of your mortgage principal or payments, or are attempting to refinance your current mortgage either in or out of the government programs described in Ch. 4, talk to a HUD-approved housing counselor before filing bankruptcy. If you're negotiating a HAMP modification, the bank will suspend the process until after you receive your discharge. Under regulations applicable to HAMP modifications, any new mortgage will contain language stating that you cannot be required to reaffirm the old mortgage debt as a condition of obtaining a modification. Also, the servicer cannot deny you a modification just because you were able to discharge the underlying debt in a Chapter 7 bankruptcy. If, however, you don't qualify for a HAMP modification (or a modification under any of the other government programs detailed in Ch. 4), your servicer may reject your modification request due to your bankruptcy under its own non-HAMP policies.

How Chapter 7 Bankruptcy Helps You

Whether or not you plan to give up your house, you can buy some time just by filing for bankruptcy. As soon as you do, foreclosure proceedings must stop—at least for a while. When you file for bankruptcy, the federal bankruptcy court automatically issues a court order called a stay. It bars creditors, including mortgage lenders, from taking any measures to collect a debt you owe unless the creditor seeks permission from the bankruptcy court to proceed, and the court grants permission after notice and a hearing.

The automatic stay immediately stops foreclosures as well as other creditor actions. If, for example, your home is due to be sold at auction on December 5 at 10 a.m., and you file for bankruptcy at 9:59 a.m. that day and notify the lender of the filing, the sale is "stayed" and has no effect even if it goes ahead after you file. But if you file at 10:01 a.m., just one minute after the sale, the sale would go through.

What Happens to Your Property in Chapter 7 Bankruptcy?

When you file Chapter 7, most types of property you own automatically become part of your "bankruptcy estate," under the control of the bankruptcy court. The bankruptcy trustee may have authority to sell some of the bankruptcy estate to pay your creditors. But every state lets you claim some or all of your bankruptcy estate as exempt, meaning you get to keep it.

As a general rule, exemption laws let you keep necessities, such as furniture, clothing, personal effects, tools of the trade, cars, books, TVs, and home computers. You can also usually keep cash or bank deposits up to a certain amount. Finally, you can keep at least some equity in the house where you're living when you file for bankruptcy; this is known as a homestead exemption. In actual practice, very few people lose property to the bankruptcy trustee.

Chapter 7 bankruptcy is what most people think about when they think about bankruptcy. It's called "liquidation" bankruptcy because it cancels your debts, but you might have to let the bankruptcy court liquidate (sell) some of your property for the benefit of your creditors.

Check Out Exemptions for Your State

The specifics of exemptions vary wildly from state to state and depend not only on the type of property involved but the amount of equity you have in it. For example, if your car is worth $20,000 but you owe $20,000 on it, you have no equity and can keep it as long as you are current on the payments. But if you owe nothing on your $20,000 car, you may have to say bye to it. For more information about exemptions in your state, visit nolo.com and in the "Bankruptcy" section choose "Bankruptcy Information for Your State."

You may have to give up other (nonexempt) property to be sold to help pay off your debts. Most people don't have any nonexempt property. But if you own luxury items outright, such as a boat, an RV, a valuable coin collection, corporate securities, an ownership interest in a business, or an expensive car in which you have considerable equity, they might be sold by the bankruptcy trustee to repay some of your debts.

Once the bankruptcy trustee (the person employed by the court to supervise your assets and pay creditors) has paid creditors whatever money is available, your remaining debt is canceled (discharged). There are certain kinds of debts, though, which can't be discharged in bankruptcy (see below).

It takes only about three months for a Chapter 7 bankruptcy case to go through court. After the court grants a Chapter 7 discharge, the party seeking to foreclose on your home is free to take the next step under your state's foreclosure laws.

Common Debts That Don't Go Away in Chapter 7 Bankruptcy

- Student loans (with rare exceptions)
- Recent back taxes (taxes first due less than three years before you file for bankruptcy for which returns were filed at least two years before your filing date)
- Back child support and alimony
- Obligations to an ex-spouse that were created or assumed in a divorce decree or marital settlement agreement
- Criminal fines and penalties (state or federal)
- Liabilities arising from willful and malicious actions such as assault or theft
- Liabilities for personal injury or death arising from drunk driving
- Debts arising from acts the creditor proves were fraudulent (for instance, misstatements on a loan application)
- Traffic tickets
- HOA (homeowners' association) fees that accrue after you file for bankruptcy

Using Chapter 7 Bankruptcy to Keep Your House

You can use Chapter 7 bankruptcy to save your house if both of the following are true:

- You are current on your mortgage payments when you file (or you can get current in a hurry)
- Your equity in the house (if any) is adequately protected by the exemption laws available to you in your state.

If you are not (and can't get) current on your payments, Chapter 7 bankruptcy will be only a temporary remedy. The lender will be able to proceed with a foreclosure within two or three months. You should instead explore Chapter 13 bankruptcy, which provides a way for you to keep your house by spreading out your missed payments over several years. (See Ch. 5.)

Staying Current on Your Payments

Suppose you are current on your payments but expect to fall behind in the very near future for one reason or another. This might be the case if your mortgage interest rate is due to reset higher, you've reached the principal cap on an interest-only loan, or you have just lost some work hours or been laid off.

In these and similar situations, filing for Chapter 7 bankruptcy may be a big help. Except for a few categories of debt, such as those mentioned above, you can eliminate virtually all your unsecured debt in about three months (and you can even stop paying them before you file). That's right, all your credit card debt, personal loans, medical debts, money judgments and car repossession deficiencies go away. Once your unsecured debt load is eliminated or greatly reduced, you will have a much better chance of being able to pay your mortgage.

CAUTION
Once you file, you may not be able to change your mind. For example, if you file for Chapter 7 and then discover that you won't be able to keep your house because it has too much equity, you probably won't be allowed to back out and dismiss your bankruptcy case. This is because your right to dismiss is based on the best interests of your creditors, and if the creditors would receive a distribution from the sale of your house, their interests may require the bankruptcy to go forward.

Protecting Your Equity

In every Chapter 7 case, the bankruptcy trustee is primarily interested in finding property belonging to the debtor that can be sold for the benefit of the creditors. Unless selling the property would produce money for the creditors, the trustee isn't interested in it. The measure of value in property that might benefit creditors is called "equity," and the primary purpose of exemptions is to protect this equity by requiring the trustee to pay you the amount of the exemption if the property is sold. Selling property that's covered by an exemption would benefit you, not your creditors, so the trustee won't sell it—and you'll get to keep it (subject to any outstanding loans against it).

All but two states (New Jersey and Pennsylvania) let you keep at least some home equity when you go through Chapter 7 bankruptcy. Protection for home equity varies dramatically from state to state; you get $500,000 in Massachusetts, $50,000 in New York, and just $5,000 in South Carolina. In 17 states, two exemption lists, one state and one federal, are available. You can pick the one that's most advantageous to you. (If you haven't resided for at least two years in the state where you file for bankruptcy, however, you must use the exemptions for the state where you resided before the beginning of that two-year period.)

If your equity is under the amount that's protected, you should be able to keep your house when you go through Chapter 7 bankruptcy.

> **EXAMPLE:** Stuart and Stephanie have built up $25,000 of equity in their house, and they've managed to stay current on the mortgage payments. But credit card and medical debts (their young son has been ill) have piled up alarmingly, and they're considering bankruptcy.
>
> They live in Maine, which lets them keep $70,000 of equity under the state's homestead exemption. If they filed for bankruptcy, the trustee would not take their house and sell it. That's because after paying off the mortgage, only $25,000 would be left—and that wouldn't be available to creditors because it's within Maine's $70,000 homestead exemption, which means it would have to be paid to Stuart and Stephanie.

If you have a lot of unprotected equity, however, the bankruptcy trustee is going to want to get at it, so that it can go to your creditors.

> **EXAMPLE:** Petra owns a house in New York, which she inherited from her grandfather. The house carries a mortgage of $300,000 but is valued at $500,000, meaning Petra has equity of $200,000. In New York state, you may protect only $50,000 worth of equity

in your house. Petra is in a jam. She can't borrow against her equity because she can't afford to pay down another loan, but she needs the protection of bankruptcy against several creditors who are threatening to sue her. She's managed to keep current on her mortgage payments, but she won't be able to keep that up if her creditors sue her and garnish her wages.

If Petra filed for Chapter 7 bankruptcy, the bankruptcy trustee would sell her house, pay off the mortgage, give Petra her $50,000 exemption and use the rest to pay Petra's creditors and the bankruptcy trustee. If there were anything left over after that, Petra would get that as well. If this is not the result Petra wants—and it probably isn't—she should not file for Chapter 7 bankruptcy.

RESOURCE

How much home equity can you keep? If you have home equity and you want to find out how much your state protects or what other property is protected under your state's exemption laws, visit Nolo.com and in the "Bankruptcy" section choose "Bankruptcy Information for Your State."

Eliminating Payments on a Second or Third Mortgage

As property values fall, second and third mortgages are frequently left unsecured. In other words, the property no longer has sufficient value to guarantee their payment.

EXAMPLE: Henry bought his house for $450,000 with a first mortgage of $400,000. The house quickly grew in value to $500,000, and Henry got a $40,000 loan, secured by the new equity. A year later, his house's value has sunk to $375,000. Now Henry's first mortgage is only partially secured, because if the house were sold now at its current value, the loan couldn't be repaid from the proceeds. The second mortgage is completely unsecured.

If you find yourself in this situation, and you are current (or can get current) on your first mortgage, you can probably keep your house and at the same time use Chapter 7 bankruptcy to eliminate the amount you owe on the second or third mortgage. This is because the bankruptcy would discharge your obligation on the promissory note. However, the liens placed on your property by the mortgage holders would remain after your bankruptcy. Even so, the liens could not, as a practical matter, be enforced unless you tried to sell the house or the house got valuable enough to make foreclosure worthwhile.

A little background may help you better understand this point. Whenever you take out a mortgage or deed of trust, two legal claims are created:

- a claim for the debt (created by a promissory note) that can be enforced by a lawsuit, and
- a lien on the property itself, which uses the property as security for the debt.

As mentioned, a bankruptcy discharge will eliminate the debt created by the promissory note, but not the lien that the mortgage or deed of trust creates on the house.

In Henry's case, the second mortgage lender is in a difficult position if Henry stops making payments on the second mortgage. The lender technically has the right to foreclose, but that wouldn't make financial sense, because a foreclosure sale wouldn't produce enough money to pay off even the first mortgage lien—and so wouldn't generate anything at all for the second mortgage lender. (The first mortgage, used to buy the house, always has priority over later ones.) As a practical matter, all the second mortgage lender can do is to sue Henry on the promissory note ($40,000), which Henry continues to owe. But if Henry files for Chapter 7 bankruptcy, he can permanently discharge his obligation under the promissory note. The lender may be left with a worthless lien on Henry's house that would be unenforceable as a practical and economic matter unless the house's value surged back up.

This is a very hard concept to understand, and if your head is swimming, you're not alone. Perhaps another example will clear it up. If you have a second or third mortgage on your house, it's worthwhile staying with this.

EXAMPLE: Three years ago, Paula borrowed $250,000 from a local bank to buy her first house, which cost $260,000. She borrowed $10,000 from her parents for her down payment. The bank loan is secured by a first mortgage on the house, while the loan from Paula's parents is a personal loan; it wasn't accompanied by a security agreement pledging the house as collateral.

Over the next two years, the value of Paula's house increased to $350,000. She took out a $35,000 home equity loan to remodel her kitchen and landscape her backyard. As with the first mortgage, the home equity loan was secured by the house. At this point, Paula still had $55,000 equity in her home ($350,000 minus the $260,000 mortgage and the $35,000 the home equity loan). If Paula had stopped paying on the home equity loan, the lender could have foreclosed; the sale probably would have produced enough money to pay off the first mortgage and the $35,000 home equity loan. Any money left over would have been returned to Paula.

But over the last few months, the value of Paula's house has sunk from $350,000 to $225,000. Paula has lost her job and can't keep making payments on the home equity loan. The home equity loan lender sends her messages threatening foreclosure, but a HUD-approved housing counselor tells Paula that a foreclosure action is highly unlikely because the lender would get nothing from the sale—every penny from the foreclosure sale would go toward paying off the first mortgage.

After a while, the home equity lender sues Paula to recover the amount of the loan. Paula files for Chapter 7 bankruptcy and gets a discharge of all her debts, including the unsecured loan from her parents and the debts owed on her first mortgage and the home equity loan. The lawsuit filed by the home equity lender against Paula is dismissed. However, the bankruptcy doesn't affect the liens that the mortgage lender and home equity loan lender have on Paula's home. Just as before the bankruptcy, as long as the value of the house isn't enough to pay any portion of the home equity loan if the house were sold at a foreclosure sale, foreclosure by that lender is out of the question.

Years later, property values shoot up again, and Paula's house is worth about $300,000. The home equity lender moves to foreclose on the property because there is now enough equity to pay off both the first mortgage ($250,000) and the $35,000 home equity loan.

TIP

In some states, the lender might be barred from filing both a foreclosure and a lawsuit for the balance due. Some jurisdictions, like California, have a "one-action" rule. Such rules bar a lender from switching to a foreclosure if it has already filed a lawsuit to collect on the loan.

Using Chapter 7 Bankruptcy to Delay a Foreclosure Sale

The instant you file for bankruptcy, all foreclosure proceedings must cease. This means that if you file for bankruptcy at 11:59 am, a foreclosure sale at 12:00 pm would be void. Because of this instant relief, many people turn to bankruptcy as a last resort when their efforts to work something out with their lender have failed to materialize. As mentioned, a Chapter 7 bankruptcy filing will give you two or three months of relief before the foreclosure can proceed again, but it's definitely not a permanent fix.

As a general rule, I recommend against filing Chapter 7 bankruptcy if you have little or no debt that would be discharged and your only reason for filing is to buy some extra time in your house. You won't be able to get another Chapter 7 discharge for eight years, so why waste it just to get a little extra time? (I know, I know, it's easy for me to say this.) However, if you are facing foreclosure, you also probably have some serious debt issues. If your Chapter 7 would eliminate that debt as well as buy you some more time in your home, the equation changes and Chapter 7 bankruptcy becomes a valid option.

Don't file for bankruptcy if your main reason is to buy some time for a short sale. (A short sale is one that yields less than you owe on the house.) There is not much reason for the short sale if you have to file for bankruptcy to get it done, because a big reason to do a short sale is to come out of the situation with marginally better credit than with a bankruptcy. (See Ch. 8 for more on short sales.)

How Much Time You'll Get

A Chapter 7 bankruptcy takes about three months (sometimes a few weeks more) from the date of filing to the date of discharge (cancellation) of your debts. Unless the judge gives the lender permission, no foreclosure sale can take place during that time.

The lender can, however, file a formal request (motion) asking the bankruptcy court to lift the automatic stay and let the foreclosure sale proceed. Lenders usually must provide at least 25 days' advance notice of the hearing on their motion unless they get the judge's permission to shorten that time. Generally, the lender must hire a lawyer to file the motion, so it is a relatively expensive procedure. For this reason, some lenders skip the expense, let the bankruptcy proceed and simply reschedule the foreclosure sale once it's complete. This leaves your three- to four-month delay intact.

A lender who does think it's worthwhile to ask the court to let the foreclosure go ahead usually files a motion 30 to 45 days after you file. A court hearing on the request will be scheduled about 25 to 30 days later. The court will likely grant the motion to lift the stay unless you can show that any of the following apply:

- The proposed foreclosure is illegal in some way.
- The lender hasn't complied with state procedural requirements (see Ch. 7).
- The party bringing the foreclosure hasn't produced the necessary paperwork or evidence to show it has authority to seek the foreclosure.

If the court lifts the stay, the lender will then be free to resume the foreclosure process. If the court refuses to lift the stay, then the foreclosure will be stalled until you receive your bankruptcy discharge.

If you have been doing the math, you'll see that even if the stay is lifted, it makes little difference. Instead of a three- to four-month delay, you'll have a two-and-a-half- to three-month delay. From the lender's standpoint, it's rarely worth it.

After the discharge (or after the court lifts the stay), the lender can proceed with the foreclosure. Unlike Chapter 13 bankruptcy, Chapter 7 doesn't force the lender to let you make up your missed payments over time or preserve your right to keep ownership of your house.

The Husband and Wife Double-Down

If you are married, you can buy a few extra months if each of you files separately, one after the other. For example, assume Justin and Zoe own a house with no equity and Justin loses his job. They immediately stop making their mortgage payments. Justin files for Chapter 7 bankruptcy four months later, shortly before the property is due to be sold. When he receives his bankruptcy discharge, Zoe files her Chapter 7 case, which lasts another three months. (See Ch. 9 for more on how to stay in your home payment free and build a nest egg for the future.)

Timing Your Filing

Sometimes you don't have the luxury of deciding when to file for Chapter 7 bankruptcy. If your wages are about to be garnished, you'll most likely file as soon as possible. However, if there's no emergency, it sometimes helps to wait until your filing has the best possible effect on delaying your foreclosure sale.

For example, if you are in California, which has a 90-day notice of default period before a foreclosure sale can be scheduled, you will get more delay out of filing just before the 90-day period has expired than if you filed earlier. That's because filing for bankruptcy doesn't stop the 90-day notice period from running; it delays only the actual sale date. So if you file just before the sale can be scheduled, you can put off the sale for months. But if you file during the early part of the notice period, all or part of your bankruptcy will be pending while the notice period is running, and the bankruptcy will have little or no delaying effect during that period.

EXAMPLE: Fred receives a notice that his house will be sold in a foreclosure auction in 120 days. He files for Chapter 7 bankruptcy 15 days later and receives his discharge 90 days after that. Fifteen days later, the foreclosure auction proceeds on schedule. Fred is unhappy because his bankruptcy had no effect on the foreclosure timing; it didn't prevent the 120-day notice period from winding down. Had Fred waited a bit and filed his bankruptcy shortly before the scheduled auction date, the auction would have been delayed until he received his discharge 90 days later, or the foreclosing party obtained permission from the judge to reschedule the auction.

Keeping the Money You Saved Before Filing for Bankruptcy

If you're sure you'll be giving up your house sooner or later, it makes excellent financial sense to keep living in it and give it up later. If you are current on your mortgage when you make this decision, you'll likely be able to save at least three or four months' worth of mortgage payments before foreclosure proceedings even begin. And depending on how long you have before the actual sale, you will probably be able to save at least several more months' worth of mortgage payments. (More on this in Ch. 9.)

If you would like to file for Chapter 7 bankruptcy and delay the foreclosure sale even further, you should first figure out whether you'll be able to keep what you've saved before you file, or whether you'll have to give it up to be used by the trustee to pay down your unsecured debt. This issue doesn't arise for any money you save after you file your Chapter 7 bankruptcy; it applies only to what you have in the piggy bank on the day you file.

You can keep your savings through the bankruptcy process if you can claim it as exempt. Every state has its own rules about how much money is exempt from creditors—in other words, how much you are allowed to keep when you go through bankruptcy. And there is a separate set of federal exemption rules; in states that allow it, you may pick whichever system works best for you.

For example, in California, under the exemption system that just about everybody uses when there is no home equity to protect, you can protect roughly $23,000 worth of any type of property, including cash in a bank account. You can also keep such commonly owned items as household furnishings, motor vehicles, tools of the trade, and personal effects. So, if you have $10,000 in the bank, you could keep that $10,000 and still have an additional $12,000 worth of protection for other property that isn't already specifically exempted.

To find out how much money you are allowed to keep when filing for Chapter 7 bankruptcy, check your state's page in the appendix.

It may be that the exemptions available to you in your state won't let you keep the cash you've saved as well as all your other property. In that case, you'll have to pick and choose what property you keep and what you give up. For example, if you have $50,000 worth of home equity, and your state makes you choose between the home equity and your savings account, you may have to give up the savings account. In the end, the only way to know for sure how much property (and cash in the bank) you can keep in a Chapter 7 bankruptcy is to apply the exemptions that are available to you and see how it comes out. You can do this by looking up the exemptions for your state at www.legalconsumer.com.

> **EXAMPLE 1:** Jon lives in California. He has no home equity. He has not been paying his $2,500 mortgage for seven months before he files for bankruptcy to stave off a scheduled foreclosure sale and has put $2,000 a month in a bank account, giving him savings of $14,000. In addition to hand-me-down furniture and normal personal effects, Jon's only other property is a classic 1967 Chevrolet Camaro Rally Sport, in perfect shape, easily worth $20,000.
>
> In one of the two available exemption systems in California, Jon is entitled to exempt $4,800 worth of motor vehicle equity and $25,340 of any other type of property (the wild card exemption). Jon wants to hold on to his Camaro but will have to use $15,200 of the wild card exemption to supplement the $4,800 motor vehicle exemption to fully exempt it. That leaves him $10,140 from the wild card exemption. Because there is no specific exemption for a bank saving account (as

there is for a motor vehicle, for example), Jon will be able to exempt only $10,140 of his savings. He'll have to give up the rest ($3,860) as nonexempt property, to be used by the bankruptcy trustee to pay down his unsecured debt. If he is eligible to make retirement plan contributions, he might be able to exempt his cash that way.

EXAMPLE 2: Amy lives in Massachusetts in a house she inherited. She has home equity of $200,000, but she doesn't have enough income to borrow against her equity and she has a lot of credit card debts to deal with. Bankruptcy seems like the best way out. Amy checks nolo.com and learns that the Massachusetts homestead exemption fully protects her equity. Unfortunately, the Massachusetts exemption system provides very little protection for savings, so if Amy has saved money before filing for bankruptcy, she'll have to give it up (unless she can legally deposit it into a retirement account).

If Amy had no home equity she needed to protect, she could use the federal exemptions (an alternative system to the Massachusetts state exemptions) to protect her savings, because they provide $12,725 protection for any type of property (including a bank account) for single filers and $25,450 for joint filers.

The Chapter 7 Bankruptcy Process: An Overview

Chapter 7 bankruptcy is a very straightforward process. It typically consists of six steps:

Step 1: Before filing, complete a mandatory credit-counseling course by phone or online.

Step 2: File the official bankruptcy forms (fillable forms are available online) listing all your property and creditors and providing information about your financial transactions during the previous two years.

Step 3: Mail the bankruptcy trustee, who handles the case for the court, a copy of your most recently filed income tax return, plus any other documents the trustee asks for.

Step 4: About 30 days after you file, attend a creditors' meeting, usually the only personal appearance you'll have to make. The creditors' meeting occurs in a small hearing room and is conducted by the trustee. Creditors seldom appear. At this meeting, you are required to answer (under oath) any questions the trustee has about the information in your papers, or provide other information the trustee thinks is relevant. A typical meeting lasts five minutes or less. You are not required to have a lawyer represent you at this meeting—you will have to answer the trustee's questions directly, whether or not you have a lawyer with you.

Step 5: No later than 60 days after the creditors' meeting, you must attend mandatory budget counseling (by phone or online) and file a simple form telling the court that you have completed it along with a certificate of completion from the counseling agency.

Step 6: Remain in a holding pattern (don't operate a business with inventory or sell or give away any property without the trustee's permission) until the court sends you a written discharge of your debts. That will come about 60 to 75 days after the creditors' meeting. During that period, creditors can, but seldom do, object to your getting rid of a debt. The trustee arranges for you to turn over nonexempt property, if you have any, but most people who file for Chapter 7 bankruptcy don't have any nonexempt assets.

The Chapter 7 Bankruptcy Timeline	
Before you file	Mandatory credit counseling
Filing date	Papers filed to start the bankruptcy
About a month after you file	Creditors' meeting held
Up to 60 days after the creditors' meeting	Mandatory budget counseling
60 days after the creditors' meeting	Court sends written discharge of your debts

Do You Qualify for Chapter 7 Bankruptcy?

When radical changes in the bankruptcy law were implemented in 2005, a new urban legend was born to the effect that almost no one could file for Chapter 7 bankruptcy anymore. Not true. In fact, pretty much anybody who could file before 2005 can file now.

To qualify for Chapter 7 bankruptcy, you must pass either the income test or the means test. Here is how they work.

The Six-Month Gross Income Test

You may qualify for Chapter 7 bankruptcy if your annual gross household income (12 times your average monthly gross income in the six-month period prior to the month in which you file for bankruptcy) is below the annual median household income for your state.

A household is defined by most courts as all members of an economic unit; that is, an arrangement where income and expenses are shared for the benefit of all. For example, domestic partners and their children are one economic unit, as are groups of people living together as "families." Roommates, on the other hand, are typically not considered an economic unit, assuming they handle their income and expenses separately and only share the rent. Similarly, arrangements in which a debtor lives with his or her parents, but the income and expenses are not shared, are not considered economic units. A few courts reject the economic unit definition of "household" and instead look to the tax rules. In these courts, if a member of the household is not a dependent of the bankruptcy debtor for tax purposes, he or she would not be considered part of the household.

To see whether or not you qualify under this income test, add up all your gross income for your household for the six calendar months immediately preceding the current month. Then multiply the total by two.

Figuring Your Gross Income

Total household income for last six calendar months $_____

×   _____ 2

Average annual income   = $_____

Then compare this figure to the median household income for your state. You can find the most current figures (they change at least once a year, sometimes more) on the website of the U.S. Trustee at www.justice.gov/ust (choose "Means Testing Information" and then click on the appropriate date range under "Data Required for Completing Form 22A and 22C").

If you pass the means test, you are halfway there. You also have to provide information about your current income and living expenses (called Schedules I and J). You should be fine if your current living expenses are reasonable, necessary, and use up virtually all of your monthly income. If you have more income per month than you really need for living expenses, the trustee might seek to dismiss your case.

> **EXAMPLE:** Preston and Megan live in Kansas with their three children. In September they examine their gross income from all sources (which includes bonuses, commissions, overtime, and even lottery winnings) for the months March through August. Their total income for that period is $36,600. They multiply that figure by two to arrive at an annual figure of $73,200.
>
> They find that Kansas has a median annual household income of $76,402 for a family of four. They add the additional allowance of $8,100 for the fifth member of their household to arrive at a figure of $84,502. Their annual gross household income is less than the Kansas median annual household income, which means they pass the income test and can file for Chapter 7 bankruptcy.

TIP

If you wait, you may qualify later. If your income is higher than the median income for your state based on your gross income for the previous six months, but your income has recently gone down, you might consider waiting for another month or two to file. The delay may render your income for the new six-month period low enough to produce an average below your state's median.

The Means Test

If your household income is above the median for your state and household size, you may still be able to file for Chapter 7 bankruptcy if you pass what's called the means test. You'll have to show that your expenses and allowable deductions leave you with inadequate funds to repay a substantial portion of your unsecured debts. (An unsecured debt is a debt that isn't attached to particular collateral—for example, credit card debt.)

You can take the means test for free at www.legalconsumer.com by entering some basic information about your income and expenses. If you pass, you can file for Chapter 7 bankruptcy. If you don't pass, that means the court may consider you to have enough money to pay back at least some of your debts, perhaps by filing for Chapter 13 bankruptcy. But check with a bankruptcy lawyer first. Many experienced bankruptcy lawyers know strategies that might help you pass the means test, legally.

The Actual Income and Expenses Test

Even if you pass the income or means test, some bankruptcy courts will require you to file for Chapter 13 bankruptcy rather than Chapter 7 bankruptcy if, looking forward, your actual income will exceed your actual expenses by more than about $200 a month. This determination is based on the income and expense schedules that must be filed with every bankruptcy.

Will You Need a Lawyer?

Will you need a lawyer to represent you in Chapter 7 bankruptcy? Opinions on this differ. Surprised? Don't be. Put any two lawyers in a room, and ask them the same question. You will probably get four different answers.

Those who feel you can go it alone point to the fact that for the vast majority of filers, there's no court appearance (although you will have to appear at the meeting of creditors) and no legal advocacy is needed.

If you do decide to represent yourself, be aware that the legal system holds you to the same legal standards as those expected from a licensed attorney. You are responsible for knowing and correctly following the laws and for completing your paperwork properly. When you appear at the meeting of creditors, the trustee will not provide you with legal advice or help. Instead, the trustee will scrutinize your case looking for assets to take and/or reasons to have it disallowed.

If you file under the wrong chapter or make other mistakes, you will bear the consequences. For some mistakes, you may need to amend your papers and attend one or more extra creditor meetings. But other mistakes can be much more costly. For example, the trustee or your creditors may ask the court to deny your bankruptcy or you might lose assets or other valuable legal rights.

A good lawyer can help you successfully navigate the bankruptcy system. In addition, your attorney can advise you on how to keep your home or, if you must give it up, how to stay there longer. If you think you might want to represent yourself, first get a good do-it-yourself book and read it carefully, so you know what you are taking on (Ch.10 has some recommendations). It may also make sense to meet with a bankruptcy attorney (many will provide an initial consultation for free), to see if your case has any tricky issues and to find out how much representation would cost.

Fighting Foreclosure in Court

I f you're in a state that requires foreclosures to go through court (see Chapter 2 and the appendix to find out if you live in a judicial foreclosure state), you'll have the right to present your objections to the foreclosure to a judge for review. If you're in a non-judicial foreclosure state, you'll have to file an action in court against the foreclosing party (or file bankruptcy) to have a judge review the foreclosure. And, at least in California, you may not be able to obtain judicial review from a state court judge if you don't have some evidence already in hand that something is wrong with the foreclosure or mortgage (in other words you can't go to court in order to discover wrongdoing). See "State Courts May Refuse to Review Nonjudicial Foreclosures" below.

In judicial foreclosure states, you may have a decent shot at delaying or stopping a foreclosure, even if you don't file for bankruptcy, in any of the following situations:

- The foreclosing party brought the foreclosure based on false information (for example, your payments were credited to the wrong party and you were never behind, or the lender substantially overstated the amount you had to pay to reinstate your mortgage, depriving you of your reinstatement rights under state law).
- You can prove that the foreclosing party didn't follow state procedural requirements for bringing a foreclosure (for example, by failing to properly serve on you a notice of default required by state law).
- The foreclosing party isn't legally entitled to bring a foreclosure action (for example, state law says that only the actual holder of the promissory note can foreclose on the mortgage and the foreclosing party does not meet that description).
- The person signing the affidavits in support of the foreclosure did not have personal knowledge of the information in the documents (in other words, the person signing the affidavits was a robo-signer).
- The notary public attesting to the validity of a signature in the documents did not follow regulations governing notarization.

- Mortgage Electronic Registration Systems (MERS) is involved in the property's chain of title and your state's recording or assignment laws were violated as a result.
- The original lender or mortgage originator engaged in unfair lending practices through fraudulent behavior or by violating a state or federal law with regard to certain mortgage provisions or disclosures to borrowers.

RESOURCE
More on going to court. For detailed information on the approaches to fighting foreclosure in court that are covered briefly here, get *Foreclosure Defenses: Non-Bankruptcy & Bankruptcy Remedies*, by Craig Triance and Richard West (The King Bankruptcy Practice Series).

As you'll see, to successfully fight a foreclosure in court you will probably need to hire an attorney to represent you. The foreclosing party will have an attorney, and trying to do battle with an attorney in court when you aren't one yourself can be an exercise in futility. If you absolutely have to represent yourself, though, there are resources that can help you, and they're discussed in Ch. 10.

You Can Sue for Money, Too

A number of state and federal laws also give you the right to sue violators for compensation for your monetary losses. But the violations don't mean you can stop the foreclosure itself. The reason? Mortgages have become investment vehicles, and for the system to work, investors must be able to rely on the legitimacy of their investments. If all bad behavior by a mortgage broker, servicer, or lender could retroactively be used to devalue an investment, investors would never invest.

For instance, say that a mortgage broker recklessly encouraged you to sign up for a mortgage you couldn't afford, telling you that you could refinance in a year or two and make the mortgage more affordable then.

You Can Sue for Money, Too (continued)

You might think that a court would make things right by denying the foreclosure and ordering the lender to rewrite your loan to make it affordable. Unfortunately, this sort of relief is usually not available. However, if you can cast doubt on the legality of your mortgage or the foreclosure proceedings, you may have the leverage against your lender you need to negotiate a reduction in the amount of principal you owe under your mortgage. See "The Lender Didn't Follow State Foreclosure Procedures or Mortgage Terms Governing Foreclosures" and "The Foreclosing Party Can't Prove It Owns the Mortgage," below.

The legal doctrine of "promissory estoppel" is another tool borrowers are using to seek monetary damages from banks that broke their promises to homeowners. Under promissory estoppel, someone who makes a promise is prevented (estopped) from reneging on that promise if the person to whom the promise was made reasonably relied on the promise by taking some action (or failing to take action) and suffered monetary damages as a result.

In a pending class action lawsuit, the named plaintiff claimed that her lender promised her a permanent mortgage modification if she completed a trial period during which she made modified payments to the bank. The plaintiff made the payments required during the trial period, but the bank refused to give her the permanent modification as promised. The homeowner complained that she had reasonably relied on the bank's promise, made the payments, and suffered money damages (the amount of the modified payments, which she would not have made without the bank's promise of a permanent modification) when the bank reneged on its promise.

In another case, a homeowner decided to forgo filing for Chapter 13 bankruptcy to prevent foreclosure in reliance on her bank's promise to "work with her" to reinstate her mortgage. The bank failed to deliver on its promise and instead foreclosed on the house. The trial court tossed out the lawsuit for money damages, but the court of appeals reversed, holding that the lawsuit should be allowed to go forward under the doctrine of promissory estoppel. (*Aceves v. U.S. Bank*, 192 Cal. App. 4th 218 (2011).)

How Long Can You Delay the Sale of Your House?

As you might expect, contesting a foreclosure in a judicial foreclosure state is very different than doing so in a nonjudicial foreclosure state. (If you don't know which kind you're likely to come up against, see Ch. 2 or your state's page in the appendix.) And the amount of delay you're likely to get depends on the procedure, too.

Judicial Foreclosures

In judicial foreclosures, just filing an answer to the foreclosure petition or complaint might give you several additional months. This is because once you contest the case, you're entitled to your day in court. So the court will set a date for a hearing at which the judge will hear your argument about why the foreclosure should not go forward.

It's impossible to generalize how long it will take to get your hearing; some states and courts are faster than others. But it's likely to take anywhere from two to six months. And the first hearing may not be the end of it. If you have solid evidence of wrongdoing by the foreclosing party, you may be able to force a type of trial at which you and the foreclosing party will be expected to produce witnesses that the judge can question and that the parties can cross-examine.

If you don't respond and let the case go by default, you are looking at a month at the most before the court issues a foreclosure judgment. In most states, the judge then orders a sale to be held. In Connecticut or Vermont, however, the judge can transfer title then and there, without a sale.

Nonjudicial Foreclosures

In nonjudicial foreclosure states, the only way to raise a defense to the foreclosure (other than filing for Chapter 13 bankruptcy) is to file an action in state court seeking a court order (temporary injunction) holding up the sale until you have gotten a chance to argue your case. In most states you must post a bond (a kind of insurance policy) to protect the owner from financial losses during the delay caused by the case. This requirement alone can be expensive and might defeat the purpose of your bringing the case if your primary goal is to buy some extra time to live in your house payment free.

Also, if you must hire a lawyer for this court process, your costs will be considerable—maybe several thousand dollars. Your case may be dismissed just a month or two after you file it, meaning you will have spent a lot of money for very little delay. Of course, if you have a good shot at saving your house, the risk may be worth it.

> TIP
> **Delaying foreclosure with a foreclosure mediation program.** If your state or county has an official foreclosure avoidance mediation program, by participating you may be able to delay the foreclosure and force the lender to discuss loss mitigation options with you. You can learn more about these programs in Ch. 4.

When It May Be Worth Fighting

If it's clear that the foreclosing party failed to follow the law and that as a result, you were deprived of an important right, it may be worth it to go to court and contest the foreclosure. After all, if you could get the foreclosure lawsuit dismissed or significantly delayed, you may be able to stay in your house much longer than you would otherwise. And that, of course, could have significant financial and emotional benefits. (See Ch. 9.)

Often, however, you can't really tell whether a foreclosure is illegal unless you have access to internal bank documents. You most likely won't be able to access these documents unless you file a lawsuit and seek production of the documents in what are called "discovery" proceedings, such as depositions, interrogatories, and motions to produce documents. At least one California case has precluded this strategy, ruling that courts in California should not intervene in foreclosure proceedings unless there is actual evidence of wrongdoing prior to the filing of a lawsuit. See "State Courts May Refuse to Review Nonjudicial Foreclosures," below.

Other Strategies for Fighting Foreclosure

This section lists the most common circumstances in which you may want to contest a foreclosure in court. But there are others. Over the years, attorneys have come up with a panoply of theories to contest foreclosures, drawing on the common law—law fashioned in cases decided by our courts. None of these theories are widely used; however, it's possible that one might be useful in your case.

For example, you might be able to block foreclosure by arguing that your loan terms are unconscionable—that is, so unfair that they shock the conscience of the judge. In one case, for example, the borrower spoke very little English, was pressured to agree to a loan that he obviously couldn't repay, was not represented by an attorney, and was unaware of the harsh terms attached to the loan (such as an unaffordable balloon payment).

Check *Foreclosures*, by John Rao, Odette Williamson, Tara Twomey, Geoff Walsh, Andrew G. Pizor, Diane E. Thompson, Margot Saunders, and John W. Van Alst (National Consumer Law Center), for more information on these common law defenses.

You're on Active Duty in the Military

If you're on active military duty, you have some special protections under the Servicemembers Civil Relief Act (SCRA). Foreclosure on a mortgage you took out before you were on active duty must be a judicial foreclosure, no matter what the custom is in your state. You can waive this requirement, but the waiver must be in writing and be executed while you are on active duty or afterwards. The right to a judicial foreclosure can't be waived beforehand.

If a foreclosure is begun against you while you're on active duty, you can stay (postpone) the action for a period of not less than 90 days by requesting it from the court in writing. (See Ch. 4 for more detail on these rules.)

The Lender Didn't Follow State Foreclosure Procedures or Mortgage Terms Governing Foreclosures

Because every foreclosure means that someone loses a home, many courts require the foreclosing party to strictly follow state law and respect the terms of the mortgage or deed of trust. If they don't, you can call them on it.

But if the foreclosing party makes a trivial violation of the rules, the judge will probably let it go. Virtually all judges overlook errors that are inconsequential, such as the misspelling of a name. And the statutes of some states specifically provide that certain procedural errors (often failure to provide required notices) will not affect the right of the foreclosing party to obtain the foreclosure.

Similarly, if the foreclosing party's error doesn't actually cause you any harm, it's probably not worth fighting over. Most courts will overlook a violation that is technical in nature and doesn't deprive you of a fair procedure, on the principle of "no harm, no foul." For example, say the lender failed to record the notice of default in the local land records office (a typical requirement) on time, but you got your required notice on time. The court might well decide that the failure to record didn't harm you and allow the foreclosure to proceed.

More serious violations will get a more serious response from the court. For example, if the lender failed to send you a notice of default as required by state law, the lender might have to start over, because the lack of adequate notice deprived you of valuable time to resolve the problem. (You might have negotiated with the lender, gotten refinancing, or taken advantage of state rules permitting reinstatement or redemption of the mortgage.)

Typical Foreclosure Requirements

In most states, the foreclosing party must take one or more of the following steps, depending on the state and the type of foreclosure (judicial or nonjudicial). If the lender missed a step, you may able to contest the foreclosure. Typically, in a nonjudicial foreclosure, the lender must:

- mail you a notice of default, telling you how much time you have to reinstate the mortgage
- record the notice of default in the local land records office
- mail you a notice telling you the date the property will be sold, and
- mail you a notice telling you how long you have to redeem your mortgage (by paying it off).

In a judicial foreclosure, the lender typically must:

- mail you a notice telling you that foreclosure proceedings will soon be started in court
- serve you with a copy of the complaint to foreclose, and/or
- publish notice of the intended foreclosure sale in a local newspaper for a particular number of weeks before the sale.

All of these notices have time limits and specific content requirements. For instance, a notice might have to describe the property, the amount due on the mortgage, the amount necessary to reinstate the mortgage including costs and interest, and information on the person you can contact to discuss the notice. (See Ch. 2 and your state's page in the appendix.)

The Foreclosing Party Can't Prove It Owns the Mortgage

A mortgage (or a deed of trust) consists of two basic parts: (1) a promissory note setting out the terms of the loan, and (2) a security agreement making the real estate collateral for the loan and setting out the terms under which a foreclosure may occur in case of a default. In federal courts and some state courts, only the holder, or owner, of the original promissory note—or a valid written assignment of the note—may initiate and prosecute foreclosure proceedings.

If your mortgage, like many, has traveled across the world and been owned by many different entities, proving just who owns the promissory note can be difficult for the last holder in the chain of title. Because mortgages are frequently bought and sold electronically, the only proof of ownership is a chain of assignments from one owner to the next. These assignments might never have been put down on paper, but rather kept in computer databases. The original promissory note that you signed is stored somewhere, but it can be difficult for a foreclosing party to actually come up with it, or even a copy of it.

Some attorneys representing homeowners have been successful in delaying or derailing foreclosures brought in federal court on the ground that ownership has not been satisfactorily established. The legal theory involves a concept called "standing"—that is, who has the right to bring a lawsuit in the federal court. To have standing to sue about a contract, you must have an ownership interest in the contract and have suffered some loss. In several recent cases in federal courts, the foreclosing parties were unable to establish these facts, and so the courts dismissed the foreclosure complaints.

Because these cases were decided in federal court, there is currently no good information on what type of proof of ownership would be acceptable in state courts, which frequently have different rules about standing to sue. For example, in Ohio and many other states, the Uniform Commercial Code (UCC) gives a long list of persons connected with a loan the right to sue to enforce its terms. In those states, it may be hard to get a foreclosure thrown out by arguing that the wrong party brought it. On the other hand, the Massachusetts Supreme Judicial Court affirmed a lower court's invalidation of a foreclosure sale where the lender was unable to prove that it was the owner of the mortgage at the time of the foreclosure. (*U.S. Bank Nat. Ass'n v. Ibanez*, 458 Mass. 637, 941 N.E.2d 40 (Mass., 2011).) This case has resonated with the courts of some other states, such as Michigan, with similar laws governing foreclosure and mortgages.

What Is MERS?

Generally, each time a mortgage is sold from one bank to another, an assignment (which is a document showing that the mortgage has been transferred) is prepared and recorded in the county land records. The assignment transfers all of the interest the original lender had under the mortgage to the new bank. Mortgage Electronic Registration System, Inc. (MERS) is a company that was created by the mortgage banking industry in the mid-1990s to simplify this process. MERS is not a lender, a servicer, or an investor. Rather, it is essentially a large electronic database of mortgages and mortgage transactions. Mortgage documents typically refer to MERS as the "mortgagee of record" and "nominee," or agent for the purpose of making future transfers to other entities.

Like a lot of what has transpired in the mortgage industry, it's hard to get a handle on how MERS works and what exactly is wrong with it. Fortunately, cogent testimony offered by Christopher Peterson, Professor of Law at the University of Utah, before the House Judiciary Committee casts much light on the subject. (You can find a transcript of Peterson's testimony at http://judiciary.house.gov/hearings/pdf/Peterson101202.pdf.)

MERS is what fostered the real estate boom by supposedly facilitating the electronic transfer of mortgage ownership among banks and investors. Mortgages of various risk levels were packaged in a variety of forms, such as real estate trusts, securitized mortgage bonds, and other miscellaneous financial derivatives, and these transactions were supposedly recorded in the MERS database.

Most of the financial entities dealing with mortgages were and are members of MERS. Under the MERS rules, they were also agents authorized to effect transfers, or assignments, to other members. These transfers were usually not recorded in county land records offices, because (according to MERS) MERS remained the mortgage holder of record (or the beneficiary on a deed of trust) acting as nominee for the lender. Basically, MERS acts as a stand-in for the loan holder, tracking mortgages as they are transferred, thereby eliminating the need to record every assignment with county clerks. Thus, not only does MERS facilitate transfers of real estate interests, it saves the real estate and banking industries millions if not billions of dollars in local fees by eliminating all those transactions that would otherwise have to be recorded, at an average pop of

What Is MERS? continued

$35 per transaction. Avoiding the need to record (and avoiding these recording fees) was a major reason for creating MERS in the first place.

Some counties even have pending lawsuits against MERS claiming they are out millions of dollars in recording fees that the company helps banks avoid. However, whether or not these suits will succeed is uncertain because there have already been several instances where MERS obtained dismissals of similar suits when courts decided that the laws in those jurisdictions did not require MERS to record assignments.

Additionally, several courts have rejected borrowers' challenges to MERS' role as a nominee. For example, the Ninth Circuit Court of Appeals recently affirmed an order dismissing claims against MERS pertaining to its assignment of a mortgage to a foreclosing lender. The District Court held, and the Court of Appeals affirmed, that MERS as a nominee had authority to act (including assigning its rights in the mortgage), was a legitimate organization, and that the mortgage the borrowers signed put them on notice of MERS' role in home loan transactions. Similar decisions have been reached in other districts as well.

MERS' status as a nominee for the lender has also led to considerable litigation over whether or not it has standing to initiate a foreclosure in its name as the plaintiff in a judicial foreclosure or as a beneficiary in nonjudicial foreclosure proceedings. For example, the Maine Supreme Court held in 2010 that since MERS does not own the promissory note, it lacks standing to begin foreclosure proceedings in that state (*Mortgage Electronic Registration Systems, Inc. v Saunders*, 2 A.2d 289 (Maine 2010)). The Supreme Court of Minnesota, on the other hand, decided in the case of *Jackson v. Mortgage Electronic Registration Systems, Inc.*, 770 N.W.2d 487 (Minn. 2009) that MERS does have standing to foreclose.

As a result of this type of litigation, MERS instituted a significant policy change in 2011, prohibiting all members from conducting foreclosures in its name. Consequently, there shouldn't be any more new MERS foreclosures, even in states that previously allowed them. However, there are still some foreclosure proceedings pending throughout the county that were initiated in MERS' name prior to the 2011 rule change.

If MERS shows up in your foreclosure case, you will want to be familiar with cases involving MERS. See Ch. 10 for more information on doing your own legal research.

Cases about the ownership of mortgages and promissory notes and the legality of foreclosure proceedings can be difficult to file and argue, and you may not get very far if you do it on your own. On the other hand, some federal courts are friendlier to self-represented people than are state courts, and Nolo has an excellent book on representing yourself under the federal rules of civil procedure. See *Represent Yourself in Court*, by Paul Bergman and Sara Berman (Nolo).

State or Federal Court?

Most judicial foreclosure lawsuits are brought in state court. But in the last couple of years, foreclosing parties have started to use the federal courts to avoid the delays and inefficiencies of state courts. Any action that can be brought in state court can also be brought in federal court if the parties in the case are from different states (you're in Missouri and the foreclosing party is based in New York, for example) and the amount in controversy exceeds $75,000. Federal courts may be faster (which is not what you want if it means you'll lose your house quicker), but they may also be less forgiving of procedural errors by the foreclosing party than are state courts, which will work to your advantage.

The Mortgage Servicer Made a Serious Mistake

Mortgage servicers make mistakes all the time when they're dealing with borrowers. A study done by law professor Katherine M. Porter showed that in 1,700 Chapter 13 bankruptcy cases, a majority of the claims submitted by mortgage owners had serious errors. (*Misbehavior and Mistake in Bankruptcy Mortgage Claims*, Texas Law Review 2008.) You may be able to fight your foreclosure based on this kind of mistake—for example, because the mortgage servicer imposed excessive fees or told you that you owed more than you really did.

What to Look For

Many errors occur when a lender or mortgage servicer tells you how much you must pay to reinstate or redeem your mortgage. Many states let you reinstate a mortgage within a certain period of time by getting current on your mortgage payments, including costs, attorneys' fees, and interest. And even if a state doesn't specifically provide a period in which you can reinstate the loan, the mortgage documents may themselves allow it. (See Ch. 2 and your state's page in the appendix.)

In either case, when you receive notice of an impending foreclosure and are told how much you would need to pay to reinstate the mortgage, the amounts must be reasonably accurate and must be justified by language in the mortgage documents. For example, your lender can't require you to pay a fee for a monthly reappraisal or inspection of the property if the mortgage documents don't provide for it, if you were current on your payments when the inspection was made, or if the overall number of inspections or the inspection fee itself is obviously unreasonable. You could properly contest the foreclosure on the ground that the notice you received deprived you of the right to reinstate your mortgage because of the excessive fees.

> **EXAMPLE:** Henry receives a statutory notice of default that tells him he'll have to make up three missed payments and pay costs of $2,000. The costs include $800 for a reappraisal of the property and $1,200 for six drive-by property inspections at $200 a pop. While he could make up the missed payments, he can't afford the costs so he doesn't reinstate the mortgage within the time allowed in the notice. The lender starts a foreclosure lawsuit.
>
> A mortgage broker advises Henry that the reappraisal and inspection fees are a rip-off, so Henry contests the foreclosure on the basis that the notice of default was faulty. The court agrees and delays the foreclosure for a month to give Henry time to reinstate the mortgage without paying the inflated fees. If Henry doesn't reinstate on time, the foreclosure will go forward.

Determining whether or not your mortgage agreement allows a particular cost or procedure requires careful reading of the document. The fact is, mortgages are often almost undecipherable—you need an expert to make sense of them. The biggest area of contention is the amount the lender charges the homeowner for attorneys fees paid by the lender for work on the default notice and foreclosure documents. As a general rule, such charges must be reasonable, though some state laws specifically limit the amount of attorneys' fees that can be charges in a foreclosure.

If the mortgage has been bought by Freddie Mac, Fannie Mae, or the FHA, there are limits on what attorneys can charge for services related to mortgage defaults or foreclosures. Limits also apply to fees charged by mortgage servicers. If the fees exceed these limits, and reinstatement of the mortgage is conditioned on payment of the fees, the result depends on the kind of foreclosure proceeding:

- **In a judicial foreclosure,** the judge could dismiss the foreclosure proceedings and either reinstate the mortgage or require the lender to start over. Or, in some states, the judge could delay the foreclosure, giving you more time to reinstate.
- **In a nonjudicial foreclosure,** a violation of attorneys' fee limits may be the basis for you to ask the court for an order (injunction) halting the foreclosure proceedings.

In addition to errant attorneys' fees, the most common errors that may have been made by your mortgage servicer—and that may lead a court to stop a foreclosure—are:

- misapplying your mortgage payments to the wrong account
- buying insurance on the property and billing you for it even though you already carried (and were current on) the insurance required by your mortgage agreement
- failing to pay your property tax, resulting in your owing fines to the government, even though you were paying into an escrow account and the servicer was responsible for paying the taxes
- charging you late fees and property inspection fees even though you were current on your mortgage payments, and
- engaging in coercive collection practices and falsely claiming that certain amounts are due.

How to Get Information About Errors

The more information you can wrest from your mortgage servicer, the better. A federal law called the Real Estate Settlement Procedures

Act (RESPA) provides a way for you to challenge common kinds of errors such as improper charges, improper calculation of interest, or the failure to credit payments properly. It also gives you a way to get the information you need to make such a challenge.

Your first step is to send the servicer what's known under RESPA as a qualified written request identifying the borrower and the account and the information you're after. A sample is shown below.

Within 20 business days of receiving the qualified written request, the servicer must provide you with written acknowledgement that your request was received.

Within 60 business days, the servicer must provide the information you requested or explain why it is not available, plus give you the name and contact information of someone you can follow up with. Effective January 10, 2014, these time frames will be shortened. Pursuant to the Dodd-Frank Wall Street Reform and Consumer Protection Act, a mortgage servicer must acknowledge receipt of a qualified written request within five days and respond within 30 days. The 30-day period may be extended for an additional 15 days if the servicer notifies the borrower within the 30-day period of the extension and the reasons for delay in responding.

While this process is going on, the servicer cannot report to a credit bureau as overdue any payment relating to your qualified written request. However, foreclosure proceedings may continue (if you are requesting this information after the foreclosure has begun).

If the servicer you are requesting information from has transferred your account to another servicer, your qualified written request must be sent no later than a year after the transfer.

If the servicer fails to comply with the act, you can sue and ask for statutory damages of $2,000 (this amount was increased from $1,000 by the Dodd-Frank Act), reimbursement for your attorneys' fees, and compensation for your other losses. However, none of these remedies will help you stop the foreclosure. On the other hand, knowing that these remedies exist may help prod the servicer into giving you the information you've asked for.

Sample Qualified Written Request

Elmer Budd

401 North State Street

Frisco, TX XXXXX

December 2, 20xx

VIA CERTIFIED MAIL

A & B Mortgages

1111 Black Lane

San Rafael, CA 95555

Attn: A & B Mortgages Loan Accounting Department

Re: Countrywide # 0987654

Dear Sir or Madam:

A & B Mortgages is the servicer of my mortgage loan at the above address. I dispute the amount that you claim I owe. I am making this qualified written request under the Real Estate Settlement and Procedures Act, asking that you send me detailed information about how you have handled my loan.

Specifically, I request:

- a complete payment history, including but not limited to the dates and amounts of all the payments I have made on the loan to date
- a breakdown of the amount of claimed arrears or delinquencies
- an explanation of how the amount you claim I owe (on the monthly billing statement) was calculated and why this amount was increased to $5,600 on November 6, 20xx
- the payment dates, purpose of payment, and recipient of any and all foreclosure fees and costs that have been charged to my account

Sample Qualified Written Request (continued)

- the payment dates, purpose of payment, and recipient of all escrow items charged to my account since January 20xx, the date A & B Mortgages took over the servicing
- a breakdown of the current escrow charge showing how it is calculated and the reasons for any increase within the last 24 months, and
- a copy of any annual escrow statements and notices of a shortage, deficiency, or surplus sent to me within the last three (3) years.

Thank you for taking the time to acknowledge and answer this request as required by the Real Estate Settlement and Procedures Act (Section 2605(e)).

Very truly yours,

Elmer Budd

Elmer Budd

The Independent Foreclosure Review

In response to the foreclosure crisis of the late 2000s when loan servicing errors were common and egregious, the Office of the Comptroller of the Currency (OCC), the Office of Thrift Supervision (OTS), and the Board of Governors of the Federal Reserve System (FRB) required certain mortgage servicers to hire independent consultants to review foreclosures that were initiated, pending, or completed during 2009 or 2010.

The "Independent Foreclosure Review," which began in 2011, allowed eligible borrowers to request a review of a foreclosure on a primary residence that was in progress at any time in 2009 or 2010 if they believed they suffered financial injury as a result of errors. Under the program, if an independent consultant found errors, then the servicers would be required to financially compensate the borrower or otherwise remedy any mistakes.

However, fewer borrowers than anticipated requested reviews, plus the reviews took considerably longer and were much more costly than expected. Consequently, in January 2013, 13 mortgage servicers and federal bank regulators reached an agreement that ended the Independent Foreclosure Review for those servicers participating in the settlement. (The participating servicers are Aurora, Bank of America, Citibank, Goldman Sachs, HSBC, JPMorgan Chase, Morgan Stanley, MetLife Bank, PNC, Sovereign, SunTrust, U.S. Bank, and Wells Fargo and their affiliates. At the time of writing, the Independent Foreclosure Review process continues for Ally, Everbank, and OneWest.) The terms of the settlement include an estimated $3.6 billion in direct cash compensation to nearly 4.2 million eligible borrowers and $5.7 billion in additional mortgage assistance, such as loan modifications and forgiveness of deficiency judgments.

For borrowers whose mortgages were serviced by 11 of the 13 settling servicers (all except Goldman Sachs and Morgan Stanley), payments ranging from $300 to $125,000 began on April 12, 2013, with more than 90% of the total payments to borrowers at those 11 servicers scheduled to be sent by the end of the month. The remaining checks, which require additional borrower information, should go out in mid-2013. (At the time of writing, information about payments to borrowers whose mortgages were serviced by Goldman Sachs and Morgan Stanley had not been announced.)

The Independent Foreclosure Review, continued

In most cases, borrowers will receive a letter with an enclosed check sent by the paying agent—Rust Consulting, Inc. Initial reports indicated that some of the checks distributed by Rust bounced due to unavailable funds, but regulators say the problems that led to some checks being rejected have been resolved.

If you have questions, call the toll-free Independent Foreclosure Review number at 888-952-9105. You can also go to the Office of the Comptroller of the Currency's website, www.occ.treas.gov (click on "Independent Foreclosure Review") or the Federal Reserve's website, www.federalreserve.gov (click on "What You Need to Know: Independent Foreclosure Review") for more information on the settlement.

The Lender Engaged in Unfair Lending Practices

You may be able to fight your foreclosure by proving one or more violations of federal or state laws designed to protect you against illegal lending practices.

Two federal laws protect against unfair lending practices associated with residential mortgages and loans: the Truth in Lending Act (TILA) and the Home Ownership and Equity Protection Act (HOEPA). Both allow you to sue for money damages, including a refund of any financing costs you paid. Both of them also let you cancel your mortgage under some circumstances. Canceling the mortgage would usually work to defeat the foreclosure, if you could arrange for a refinance to return the remaining loan principal to the lender.

As powerful as these statutes may sound, most lenders are aware of them and either comply with their requirements or structure their loans so that they don't apply. Still, your case may be the exception.

The Right to Rescind the Loan

For the purpose of fighting a foreclosure, the most important provision of these laws is that you may, for some types of loans and some types of violations, be able to retroactively cancel or rescind your loan. This is referred to as the right to an extended rescission.

Both laws require a lender to give you a three-day rescission period when you take out the loan. But your right to rescind is extended for three years if it later comes to light that the lender violated an important part of the law. Even better, the three-year period is itself extended in the event of a foreclosure. So, if one or both of these laws cover the mortgage being foreclosed on, and you can show a material violation of these laws, you can cancel the loan and by doing that defeat the foreclosure. But those are a couple of big "ifs." Let's take them one at a time.

What Loans Are Covered

The right to extended rescission applies only if you did *not* use the mortgage loan to buy or build your primary residence. So a first mortgage, which you used to buy your house, is not covered. But a home equity loan, equity line of credit, or refinancing loan would be covered. (The law is aimed at predatory lenders who use loans to skim the equity from borrowers' homes, particularly those of older, minority, and low-income homeowners.)

But lenders of second or third mortgages rarely foreclose—so the right to rescind is unlikely to help you with foreclosure. It might, however, help you if you refinanced your first mortgage and the holder of the new mortgage is foreclosing.

HOEPA applies only to (1) loans that are closed-end consumer credit—that is, loans that are repayable under specific repayment terms over a specified term, and (2) loans that fall into at least one of the following two categories:

- The loan is a high-cost mortgage that has an annual percentage rate (APR) that is at least 10% above the rate for U.S. Treasury securities of a comparable term. For example, if the yield on a 15-year Treasury bond is 6%, an APR of 16% on a 15-year loan will qualify. For first-mortgage loans made after October 1, 2002, the loan's APR must be at least 8% above the Treasury rate. The APR trigger for junior liens remains at 10%.
- The loan has up-front fees and charges (including broker fees and, as of October 1, 2002, premiums and other charges for credit insurance) that are at least 8% of the loan amount or about $625 (this amount changes annually with the Consumer Price Index), whichever is greater.

Upcoming Changes to HOEPA

Starting on January 10, 2014, pursuant to the Dodd Frank Wall Street Reform and Consumer Protection Act, the coverage of HOEPA will expand. Under rules promulgated by the Consumer Financial Protection Bureau, most types of mortgage loans secured by consumers' principal dwellings, including purchase-money mortgages, refinances, closed-end home equity loans, and open-end credit plans (home equity lines of credit or HELOCs) are potentially subject to HOEPA coverage.

Also, the APR threshold triggering HOEPA's coverage for a first-lien mortgage will be lowered to 6.5 percentage points over the applicable average prime offer rate, down from 8 percentage points. Likewise, the total points and fees threshold for loans greater than $20,000 will be lowered to 5% of the transaction amount, down from 8%. And, for subordinate or junior mortgages, a transaction is a high-cost mortgage if the transaction's APR exceeds the applicable average prime offer rate by more than 8.5 percentage points.

Additional new restrictions for HOEPA loans include prohibitions on balloon payment features (subject to some exceptions), prepayment penalties, and the financing of points and fees.

What Is a Material Violation of TILA and HOEPA

To be able to rescind your loan, you must also show that the lender materially violated the law—in plain English, that it violated a significant provision of the law.

Material violations of TILA. Lenders violate this law when they don't make the disclosures it requires, including the annual percentage rate, the finance charge, the amount financed, the total payments, the payment schedule, and more. Typically, these terms are found in a document called a truth in lending disclosure statement. The numbers on this disclosure statement must be accurate to within very narrow tolerances. Depending on the type of loan, the disclosed annual percentage rate (APR) must be within one-eighth of one percentage point of the actual APR. The total finance charge cannot be understated by more than $100 in most cases and by not more than $35 if the creditor has started foreclosure proceedings.

Material violations of HOEPA. The violations must be something that deprived you of the benefits of HOEPA. A lender that makes a HOEPA loan must comply with various notice provisions. The lender is also prohibited from including certain mortgage terms, such as balloon payments in loans with terms of less than five years, negative amortization, and making loans requiring more than two payments to be paid in advance from the loan proceeds.

Who Can Be Held Responsible for TILA and HOEPA Violations

TILA and HOEPA apply not only to the original lender or mortgage originator, but also to any person or entity who became an owner through an assignment. In other words, downstream mortgage holders are held accountable for the sins of the original lenders. Downstream mortgage holders can escape liability only if they can demonstrate that a reasonable person exercising ordinary due diligence could not have determined that the loan was covered by HOEPA.

How to Rescind a Loan

To rescind a loan, you must give the lender (not the mortgage servicer) a written notice of rescission. If the rescission is successful, the lender must return everything you paid except for payments of loan principal, and you must return the portion of the loan principal that has not yet been repaid. In other words, when you rescind a loan, you can get out from under the loan (and the foreclosure), but you can't keep the loan proceeds. You'll need to refinance to repay the principal.

RESOURCE

More information on TILA and HOEPA. Any attorney you hire to fight your foreclosure should be intimately familiar with TILA and HOEPA and know how those laws may help you in fighting your foreclosure. If you are representing yourself, I recommend that you buy a copy of *Foreclosures*, by John Rao, Odette Williamson, Tara Twomey, Geoff Walsh, Andrew G. Pizor, Diane E. Thompson, Margot Saunders, and John W. Van Alst, published by the National Consumer Law Center (www.nclc.org).

You Have a High-Cost Mortgage

A number of states have special protections for people facing foreclosure on high-cost mortgages. (For specifics, see Ch. 2.)

If your state has a high-cost mortgage statute, and the lender has violated any of its provisions, you might be able to raise that violation as a defense in your foreclosure case. If your state has a high-cost mortgage statute, there's a brief summary on your state's page in the appendix, including any provisions that might help you fight your foreclosure.

How to Fight a Foreclosure

How hard it is to fight a foreclosure depends to a great extent on where you live. If your state requires the foreclosing party to sue you (this is called judicial foreclosure), then it's easier (and less expensive) to jump into the existing lawsuit. If, in your state, foreclosures proceed without court supervision (nonjudicial foreclosure), then you'll have to bring your own lawsuit—a more worky and costly process, especially in California. (To see which procedure is followed in your state, check the list in Ch. 2 or your state's page in the appendix.)

If You're in a Judicial Foreclosure State

In these states, the foreclosing party must bring a lawsuit to get the foreclosure started. You will be notified of the foreclosure lawsuit when papers called a summons and complaint are delivered to (served on) you. The papers will advise you of the lawsuit and give you a period of time within which you must respond if you choose to contest it.

And, significantly, the foreclosing party will have the burden of proving to the judge that the foreclosure is justified under the terms of the mortgage.

Whether or not you respond is up to you. Either way, the mortgage holder will be required to prove that the foreclosure is legal (although if you don't respond, the chances are excellent that the foreclosure will go through). The proof will typically consist of a thick bundle of documents purportedly containing various papers that you signed when obtaining or refinancing your mortgage. There will also be notices, signed agreements, internal accountings of payments both made and missed, and written statements under oath (called declarations or, if sworn before a notary public, affidavits) from lender and mortgage servicer officials who claim to have knowledge of:

- your missed payments
- the lender's compliance with your state's laws regarding foreclosure procedures, and
- the circumstances through which your lender came to own the mortgage.

As a general rule, if you don't point out errors or omissions in the paperwork, the court will accept the papers as evidence that will support a foreclosure judgment and order for sale.

If you do respond, you will have the opportunity to tell a judge just why you think the papers are wrong and that foreclosure is not warranted. To contest the foreclosure, you can file a very simple form, called an "answer" in most places. In it, you state your factual and legal arguments for opposing the foreclosure.

If you have evidence of your own regarding these issues, you also can file your own sworn statements. For example, if the lender claims that you missed five payments, but you can prove (typically with canceled checks) that you missed only one, you would submit a statement under oath to that effect and attach your canceled checks.

The court will set a date for a hearing, at which the judge will hear arguments on the paperwork submitted by both sides. After the hearing, the judge may:

- make a decision based solely on the paperwork
- postpone the hearing for a month or two to give the parties time to gather more information (for example, if the paperwork filed by the foreclosing party doesn't show authorization to bring the foreclosure lawsuit, the judge may continue the hearing for a month so that the foreclosing party can bring in additional documentation), or

Were the Affidavits in Your Foreclosure Case Robo-signed?

As part of the foreclosure process in the 25 or so states that require judicial foreclosures, the plaintiff must prove that it owns the mortgage in question and that the defendant defaulted on that mortgage. Typically, the lender proves these two things by submitting documents and a written statement signed under oath (called an affidavit) by a person (usually a bank employee) who has reviewed the documents and who has some personal basis for believing the facts in those documents to be true. The idea is to prevent foreclosures on homes where the foreclosing bank cannot prove that it actually owns the mortgage (which is more common than you might think) or where the homeowner is not actually in default to the degree asserted in the foreclosure papers.

In 2010, it came to light that several large banks routinely used affidavits signed by employees who did not personally review the documents and who had no basis for believing that the homeowner was in default or that the bank owned the loan. Financial giants like Bank of America, Chase, Wells Fargo, and GMAC had hired foreclosure mills to carry out their foreclosures. Employees of those foreclosure mills have testified that they signed many thousands of affidavits a month, spending about 30 seconds on each affidavit, and that they didn't have a clue regarding the veracity of the affidavit or the documents in question—hence the name "robo-signers."

Foreclosures are not legal if the paperwork isn't in order. This means that if the affidavit submitted in support of a foreclosure is false—and any affidavit completed by a robo-signer is false by definition—the foreclosure is invalid. Of course, the reality is that banks previously foreclosed on thousands of properties based on false affidavits. But once the issue of robo-signing came to light, many banks imposed a moratorium on foreclosures while they reviewed hundreds of thousands of cases for potential paperwork errors and to adjust their internal procedures to fix the problem.

Were the Affidavits in Your Foreclosure Case Robo-signed?, continued

In addition, some states have passed laws that impose severe penalties for robo-signing. For example:

- California law imposes a civil penalty up to $7,500 per loan on lenders or servicers that record or file multiple, unverified documents.
- In Nevada, a bank must record a signed affidavit containing certain information regarding the loan as part of the foreclosure otherwise it is subject to damages ($5,000 or treble actual damages) and criminal penalties.

Plus, Lender Processing Services Inc. (LPS), a company at the heart of the robo-signing debacle, recently reached a $127 million multistate settlement to resolve claims of improper foreclosure practices, including robo-signing. During the foreclosure crisis, LPS and its subsidiaries allegedly executed thousands of documents that may have had defects such as unauthorized signatures, improper notarizations, and inaccurate information. The settlement, which involves 46 states and the District of Columbia, requires LPS to review and correct faulty foreclosure documents that were executed between 2008 and 2010 and imposes significant reforms against robo-signing practices by the company.

As a result of all this, there are far fewer instances of robo-signed documents being used in support of foreclosures today, though this is not to say that it never occurs. The good news is that in judicial states, judges now take a much closer look at the affidavits and underlying paperwork and will refuse to sign off on a foreclosure if the documents are suspicious (though the foreclosure will probably continue once the paperwork is in order). In nonjudicial foreclosure states, a homeowner can bring a lawsuit to stop a foreclosure if false affidavits were recorded as part of the foreclosure process.

- decide that the information in the paperwork is inadequate and schedule an "evidentiary" hearing a month or two later at which the parties will present their cases through live witnesses who can be questioned by the judge and cross-examined by the other side. For example, if there is conflict over missed payments, both you and an official from the mortgage servicer would testify, and the judge would decide which of you is most likely telling the truth.

After any later hearings, the judge will either:

- order the foreclosure to go ahead (and in many states, set the sale date), or
- dismiss the case, sending the lender back to the drawing board.

In Vermont or Connecticut, a judge who approves the foreclosure can order ownership (title) to be transferred then and there.

If You Are in a Nonjudicial Foreclosure State

Because nonjudicial foreclosures proceed outside of court, you'll have to file a lawsuit to get a judge's attention. And you'll have the burden of proof because you want the judge to stop a proceeding—the fore-closure—that is already authorized by the mortgage. In fact, in a recent California case, *Gomes v. Countrywide Home Loans, Inc.,* 192 Cal. App. 4th 1149, 121 Cal. Rptr. 3d 819 (Cal. App. 4 Dist., 2011), the court ruled that a homeowner could not use the California court system to stop a foreclosure unless the homeowner already had evidence in hand showing that the mortgage or foreclosure was invalid.

You'll most likely need to hire an attorney to succeed in your law-suit, although Nolo's *Represent Yourself in Court* will provide extremely helpful guidance if you choose to do this yourself. Unfortunately, litigation in which an attorney's services are used is always expensive when you have the burden of proof. So unless the lawyer thinks you have a very good case, you may not want to bother with a lawsuit. If the only basis for your challenge is that the foreclosing party made a technical procedural violation, you'll probably gain only a few weeks of delay even if you win.

State Courts May Refuse to Review Nonjudicial Foreclosures

In a recent California case, an appeals court ruled that, in California, a borrower can't challenge a foreclosure in court unless the borrower already has evidence of errors that would justify derailing the foreclosure from its statutorily defined procedural path. (*Gomes v. Countrywide Home Loans, Inc.*, 192 Cal. App. 4th 1149, 121 Cal. Rptr. 3d 819 (Cal. App. 4 Dist., 2011).) The court's opinion relied heavily on the assumption that by signing the mortgage, the homeowner agreed to have the foreclosure proceed out of court, without judicial review. Because borrowers may find it to be impossible to get proof of wrongdoing without the discovery techniques that are only available in lawsuits, the opinion in effect insulates lenders from accountability in state court for wrongdoing. This decision may lead to an increase in Chapter 13 bankruptcy filings, due to the fact that in Chapter 13 borrowers can ask the bankruptcy judge to rule on irregularities in the mortgage and foreclosure process.

To get your day in court to challenge a nonjudicial foreclosure, you must file an affirmative lawsuit against the lender and the foreclosing agent (typically, the trustee or the mortgage servicer). In the lawsuit, you ask the court to enjoin (stop) the foreclosure proceedings until a judge can hear your reasons as to why the foreclosure shouldn't proceed.

In this kind of lawsuit, you typically ask the court for three things, in this order:

- a temporary restraining order
- a preliminary injunction, and
- a permanent injunction.

Your application for a temporary restraining order (TRO) must convince the judge that you will suffer "irreparable injury" if the judge doesn't stop the foreclosure immediately. Because you will lose your home if the foreclosure is allowed to proceed, most courts accept that a foreclosure causes irreparable injury.

TROs are typically granted without a formal notice or hearing, which means the foreclosing party may have only a day or two of notice in which to prepare a response. If no response is filed, the judge may well grant the TRO, but require you to post a bond to protect the foreclosing party from economic harm in case you lose the case down the line. A bond can be costly, assuming you can get one at all. You might be able to get the bond requirement waived if your income is low enough.

Getting the Bond Requirement Waived

The court may grant a waiver if any of the following is true:
- The delay required by the lawsuit will not cause unreasonable harm to the lender.
- The validity of your mortgage is in question (for example, the deed was not properly acknowledged or recorded).
- The lender's interest in pushing ahead with the foreclosure can be protected by some other method, such as by requiring you to make reasonable monthly payments during the course of the lawsuit.

The TRO will typically last until the date set for a hearing on whether the court should issue a preliminary injunction—which would stop the foreclosure pending a full trial on the matter. A hearing on the preliminary injunction is typically held between ten days and two weeks after the TRO is issued.

At the preliminary injunction hearing, the court will review each party's paperwork—essentially the same paperwork submitted in a judicial foreclosure hearing, described earlier. At this hearing, the court must decide whether:
- you are likely to prevail if the case proceeds to trial, and
- the injury that you would suffer from the foreclosure outweighs the injury that the foreclosing party is suffering by not getting paid (called balancing the equities).

If the judge decides these issues in favor of the foreclosing party, the TRO will end, and your motion for a preliminary injunction will be denied. While you are technically allowed to continue with your lawsuit, the foreclosure will likely proceed in the absence of a preliminary injunction. Your only remedy at this point (and it's a considerable long shot) would be to ask a higher court for an order (called a "writ") overruling the lower court's denial of the preliminary injunction.

But if the judge decides these issues in your favor, then the judge will issue a preliminary injunction. The preliminary injunction may order the foreclosing party to take corrective action—for example, by issuing a new pay-off statement and giving you a chance to reinstate the mortgage. Or it may simply keep the TRO in effect.

Because it often takes a year or two to bring a case to trial on a permanent injunction, getting a preliminary injunction is pretty much equivalent to a victory for you. Typically, the foreclosing party will either attempt to reach a settlement with you, drop the current foreclosure and begin from scratch, or meet any conditions laid down by the court and then go back into court to ask that the injunction be lifted.

The burden is on you to prove that the foreclosing party didn't comply with state laws or the terms of the mortgage. You meet this burden with the documents you file—typically, declarations or affidavits from you and various witnesses that establish the facts you believe entitle you to stop the foreclosure. For example, if you contest the accuracy or legality of the fees the foreclosing party required you to pay to reinstate the mortgage, you would attach a sworn statement to your application for a TRO or preliminary injunction, setting out the facts as you know them.

If the foreclosing party produces documents that contradict yours, then you will need to convince the judge at the preliminary injunction stage that you deserve to have the foreclosure put on hold until you can produce your full case at trial. Because most preliminary injunction hearings don't involve live witnesses, your paperwork may have to carry the day.

Due Process Suffers in Nonjudicial Foreclosures

When attempting to foreclose on your house, the lender must comply not just with your state's laws and the terms of your deed of trust. It must also comply with the due process requirements of the United States Constitution.

In the foreclosure context, this means:

- You must receive adequate notice of the proceedings that may cause you to lose your house.
- You must have an opportunity to question the legality of the foreclosure proceedings before a neutral magistrate.

By agreeing to a nonjudicial foreclosure (as a practical matter, you have no choice) when you get a loan, you give up a fundamental due process right: the right to an evaluation of the foreclosure's legality by a neutral magistrate before a foreclosure sale. To challenge a nonjudicial foreclosure in court, you almost certainly will need a lawyer. Because people facing foreclosure are almost always strapped for cash, lawyers are often unaffordable. For that reason, for many people, the ability to file an action in court challenging a foreclosure is only theoretical.

Consider Recording a Lis Pendens

Instead of seeking a TRO or preliminary injunction to delay the foreclosure sale until you can have a hearing, consider recording a "lis pendens" and filing a regular civil complaint attacking the foreclosure. A lis pendens is a simple document providing notice to the world that title to the property is a subject of litigation. As long as it is on record, any sale of the property can be undone if your lawsuit succeeds, because the buyer had notice of the controversy. Also, no title company will insure title to property subject to a lis pendens.

222222222

222222222 2

Apolog

CHAPTER 8

If You Decide to Leave Your House

Let the Foreclosure Proceed ... 179

Be Community Minded ... 181

Sell the House in a Short Sale ... 182
  Advantages of a Short Sale ... 182
  Disadvantages of a Short Sale ... 182
  Will You Be Able to Negotiate a Short Sale? ... 185

Offer the Lender a Deed in Lieu of Foreclosure ... 192
  Will the Lender Accept a Deed in Lieu? ... 192
  Fannie Mae and Freddie Mac Deeds in Lieu of Foreclosure ... 193

Avoiding Deficiency Judgments ... 194

Income Tax Liability for Deficiencies ... 195

O nce it appears that foreclosure is inevitable, many people pack up their belongings and their families and immediately look for a new place to live. They fear losing reliable shelter and want to find another home as soon as possible where they will feel secure. Staying in a house facing foreclosure can be terrifying if you think you might end up out on the street. And it may be unbearably depressing if you are reminded every day that you won't be living there indefinitely.

While these reactions to foreclosure certainly are understandable, foreclosure can actually be a time of opportunity. You will almost certainly have enough time to find a new place to live. Meanwhile, it may prove to be a big financial advantage to stay put for a while—maybe a long while.

So try to put fear and negativity aside as you assess your options to come up with the best choice for your circumstances. This chapter lays out the basic approaches to giving up your house and the advantages and disadvantages of each.

Giving Up the House: Your Options

- **Let foreclosure work for you:** Stay in the house as long as possible without making any payments, to save money for a future move.
- **Short sale:** Offer the house for sale and persuade the lender to accept the offer and let you off the mortgage.
- **Deed in lieu of foreclosure:** Persuade the lender to let you sign over the deed in exchange for cancellation of foreclosure.
- **Walk away:** Move out when it suits you and let the foreclosure proceed. Works best when your lender can't sue you for a deficiency.
- **Negotiate a mortgage modification:** Engage in negotiations, even if you think your efforts will ultimately prove unfruitful, to avoid being labeled a "strategic defaulter" when you apply for a mortgage in the future.
- **File for Chapter 7 or Chapter 13 bankruptcy:** Eliminate any deficiencies or taxes you owe as a result of the foreclosure or other remedies.

TIP
Talk to an expert to see how your choice will affect your credit.
It's not possible to really know what effect any of these actions will have
on your credit—any wisdom you hear from a credit or real estate industry
insider now is likely to be out of date when you get around to needing it. So
when you're ready to decide which approach to take, talk to a HUD-approved
housing counselor (see Ch. 4) about how it might affect your credit. But don't
let credit scores be the main consideration. It's possible to "live long and
prosper" without running on the credit hamster wheel.

Let the Foreclosure Proceed

If you don't fight the foreclosure or take any of the other steps discussed
in this book, the foreclosure will move forward on a schedule dictated
by your lender's workloads and policies, the laws of your state, and any
foreclosure moratoriums imposed by your lender due to recent foreclosure
scandals. Specific information for your state is in the appendix.

The single most important point to understand is that *you don't have
to leave your house just because the lender has started foreclosure proceedings.*
In most states, you'll probably be able to stay long enough to plan for the
future by saving all or some of the money that you're no longer putting
toward the mortgage.

> **EXAMPLE:** Joshua and Ellen got in over their heads and now can't
> afford the $3,000 monthly payments on their first, second, and
> third mortgages. They decide to let the house go. They turn to
> their state's page in the appendix to see how much time they have.
> They learn that:
>
> - They can go three months without making payments before
>   they will receive what's called a notice of default in their
>   state. This notice gives them an additional three months to
>   make things right. If they don't (and remember, they plan
>   to let the house go), they will have another 30 days' notice
>   before the house is sold.

- They can file for Chapter 7 bankruptcy and delay the sale by three additional months. Bankruptcy will also let them leave without owing the lender anything.
- After the foreclosure sale, they'll probably be able to stay in the house for at least two to three more months.

Altogether, they will have at least a year of living in the house without making payments, and if they can save at least $2,000 a month, they will have roughly $25,000 in the bank when they set out to seek new shelter. (See Ch. 9 for more details on how this all works.)

Although quickly dropping home values make it increasingly unlikely, you may have some equity left in your home. If you do, the longer you can stay in it payment free, the better chance you have of pulling some of your equity out before finding new shelter. Just do the math: If you have $20,000 equity, your payments are $2,000 a month, and you can stay in the house without making your loan payments for ten months, you will have succeeded in pulling out $20,000 in equity, so to speak.

How much time you'll get to remain in your house and how much money you can save (or, if you have any, equity you can pull out), depend on these factors:

- the amount of notice you are entitled to receive before the lender begins foreclosure proceedings
- how soon in the whole process you decide to stop making payments
- how long the modification process takes before your servicer issues a final denial and proceeds with foreclosure
- whether judicial or nonjudicial foreclosure is used in your state (judicial foreclosures usually take longer than nonjudicial ones)
- whether any foreclosure moratoriums are in effect
- how much notice your state's law gives you to leave the house after the foreclosure sale (typically, 15 to 30 days)
- whether part of your strategy involves filing for bankruptcy before the foreclosure sale, which provides an additional two to three months' delay, and
- if you file for bankruptcy, how much money you can keep under your state's exemption laws—it varies from nothing to $50,000.

All of these variables are discussed in detail in Ch. 9, and your state's page in the appendix will give you an estimate of how long you can remain in your home. The most unpredictable factor in arriving at this estimate is whether your foreclosing bank is on the ball in finding new owners for its foreclosed properties or will just let the house sit there unsold, whether or not you move out.

Walking Away From Your House

What about just walking away from your house? If you do, sooner or later the lender will foreclose on the property and sell it. You may think this won't concern you; you'll be gone, onto the next phase of your life. In fact, this may or may not be true, depending on your potential tax liability and potential liability for the unpaid part of the mortgage. Some people might be better off, emotionally, by shutting their old house out of their mind and finding new shelter in some faraway location. But for most people, this option makes the least sense.

If you want to use the foreclosure to your best advantage, you should at least consider remaining in the home for as long as possible—payment free— and consider filing for bankruptcy to rid yourself from any liabilities arising from your former home ownership. And if tax liability is an issue, you should do your best to file for bankruptcy before the foreclosure sale or be prepared to prove that you were insolvent at the time of the foreclosure sale.

Be Community Minded

The longer you stay in your home throughout the foreclosure process, the better off your lender, the ultimate purchaser, and your neighborhood will be. You've undoubtedly read articles about neighborhoods full of vacant homes, which are plagued by theft and vandalism. It's become a very serious problem.

If the owners of those homes stayed put and continued to maintain them, everyone's home values would likely be a lot higher. If you are the first one (or even the second or third) on your block to go through foreclosure, you single-handedly can be responsible for propping up the value of surrounding properties. My point is that you are earning your keep by remaining on the property until a new owner is ready to assume occupancy.

Sell the House in a Short Sale

In a short sale, you sell your house before it's auctioned off in foreclosure, usually for an amount that falls short of what you owe on it. For a short sale to work, your lenders must agree to receive less than they are entitled to under the terms of the loans you signed. Why would they do that? They aren't in the business of owning homes, and generally do a poor job of it. Also, foreclosures are expensive for lenders, who might not get all they're owed anyway.

Advantages of a Short Sale

The main benefit of a short sale is that you may get out from under your mortgage without liability for the amount of the loan that is left unpaid. You also won't have a foreclosure or a bankruptcy on your credit record. The general thinking is that your credit won't suffer as much as it would were you to let the foreclosure proceed or file for bankruptcy to get out from under any liability you might incur in the course of the foreclosure.

Your credit rating will take a hit regardless of which option you choose—short sale, foreclosure, or bankruptcy. But a short sale might mean that you could buy a big-ticket item on credit a year or two earlier than you otherwise would, or get a credit card at 15% instead of 19% interest. You will need to balance the prospect of improved credit against your opportunity to stay in your house longer and save money, as described below (and in Ch. 9). Only you can decide which path suits you better.

Disadvantages of a Short Sale

Short sales have some drawbacks when compared to letting the foreclosure happen or filing for bankruptcy.

No Chance to Stay and Save

If you sell your house, you will be expected to leave as soon as escrow closes. But if you let the foreclosure happen and stay in the house until you are formally told to leave by written notice, you can build a nest egg that you can draw on in the future to obtain good rental housing. (Again, see Ch. 9 for more about this strategy.)

It's very difficult to accomplish a short sale if you don't get started as soon as you learn about the pending foreclosure, especially if you have to negotiate with several mortgage holders. Needless to say, if you don't complete the short sale before the foreclosure sale, you'll have nothing to sell.

Potential Deficiency Judgment

The sale price is "short" of the full amount you owe to the lender; the difference between the total debt owed and the sale price is the deficiency. For example, say your lender approves a short sale in the amount of $200,000, but you owe $250,000. The deficiency is $50,000.

In many states, the lender is prohibited from getting a deficiency judgment following a foreclosure. However, most states don't prohibit the lender from getting a deficiency judgment following a short sale. (California is one of the few states that does specifically prohibit deficiency judgments following short sales.)

If you want to avoid a deficiency judgment following a short sale, you'll have to make sure that the short sale agreement expressly states that the transaction is in full satisfaction of the debt and that the lender waives its right to the deficiency.

Potential Tax Liability

A short sale may generate an unwelcome surprise: taxable income based on the amount the sale proceeds are short of what you owe. It can happen if you borrowed against your principal residence and used the money for any purpose other than acquiring or improving that property. For example, if you used the loan to buy a second house, to pay college tuition for a child, or to take a vacation, and you end up not paying it back in full, the amount your lender writes off (typically whatever amount wasn't paid back) is considered forgiven debt. Although the

Those Mysterious Credit Ratings

Nobody really knows how a foreclosure or short sale will affect your credit. Only the folks who set the credit scores can really tell you—and they won't, because certain important factors used to derive credit scores (and the criteria used in follow-up "manual" examinations) are kept confidential as a business secret.

In past years, credit grantors would subjectively assess the raw information in your credit file when deciding whether or not to grant you credit and at what interest rate. For instance, they might have seen that you did a short sale and given you a break for at least being responsible enough to sell the house rather than just walking away or giving the house back with a deed in lieu of foreclosure.

Now, however, this type of examination is made only if your credit score is low enough to trigger it. And because you already have two strikes against you because of your low credit score, the results will seldom cheer you.

Even if current information we do have about credit scores indicates that a short sale is marginally better for your credit, things might change. Credit card issuers are reporting default numbers that indicate a crash-and-burn scenario for that industry. Also, because of trillion-dollar government deficits (financed by foreign loans and the printing of money), it's not hard to see that we'll be living with inflationary pressures for some time to come. Because issuing credit expands the money supply, the government will likely rein in the credit industry to help fight inflation when the time comes.

All this means it's next to impossible to predict what role, if any, credit scores will play in the new economy. If consumer credit gets tight enough, the very concept of the credit score may be an artifact of times gone by. For now, the best and most current information on the subject of consumer credit, and how to rebuild it, can be found in *Credit Repair* by Margaret Reiter and Robin Leonard (Nolo).

concept is not at all intuitive, the IRS treats forgiven debt as taxable income, subject to regular income tax.

> **EXAMPLE:** Joan owes $150,000 on her first mortgage and $50,000 on the second, which she borrowed to pay for her daughter's first year of tuition at an exclusive Eastern college. Joan loses her job and is facing foreclosure. She arranges to sell the house for $140,000 and gets permission from her first lender to pay off the first mortgage for $135,000 and permission from her second mortgage lender to pay off the second mortgage for $5,000.
>
> The $15,000 the first mortgage holder will write off (forgive) is not considered taxable income because Joan used it to acquire the house. But the amount the second mortgage holder will write off, $45,000, is forgiven debt and considered taxable income to Joan because it wasn't used to buy or improve her principal residence.

If you face this situation and can prove to the IRS you were legally insolvent at the time of the short sale, you won't have to pay the tax (see Income Tax Liability for Deficiencies, below). Insolvency is when your total debts are more than the value of your total equity in your real estate and personal property. You can also get rid of this kind of tax liability by filing for Chapter 7 or Chapter 13 bankruptcy, if you file before escrow closes. Of course, if you are going to file for bankruptcy anyway, there isn't much point in doing the short sale, because any benefit to your credit rating caused by the short sale will be negated by the bankruptcy.

Will You Be Able to Negotiate a Short Sale?

In some areas, short sales are increasingly hard to get approved, while in others they are on the increase (or so I'm told). So even if the short sale option looks good to you, there's no certainty that you can make it work.

Is There Time?

Historically, short sale deals have often fallen apart because of the amount of time required to obtain approval from the lender. At the start of the housing crisis, so many people were requesting short sales that lenders simply were not able to keep up with the volume. Sellers and buyers often got frustrated and chose to give up on the deals before the sales were approved. Since then, many lenders have increased their personnel and streamlined the process to better keep up with increased requests for short sales.

Also, in mid-2012, the Federal Housing Finance Agency (FHFA) announced guidelines that establish strict timelines for homeowners with Fannie Mae or Freddie Mac mortgages. (To find out if Fannie Mae or Freddie Mac owns your loan, go to www.knowyouroptions. com/loanlookup or www.freddiemac.com/mymortgage.) Under the new guidelines, mortgage servicers are required to:

- review and respond to a short sale request within 30 calendar days from receipt of the complete short sale application
- provide the borrower with weekly updates if the short sale application is still under review after 30 days, and
- make a final decision to accept or deny the short sale, and notify the borrower of this decision, within 60 calendar days after receipt of the complete loss mitigation package.

Still, sometimes it is difficult to get a short sale processed in time. Short sale negotiations often occur in rushed settings because many homeowners start thinking about short sales only when they are about to lose their houses to foreclosure. And generally you've got to have a bona fide offer from a buyer before you can find out whether or not the lender will go along with it. In a market where sales are hard to come by, this can get frustrating because you won't know in advance what the lender is willing to settle for.

The Terms

Short sales are also difficult to come by if there are investors in the picture who might not approve of getting less return on their investment than they were counting on.

A short sale will benefit you only if the lenders are willing to accept the amount a buyer is willing to pay and let you off the hook for the rest. For example, if you owe $300,000 and you can sell your house for just $200,000, you are unlikely to be successful in negotiating a short sale. There's a chance, though—the lender might decide that even a 33% loss on the short sale is better than what could happen in a foreclosure, where houses can sit vacant for months and rapidly depreciate in value before being bought by a new owner.

Clearly, the closer the offer is to the principal balance of the loan, the quicker the lender will sign off on the sale. It would be nice if there were a hard and fast line for how much a lender will forgo. In fact, as foreclosures continue apace, real estate agents and HUD-approved housing counselors should have a pretty good idea of the kind of deals lenders are accepting in your area.

You'll want to work with a real estate professional anyway when you're trying to get your house sold at a price that will be acceptable to all the mortgage lenders. A real estate agent's negotiating help can be critical, because the lender may agree with the proposed offer, or it may make a counteroffer. This may go back and forth until everyone is satisfied or the deal falls through.

> **EXAMPLE:** Toby and Tyler face foreclosure on their first mortgage and decide that a short sale is their best option. They contact a real estate agent, who tells them that they should list their house for at least 75% of their mortgage debt—or $225,000—for the sale to be acceptable to the lender. The 75% figure is based on the agent's knowledge of the going rate for lender acceptance of short sales.
>
> As the foreclosure sale date grows nearer, and the house goes unsold at the 75% figure, Toby and Tyler finally get an offer that would pay 60% of their mortgage; they accept, contingent on approval by the lender. The agent takes the offer to the lender and quickly receives a rejection. The buyer raises his offer to 70%, and the lender agrees.

The Home Affordable Foreclosure Alternatives (HAFA) Program

You may be eligible to complete a short sale through the Home Affordable Foreclosure Alternatives (HAFA) program. The benefit of completing a short sale through HAFA is that you would not be responsible for the difference between what you owe on your mortgage and the amount that your home sells for. You may also receive $3,000 to help pay your relocation costs upon the successful closing of your short sale. This relocation assistance can help offset the fact that by engaging in a short sale you would probably have to move out sooner than would be the case with a foreclosure.

You may be eligible for HAFA if you meet all of the following requirements:

- You have a documented financial hardship.
- You have not purchased a new house within the last 12 months.
- Your first mortgage is less than $729,750.
- You obtained your mortgage on or before January 1, 2009.
- You haven't been convicted within the last 10 years of felony larceny, theft, fraud or forgery, money laundering, or tax evasion in connection with a mortgage or real estate transaction.

HAFA is available for mortgages that are owned or guaranteed by Fannie Mae and Freddie Mac or serviced by one of the over 100 HAMP participating servicers. Go to the Making Home Affordable website at www.makinghomeaffordable.gov (click "Get Started" and "Contact Your Mortgage Company") to find out if your servicer is a participant.

HAFA sets clear timelines to keep the process efficient. Mortgage servicers must evaluate homeowners for HAFA within 30 days after one of the eligibility criteria is met. If the homeowner is eligible, the servicer will send a short sale agreement (SSA)—a contract between the homeowner and the servicer—that will include:

- a list price approved by the servicer
- the length of time the property will be marketed for sale;
- an agreement releasing the homeowner from all future liability after the property is sold

- the amount of the monthly mortgage payment, if any, that the borrower will be required to pay during the term of the SSA
- information about the $3,000 in relocation assistance after closing, and
- an agreement that so long as the borrower performs in accordance with the terms of the SSA, the servicer will not complete a foreclosure sale.

Borrowers may also complete a deed in lieu of foreclosure through HAFA. The eligibility requirements and benefits are similar to those for a HAFA short sale.

When a Short Sale Might Make Sense

- You can sell your house for a price that the lender (or lenders) will likely sign off on.
- You don't plan to file for Chapter 7 or Chapter 13 bankruptcy (because if you're hoping a short sale will preserve your credit record, a bankruptcy would undermine that goal).
- All your lenders are willing to let you off the hook for the deficiency (the amount by which the sales price falls short of what you owe).
- You have time before the scheduled foreclosure sale to find a buyer and to explore other options (such as filing for bankruptcy). This can be a problem in states (such as Georgia and Alabama) that don't give you much notice before the sale.

Convincing Multiple Lienholders

Multiple lenders (or anyone else who has a legal claim, or lien, on your property) can fatally complicate short sales. If you have only one mortgage, you have only one lender to convince. If you have two or more mortgages (or other types of home loans or liens on your property), you must convince all of the lienholders. So the more lienholders there are in your picture, the harder it will be to obtain a short sale.

This is especially true if the property's value has substantially decreased, and a sale will probably produce little or no money for a second or third mortgage holder (typically, the holder of a tax lien, home equity loan, or line of credit). If these other lenders won't get anything out of the short sale, they won't have any incentive to release their liens (legal claims on the property) so that a new buyer can have clear title. And more important to you, they won't absolve you from liability for what you owe them—which defeats a central purpose of the short sale.

> **EXAMPLE 1:** Carlos has a first mortgage on his property of $240,000, a second mortgage of $30,000, and $15,000 out on a home equity line of credit. He can sell the house for only $230,000. All of that money would typically go toward the first mortgage. The second mortgage and line of credit lenders wouldn't get anything. They would rather let the foreclosure go through and sue Carlos for the deficiency than accept a small percentage of what they are owed and agree to not sue him for the balance. Without their agreement, he won't be able to sell the house with clear title, because the property would still be subject to the liens of the other mortgage holders.

> **EXAMPLE 2:** Johnny owes $225,000 on his first mortgage, $50,000 on his second mortgage, and $25,000 on a home equity loan. He falls behind on his mortgage payments and decides to put the house up for sale. Johnny receives an offer of $260,000. This amount will more than please the first mortgage owner, because its $225,000 loan will be paid off in full. The second mortgage owner won't be so happy because it will get only $35,000 of the $50,000 it's owed. But considering the fact that it wouldn't get anything if the house went into foreclosure ("junior" liens are wiped out in foreclosures brought by senior lienholders), it agrees to the sale.

Unfortunately, when the home equity lender hears that it won't get anything, it nixes the sale. And without all lienholders agreeing to the sale, it can't happen. So Johnny goes back and asks the second mortgage holder to take $25,000 (half of what it's owed) and offers $10,000 to the home equity lender. The second mortgage holder is even unhappier now, since its share is being reduced, but it still wants the sale to go through, so it agrees. Finally, Johnny manages to negotiate a deal where everyone gets something but not as much as they would like.

Scam Alert

More and more companies out there operate scams aimed at defrauding homeowners who are trying to put together a short sale. Make sure you are dealing with a reputable real estate company and with the company that is servicing the loan (the company to which you have been sending your payments). You should also be getting guidance from a HUD-approved housing counselor (see Ch. 4).

Here is how a scam might work. A business calling itself a mortgage company offers to buy your home in a short sale and pay off the lender. You sign the deed over to them. They convince you that they will deal with the bank (for one reason or another) and that you should move out because the lender won't participate in a short sale unless you do. Then, instead of paying the lender, they turn around and sell the house to an unsuspecting buyer (or rent it out), pocket the proceeds, and walk away when the bank moves forward with the foreclosure. You are not only out of your house, but you have paid nothing to the bank and are on the hook for the entire mortgage.

For more information on foreclosure rescue scams, see Ch. 1. Also check out Nolo's "Bankruptcy, Debt & Foreclosure" blog (http://blog.nolo.com/bankruptcy) and the foreclosure area of Nolo.com for updates. Scams are like viruses—new ones pop up every day.

Offer the Lender a Deed in Lieu of Foreclosure

If you want to simply hand over ownership of your house to the lender and get your loan canceled in exchange, you can propose something called a deed in lieu of foreclosure. If your lender agrees, it will accept a deed to your property and in exchange, promise to not initiate foreclosure proceedings or to drop them if they've already begun. You don't have to sell the house; the lender will do that for you.

Will the Lender Accept a Deed in Lieu?

Getting a lender to accept a deed in lieu of foreclosure is a hard sell these days. The problem is that the lender wants cash, not real estate—especially if it already owns hundreds of other properties that failed to sell at foreclosure auctions.

On the other hand, if the bank thinks it's a better deal to take your offer than to incur the expense of foreclosure, it will be a done deal. As with short sales, it will be helpful for you to work with a HUD-approved housing counselor. (See Ch. 4.)

Before the lender will accept a deed in lieu of foreclosure, it will probably require you to put your home on the market for a period of time (three months is typical). Banks would rather have you sell the house than have to sell it themselves. Lenders seldom have real estate services as part of their operation, and so they must contract with real estate companies to unload their properties, often at a steep discount.

You can't use a deed in lieu of foreclosure if you have multiple mortgages or if you have liens on the property such as those arising from delinquent taxes, work on your home, or money judgments. You must be able to deed clear title to the whole property. In other words, you can't do two deeds in lieu of foreclosure and split the property between the first and second mortgage lenders, or other lienholders.

Fannie Mae and Freddie Mac Deeds in Lieu of Foreclosure

Starting March 1, 2013, Fannie Mae and Freddie Mac began allowing certain delinquent and current borrowers to give up their underwater properties and cancel the debts with deeds in lieu of foreclosure (sometimes called "mortgage releases").

To qualify, borrowers who are delinquent for 90 days or more must be experiencing and able to document one of the following hardships:

- unemployment
- a reduction in income due to circumstances outside their control (for example, elimination of overtime, fewer regular working hours, etc.)
- an increase in housing expenses due to circumstances outside their control
- a divorce or legal separation, or a separation of borrowers unrelated by marriage, civil union, or similar domestic partnership
- the death of a borrower or the death of either the primary or secondary wage earner in the household
- long-term or permanent disability, or serious illness of a borrower or coborrower or dependent family member
- a disaster (natural or man-made) adversely impacting the property or borrower's place of employment
- distant employment transfer or relocation
- a business failure, or
- another hardship that is not covered above.

Borrowers who are current on their mortgages or less than 90 days delinquent qualify only if the borrower's eligible hardship involves:

- the death of a borrower or primary/secondary wage earner in the household, or
- long-term or permanent disability (or serious illness of a borrower/coborrower or dependent family member).

For borrowers who are current on their mortgages or less than 31 days delinquent, the following additional requirements must be met:

- the mortgaged property is the borrower's principal residence, and
- the total monthly debt-to-income ratio exceeds 55%.

For the most part, if a borrower meets the above requirements, any deficiency will be waived. However, in certain circumstances some borrowers may have to make a cash contribution. In addition, a mortgage servicer may approve a deed in lieu of foreclosure for borrowers who previously discharged the debt obligation in a Chapter 7 bankruptcy. Fannie Mae and Freddie Mac offer up to $6,000 to second lien holders to expedite the process and, in some cases, borrowers may receive up to $3,000 in relocation assistance.

Avoiding Deficiency Judgments

The laws of most states allow the lender to come after you for a deficiency —that is, the amount by which the foreclosure sale proceeds fall short of the loan amount. However, a few states protect homeowners from liability for deficiencies from mortgages on residential homes that were used to purchase the homes, or make it too expensive for the lender to pursue the issue. See the appendix for your state's rule.

You don't need to worry about a deficiency if either of the following applies:

- Your state's law prohibits deficiency lawsuits.
- The lender agrees, as part of accepting a short sale or deed in lieu of foreclosure, not to come after you for any deficiency.

But if your state does allow deficiency lawsuits, or you have a second or third mortgage, you could be on the hook for a lot of money even after you lose your house. You can wipe out that debt by filing for Chapter 7 bankruptcy. (See Ch. 6.)

Some foreclosure advisers will tell you that deficiency lawsuits are rare and not to worry about them. And it's true that because it's expensive to sue, lenders don't often pursue deficiency lawsuits. But, lenders are more likely to pursue deficiency judgments now than they used to be, particularly if you have substantial assets that could be recovered. In any event, it's hard to know whether your case will be the exception. Even if most don't end up in a lawsuit, do you want to take the chance? Bankruptcy is your ultimate safety net when it comes to any liability arising from your former home ownership.

Income Tax Liability for Deficiencies

If you default on your mortgage, it's likely that you or the lender will eventually sell the property for less than you owe on it. And it's possible that you might be asked to pay income tax on the difference. The theory is that you are receiving a gift of this amount, because you don't have to pay it back. (The lender is forgiving the debt.)

The IRS learns of the deficiency when it receives an IRS Form 1099C from the lender. This is a form on which a creditor reports income derived when repayment of a loan is no longer feasible—which would be the case in a short sale or foreclosure, or when the creditor writes off a debt.

Whether or not you'll owe tax depends on the circumstances. Here are the basic rules.

Loans for your principal residence. If your default is on a mortgage or another debt secured by your house, and you used the money you borrowed to buy or improve your house, you won't owe tax. (Before federal tax law changed in 2007, you might have had to pay income tax in this situation. This change in the tax law is set to expire on December 31, 2013.)

Loans for other real estate. If you default on a mortgage that's secured by property that isn't your primary residence, you'll owe tax on any deficiency. So, for example, if you walk away from a loan on your second house in the country, expect a Form 1099 in the mail. The same is true for loans on nonresidential real estate

Loans not used for real estate. Similarly, if you take out a home equity loan and take that world trip you've been dreaming of instead of using the money to improve your house, you may end up on the wrong side of a tax bill.

> **EXAMPLE:** Harry owes $200,000 on his second home, which is foreclosed on and sold at auction for $150,000. The lender files an IRS Form 1099, reporting the $50,000 difference as taxable income to Harry.

If you do face income tax liability, you have two possible ways of getting out from under it: the insolvency exclusion and bankruptcy. To use the insolvency exclusion, you'll have to prove to the satisfaction of the IRS that your liabilities exceed the value of your assets. Filing for bankruptcy works because debt wiped out (discharged) in bankruptcy is not considered taxable income. You'll have to show the IRS that you filed for bankruptcy before the event that would cause the lender to file a Form 1099C. Of course, you'll want to file for bankruptcy only if it otherwise makes sense. (Bankruptcy is discussed in Chs. 5 and 6.)

Will This Tax Break Last? Stay Tuned

The federal law (The Mortgage Debt Forgiveness Act) that makes a person not liable for paying tax on the amount of a deficiency stemming from the sale of a residence is effective through 2013. This means that whatever happens to your home mortgage during that period will not increase your income tax as long as you meet the law's qualifications. The Treasury Department recently announced that a top legislative priority for 2013 is extending the act's effective date to December 31, 2015. Check this book's companion page on Nolo.com for updates on this issue. (See Your Foreclosure Companion for the link.).

TIP

You can fight back if an unpaid loan amount is treated as taxable income. If you receive a Form 1099 attributing income to you from mortgage debt forgiveness, but you think you shouldn't owe the tax, file IRS Form 982, *Reduction of Tax Attributes Due to Discharge of Indebtedness*, with your regular tax return.

How Long Can You Stay in Your House for Free?

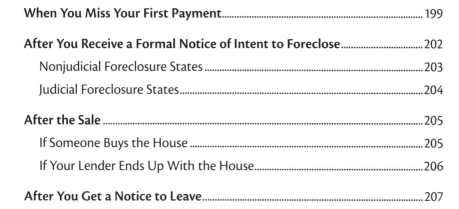

As I've mentioned throughout this book, foreclosure can actually provide a great opportunity to save some serious money. That's because legal procedures—including foreclosures—typically take many months, and because many houses don't sell at foreclosure auctions. While the foreclosure proceeding goes on, and then while the house sits vacant after a failed attempt to sell it at auction, you probably won't have to move—or make any payments for your housing.

For example, if your mortgage payments are $2,000 a month, and you stay in the house for nine months without making a payment, you could save $18,000. Of course, you might not be able to save the entire amount of your mortgage payment, but even if you saved half, you would still have a considerable amount of money in the bank when the time comes to leave.

As long as you remain, you also save the house from nine months of deterioration (and vandalism) it would suffer by being vacant. This does your community a great favor.

How long can you stay in your house payment free once you decide to give it up? There is no way to give you a precise timeline for your personal situation. Each phase of the process, from your first missed payment to your last day in the house, involves variables unique to your situation. However, the information on your state's page in the appendix will give you an idea of whether you're likely to have three months, a year, or something in between.

This chapter explains the elements of that basic timeline in more detail. Once you have a rough idea of what to expect, I highly recommend that you talk to a HUD-approved housing counselor (see Ch. 4) to get a reality check on how fast events are moving in your community. A second opinion can only help.

TIP

Filing for bankruptcy shortly before the sale date can buy you more time. If you file for Chapter 7 bankruptcy after the foreclosure sale has been scheduled, the sale will be delayed for several months while the bankruptcy is pending. If you file for Chapter 13 bankruptcy, you can probably delay the foreclosure sale for at least five or six months, especially if you hire a lawyer to navigate the tricky Chapter 13 shoals. To find out more, see Chs. 5 and 6.

When You Stay, Everybody Wins

You might feel a little guilty about staying in your house after you become unable to keep making payments on it or after it's actually auctioned off in foreclosure. But what you might not realize is that by staying, you're doing your neighbors—and probably even the lender or new owner—a favor.

It's well documented that foreclosures tend to cluster in certain communities. And when there are several empty houses in a neighborhood, it's very obvious. Lawns are overgrown with weeds or brown for lack of water; flyers pile up on porches. Maintenance is neglected. The signs of neglect quickly attract vandals, thieves, and transients. Graffiti appears on fences as copper pipe and appliances disappear from the vacant houses.

Some cities, including Cleveland, Baltimore, and Minneapolis, have actually sued lenders to recoup the costs of dealing with the problems caused by abandoned houses. The cities say they have had to pay more to their fire and police departments and have lost property tax revenue. They have also demolished some houses that were past saving and are now suing for the costs of demolition. (*National Law Journal*, May 9, 2008.) Success has varied in these types of cases.

When you stay in the house until a new owner is ready to move in, you'll help maintain its value—and that of your neighbors' houses. So let go of the guilt and remind yourself that you're doing a good deed.

When You Miss Your First Payment

If you have decided that you'll ultimately have to give up your house because your mortgage payments are no longer affordable (if they ever were), the first step toward benefiting from your foreclosure is to stop making your mortgage payments. Open up a savings account in which to deposit as much as possible of the extra money you now have.

> ### TIP
> **Don't forget about modifications.** Before bailing out on your home, find out whether you qualify for a refinance or a mortgage payment reduction under the Making Home Affordable program. You don't have to be making payments on your mortgage when you first begin the modification process, and whether or not you ultimately plan to leave, there is no harm in seeing what you can get through modification. Even if the modification fails, simply engaging in the process can buy you many precious months of payment-free shelter. See Ch. 4 for more on a Making Home Affordable modification or refinance.

Depending on where you live, and your lender's policy regarding foreclosures, you likely will be able to miss your payments for at least three months (very possibly as many as five months) before your lender starts formal foreclosure proceedings. In all but a couple of states (check your state's page in the appendix to see what kind of notice you'll get), you'll know when the lender takes the first step towards foreclosure because you will get a notice in the mail or be served with a copy of the lawsuit. If you get help from a HUD-approved housing counselor and try to work something out with your lender (even though you privately think you'll be giving up your house), you might gain a number of extra months before the lender gives up on you and starts foreclosure proceedings. (See Ch. 4 for information about HUD-approved housing counselors.)

So, from the time you decide to stop making payments until the time you receive notice that foreclosure proceedings have begun, you can live in your home for at least three months (maybe five or six) payment free. But that's not all. Keep reading.

Zombie Foreclosures: Another Good Reason to Stay in Your House as Long as Possible

Some homeowners leave their homes once a foreclosure is initiated even though they legally own their property until the day of sale and have the right to remain there throughout the process. With a "zombie foreclosure" (sometimes called "zombie title"), the homeowner moves out after foreclosure has been started, but for some reason the foreclosure is cancelled, the sale is never held, or title is never officially transferred to a new owner. As a result, certain debts continue to accrue in the owner's name and will follow him or her like the walking dead.

Often, zombie foreclosures occur in low-income areas where the lender is not anxious to assume responsibility for the upkeep of the property and wants to save on taxes, as well as other costs. If squatters occupy the property or it falls into severe disrepair, the bank may simply wash its hands of the property. In other cases, the property may have been caught up in the robo-signing scandal and the foreclosure cannot be completed. Or there may be other reasons that the lender simply doesn't follow through with the foreclosure, such as it already has too much inventory or the costs of foreclosing do not justify completing the foreclosure.

Since title is never transferred out of the homeowner's name, he or she remains liable for any property taxes, HOA dues, and maintenance on the property. Debts associated with these responsibilities can go unpaid for years and then come back to haunt homeowners who have no idea that the foreclosure process was never completed. (In some cases, the bank may not be legally required to inform the homeowner that the foreclosure has stopped or it may not be able to locate a homeowner who has moved out.)

For example, if you leave your property and title is never transferred out of your name, the following things, among others, could happen months or even years later:

- The tax collector may come looking to collect back property taxes.
- An HOA may file a lawsuit to recover unpaid assessments.
- You could be threatened with fines for not complying with housing codes and ordinances (and even face jail time in some instances if you don't meet repair deadlines).

> ### Zombie Foreclosures: Another Good Reason to Stay in Your House as Long as Possible, continued
>
> - The local government may send you a bill for yard maintenance, repairs, trash removal, and/or graffiti scrubbing.
>
> Plus, your credit score will be even more damaged due to the unpaid debt.
>
> Various sources estimate that since the housing crisis began there are roughly two million properties that went into foreclosure but never emerged from the process. It's true that in about half of those cases the homeowners are struggling to keep their homes. But just how many of the remaining million are zombie foreclosures is anybody's guess.
>
> This provides yet another reason for you to remain in your home for as long as possible. You will be much more likely to avoid becoming the victim of a zombie foreclosure if you stay through the entire foreclosure process and wait for an official notice to vacate before moving out.

After You Receive a Formal Notice of Intent to Foreclose

Before your house can be sold, you must get some sort of formal notice required by your state's foreclosure laws. (See Ch. 2.) The kind of notice you will get depends on where you live.

If you're in a nonjudicial foreclosure state, you may get:

- a notice of default (allowing you time to reinstate your mortgage by making up all the back payments) followed by a notice of sale (if you haven't reinstated your mortgage by the deadline)
- a combined notice of default and sale (stating that the property will be sold on a certain date unless you make up the missed payments)
- only one notice—a notice of sale announcing that the property will be sold on a certain date unless you pay off the mortgage, or

• in a couple of states, notice only by publication and posting.

If you're in a judicial foreclosure state, you might get a prefiling notice telling you that foreclosure proceedings will begin within a particular period. You will definitely get a summons and complaint telling you that foreclosure proceedings have been filed in the appropriate court and that you have a certain amount of time to respond.

In almost all judicial foreclosure states, if the judge orders the foreclosure sale, you'll get a notice telling you when and where the sale will take place. In Connecticut and Vermont, however, the judge can transfer title to the property as part of the judgment of foreclosure.

Will Contesting a Nonjudicial Foreclosure in Court Gain Time?

To oppose a foreclosure in a nonjudicial foreclosure state, you have to file a lawsuit. Normally, you would file a petition with the local court requesting an injunction (court order) to block the foreclosure. This might delay the foreclosure by a week or two, or longer if the court believed your argument has merit. You would have the burden of proving that the lender hadn't followed proper procedures or had made some other mistake, and it would be very difficult for you to get very far in this type of lawsuit unless you hire a lawyer. (See Ch. 7 for information on fighting foreclosure in court.)

Nonjudicial Foreclosure States

How much time you have from the first formal notice that foreclosure proceedings have started to the date your property will be sold varies widely from state to state. You can count on at least 30 days' notice before the sale (except in a few states that give you just 15 days' notice); in most states, you'll get at least 60 days. Check your state's page in the appendix to find out the precise amount of notice you are entitled to.

Gaining Time by Contesting a Judicial Foreclosure

One of the great benefits of living in a judicial foreclosure state is that you automatically have an opportunity to contest the request for foreclosure. In a judicial foreclosure, the lender (the party filing the suit) has the burden of filing all the paperwork required to prove its case. All you must do is file a written response to the foreclosure complaint or petition, attend any hearings that are scheduled, and voice your objections if you have any. Merely filing a written response will probably achieve a delay of at least several months, because a hearing will have to be set for a judge to consider the points you raise. The more foreclosures that are occurring in that particular court, the longer it will take.

If you are able to convincingly allege one or more defects in the foreclosure process, you may be able to use these facts as leverage against the lender to negotiate an acceptable modification, even a reduction of the principal if you are underwater on your mortgage. In other words, you don't necessarily have to "win" in the court to get what you want.

If you are contesting the foreclosure to try to stay in your house permanently, you almost certainly will want to hire a lawyer because of what's at stake. But if your only goal is to slow the process down so you can stay in your house a little longer and save some money, you likely can accomplish this mission without a lawyer. (Ch. 7 explains in considerable detail how you can challenge the legitimacy of a foreclosure.)

Judicial Foreclosure States

If you are in a state where foreclosures go through court (see your state's page in the appendix), you typically will receive ten to 30 days' notice of the lender's intent to file a foreclosure action. Once it's filed, you will have 20 to 30 days to respond. If you file a response contesting the foreclosure action, it may take several months or even longer before the judge rules on whether to grant the foreclosure. Even if you don't contest the foreclosure action, the sale usually won't take place until at least a month after the judge issues the foreclosure order.

So you'll likely have a minimum of two months from the first notice of intent to file the case to the date the court orders the sale to take place. You'll have at least double that amount of time if you decide to oppose the foreclosure in court.

After the Sale

After the foreclosure sale, when a new deed has been recorded with a new owner's name on it, you go from homeowner to tenant. A commonly held belief is that you aren't legally a tenant unless you enter into a formal landlord–tenant relationship and agree to pay rent. In fact, with a couple of exceptions, you are considered a tenant (typically termed a "tenant at will" or "tenant by sufferance"). You are entitled to remain in your home until you are evicted using the same court procedures that apply to other tenants—except that you may not get as much notice that you must leave.

The first step toward eviction the new owner must take is to send you a written notice stating that you must move out. (See your state's page in the appendix for the rules on what kind of notice you are entitled to in your state.) How soon you are likely to get such a notice depends on who owns your house after the foreclosure sale: a new buyer or the lender.

If Someone Buys the House

If, at the foreclosure sale, your house is sold to a new owner, that new owner will likely want possession of the property as soon as possible. You may receive a termination notice days or weeks after the auction or sale, just to get the process moving. Exactly when you can expect this termination notice will depend on the new owner's agenda and the experience the new owner has in removing tenants.

If the new owner wants to occupy the house and has experience in evicting tenants, you can expect the notice to come sooner rather than later. If, on the other hand, the new owner is a business that buys and resells foreclosed homes, there might be a significant delay before you get a termination notice, just for bureaucratic reasons. And if the new owner is a novice in buying foreclosed homes and has no experience in evictions, you can expect a delay while the new owner finds a property management firm or lawyer to do the work.

Cash for Keys: Getting Paid to Move Out Voluntarily

Your termination notice may be accompanied by an offer to pay you a lump sum if you leave the property by a certain time and leave it in good condition. Some former homeowners report offers as high as $2,000, which, from the new owner's perspective, is cheap compared to what it would cost the owner if you dug in your heels and made a formal eviction necessary. Also, experience shows that unhappy former homeowners can do a remarkable amount of damage to a house if they think the new owner is being unreasonable.

Not all buyers of foreclosed properties are enlightened enough to make this sort of offer and may be willing to spend hundreds or even thousands of dollars in lawyer fees to get you out. That said, you should always be willing to propose a move-out bonus if the new owner doesn't. And if the new owner does propose one, you shouldn't be shy about negotiating for a higher amount.

If Your Lender Ends Up With the House

If the property is not sold to a new owner at the foreclosure sale (that is, nobody makes an acceptable bid), your lender will end up with title to the property. If this happens, you may have as many as three—or possibly six—months longer to remain in your home payment free. It depends on the following factors.

How ready your lender is to sell. Most lenders have little or no expertise in selling homes, so they bring in real estate agencies to handle those transactions. Your lender may already have a standing relationship with a real estate agency, but if it has to hunt for one, it can take a considerable period of time.

How easy it is to sell the house. Selling foreclosed properties can be difficult, especially when prices are falling and home values are uncertain at best. If your house is in an area where values are relatively stable, and it is in saleable condition, the real estate agency will likely want you out yesterday, because the conventional wisdom in real estate circles is that vacant houses are easier to sell. Paradoxically, if there are a lot of vacant homes in your area, it will be harder to sell your home. If your neighborhood has a glut of homes for sale—whatever the reason— the real estate agency may not be in such a hurry to get you out, because in those circumstances vacant homes rapidly depreciate in value. In fact, you may be able to negotiate a lease that allows you to remain in the house and pay rent. Because the lender would benefit by keeping the property occupied, at least until property values stabilize, you may be able to arrange very favorable terms.

How many foreclosed houses are on the lender's books. If your lender has more foreclosed properties than it knows what to do with, the property may sit for even longer than six months. But if the lender owns few foreclosed properties, your continued occupancy will be more noticeable and so more likely to generate action to get you out.

After You Get a Notice to Leave

When you get a notice demanding that you leave the house, it tells you how long you have to vacate the property. In most states, you'll have between five and 30 days. (Check your state's page in the appendix for specifics.) In most states, once the time period runs out, you still can legally remain in the house until a sheriff physically evicts you under authority of a court order. With few exceptions, to get that court order, the new owner will have to file an eviction lawsuit (commonly called an unlawful detainer or forcible entry and detainer action). This eviction procedure can often take several months, giving you some additional time in your house payment free.

But forcing the landlord to take you to court has its downside. I usually advise people to be prepared to move at the end of the period set out in the written notice to leave rather than wait until the new owner goes to court and gets an eviction order. If you are sued, it's a matter of public record and can hurt your ability to rent or lease in the future. You'll already have bad credit as a result of the foreclosure (or bankruptcy, if you go that route), and many landlords subscribe to private databases that screen prospective tenants for being on the wrong end of previous eviction lawsuits. That fact above all others can lead a prospective landlord to reject your application for a lease or rental agreement.

Another reason to avoid an eviction lawsuit is that if the new owner sues you for eviction, you might also end up on the hook for the rental value of the property for the period you remained in the house after the ownership change. This amount would be what the court determines is the fair rental value of the home. For instance, if comparable homes in the area rent for $1,000 a month, the judge might be willing to give the new owner a judgment against you for that amount. This kind of lawsuit would fly only if the new owner made a formal demand for reasonable rent going forward (which is rare), and you refused to pay it.

If you do face such a demand, you have at least two powerful arguments against it. To begin, in a time of rapidly declining home values, it's next to impossible to assess the true rental value of a home, especially if there are a lot of vacant homes in your neighborhood due to foreclosures. Even if a judge felt that a fair rental value could be determined, you could argue that any rent you owed was more than offset by the fact that you maintained the house and that by staying there you prevented it from depreciating in value. This argument would work better if the new owner were your old lender; if a new owner wanted to move in but couldn't because you refused to leave; the house wasn't at risk of being vacant and neglected.

TIP

Consider filing for bankruptcy. When you're pretty sure you're going to have to give up your house, your prime concern becomes living there payment free for as long as possible. You may be able to extend that time if you file for Chapter 7 or Chapter 13 bankruptcy. Check out Chs. 5 and 6 to find out whether you are eligible, whether you would benefit from filing for reasons other than delaying foreclosure, and other important information.

Eviction Procedures in a Nutshell

- Generally, if you don't leave by the deadline set out in the termination notice, you must be personally served with a summons and eviction complaint (the new owner must go to court to get you out).
- You have the right to contest the eviction complaint before a judge (by filing a formal written response to the eviction complaint).
- After notice and a hearing, the court issues an eviction judgment.
- The court issues an order giving you a few days to move before the sheriff is allowed to remove you. (In a few judicial foreclosure states, the court order authorizing the sale also authorizes the sheriff to evict you after the sale, after a required brief notice is served on you. See your state's page in the appendix.)

Resources Beyond the Book

A t some point, as you make your way through the foreclosure process, you're going to want help from a human being. Someone who knows the territory—a lawyer who's familiar with what local judges will approve or a real estate agent who can tell you how quickly your house will likely sell—can be an invaluable guide. This chapter provides a little guidance about who can help you, where to find them, and how to choose someone who will best suit your needs.

But sometimes you need help from other sources, perhaps because you can't afford an expert's fee, you don't like the answer you got, or you would rather get on top of the information yourself. So I'll also steer you to some books and websites that can provide information and guidance.

Finally, this chapter introduces some techniques for finding the foreclosure-related laws listed on your state's page in the appendix. Virtually all of these laws can be accessed online, in a law library, and quite often in a general public library.

HUD-Approved Housing Counselors

I strongly suggest that you find a HUD-approved housing counselor. These counselors can help you assess your mortgage situation and, if possible, negotiate a solution with your lender that will keep you in your house. Lenders—which suffer economically from foreclosures and benefit if something can be worked out—are a principal source of funds for these agencies. (See Ch. 4 for an in-depth discussion of finding and working with a HUD-approved housing counselor.) Consider contacting one of the following:

- The federal Department of Housing and Urban Development (HUD) has a list of approved counselors. You can find a HUD-approved counselor at www.hud.gov (click "Talk to a Housing Counselor") or by calling 800-569-4287.
- The Homeownership Preservation Foundation website, www.995hope.org, offers free online counseling, among other things. Or you can call 888-995-HOPE and talk with someone.
- The Homeowner Crisis Resource Center, www.mortgagehelpnow. org, will link you up with a local nonprofit foreclosure prevention specialist who may or may not be HUD approved.

As the number of foreclosures—and the variety of programs offered through the federal Making Home Affordable program—continue to increase, the burden on HUD-approved housing counselors grows proportionately. Although new counselors are constantly being trained, their numbers appear to be lagging behind the need for them. What this means is that it may take you a while to find a counselor to work with. Rather than remain patient, some homeowners become convinced that they will have to pay a company to step in to help them. This is almost always a mistake. The pace of modifications is dictated by the mortgage servicers, and there is no proof that private companies offering modification assistance can get the job done any faster than a HUD-approved housing counselor. Worse, there is plenty of evidence that the forms of help these modification companies offer are scams in which homeowners spend large sums of money in exchange for few or no results.

Real Estate Brokers

Real estate brokers and agents can be indispensable if you are facing foreclosure and want to do a short sale. The major difficulty in doing a short sale is that you must get a solid offer from a potential buyer before your lender will tell you whether or not it will accept the terms. A local broker or agent who is familiar with a particular lender's practices will have a good idea of what kind of terms the lender will accept.

The broker can also negotiate with your lender for the final terms. Pushing a short sale through can require experience with the lender (or lenders) and experience in negotiating real estate deals.

If you don't already have a broker or agent you trust, ask around for reliable names. Most communities have real estate firms with well-respected brand names, and I see no reason not to trust agents working for those companies.

Real estate brokers and agents are subject to regulation by every state. To find out whether your broker or agent is licensed, check the website of your state's real estate regulatory agency.

Mortgage Brokers

If you wish to refinance, a mortgage broker can help you find the best loan (or any loan at all). Like real estate brokers and agents, mortgage brokers are regulated in all but one state, and licensed in most. You usually can find out whether a particular mortgage broker is licensed by visiting the website for your state's regulatory agency.

Mortgage brokers, as a group, have taken a lot of heat for the housing slump. Honest and ethical brokers are lumped in with the ones who misrepresented to their customers the nature of the loans they were getting and who handed out loans to people who couldn't afford them. Unfortunately, during the housing bubble, unethical mortgage brokers easily out-competed those who were ethical, because by all accounts it was comparatively easy for just about anyone to get a mortgage. In fact, the fault is better laid at the doorstep of the banks, which themselves were usually just intermediaries for Fannie Mae, Freddie Mac, and Wall Street investors who bought mortgages on the say-so of rating agencies.

It's also hard to blame mortgage brokers for the generally held belief that real estate prices would continue to appreciate forever. After all, the high wizards of our economy—including Alan Greenspan himself—saw no reason to worry.

My advice is to use mortgage brokers for what they are best at: finding a source of refinancing at the lowest available interest rate. But when it comes to understanding how the mortgage works and whether or not you can afford it, keep the old Latin phrase *caveat emptor* (let the buyer beware) firmly in mind.

Lawyers

I am a firm believer in do-it-yourself law, but I also think that the learning curve for some tasks is just too steep for many people to handle—especially given the other problems in their lives. If you realistically think you can keep your house (see Chs. 3 and 4), hire a lawyer if you can possibly afford it. If you are only trying to delay the inevitable, hire a lawyer if you can, but also consider handling the case (or most of it) by yourself.

I think you almost certainly will need a lawyer if you are determined to keep your house by:

- fighting a foreclosure in court, or
- filing for Chapter 13 bankruptcy and making up missed payments over several years.

You will probably benefit from having a lawyer if you realize that you'll probably lose the house sooner or later, but you want to delay the foreclosure and stay in your house as long as possible by:

- fighting a foreclosure in court, or
- filing for Chapter 13 bankruptcy.

When can you go it alone? Having a competent lawyer to represent you can always be to your benefit, but the amount you'll have to pay for one can often outweigh the benefits. With that in mind, you might sensibly choose to represent yourself if:

- you are filing for Chapter 7 bankruptcy to delay your foreclosure by a few months, or
- you are filing for Chapter 7 bankruptcy to get rid of your other debts so your mortgage will be more affordable or so that you'll emerge from your foreclosure with a fresh start.

What Type of Lawyer Do You Need?

Most lawyers who represent people in foreclosure actions specialize in real estate transactions, consumer protection, or bankruptcy. As the number of foreclosures grows, so does the number of lawyers who have expertise in all three areas.

How do you know what expertise a lawyer has? Your best shot is to pop the question directly. Ask "Do you have the experience necessary to help me with my foreclosure?" or "How many foreclosure cases have you handled, and what were the results?" This approach may seem naïve, but my sense is that most lawyers appreciate this approach and will give you honest answers.

As a general rule, if you want to keep your house but you have concluded that you don't want to file for bankruptcy, a real estate lawyer may be the best choice. A real estate lawyer will be comfortable analyzing the lender's paperwork and negotiating with the lender to keep you in your house. On the other hand, if it looks like you won't be able to work something out with the lender, a bankruptcy lawyer is likely your best choice. Bankruptcy is a highly technical area, and few non-bankruptcy lawyers know the tricks of the trade.

How to Find the Right Lawyer

If you are looking for a lawyer, it's worth it to shop around. Here are some tips.

Start with personal referrals. This is your best approach. If you know someone who was pleased with the services of a real estate or bankruptcy lawyer, call that lawyer first.

See whether you can get free or low-cost help. Many law schools sponsor clinics that provide free legal advice to consumers. And many places have senior law projects, with lawyers who will, without charge, help people over 55 with debt and foreclosure issues. To find something near you, do an online search for "senior legal services" in your area. Many parts of the country also have functioning legal aid offices that will help people who qualify—who are poor enough—deal with foreclosures. And if you don't qualify, you may get a quality referral to a lawyer who won't charge you as much as others in the community might.

Be careful with lawyer referral panels. Most county bar associations will give you the names of lawyers who have expertise in fighting foreclosures. But some bar associations may not do much screening of the lawyers they list. Ask about this when you call.

Check out online directories. Both bar associations and commercial websites provide lists of real estate lawyers online, usually with a lot more information about each lawyer than you're likely to get in a yellow pages ad. Start with the lawyer directory on the Nolo website (www. nolo.com). It sets the standard for providing information about how the lawyer goes about the practice of law. Use Google to find other lawyers for your state or city.

Look for a bankruptcy expert. To find a good bankruptcy lawyer, consider using the membership directory of the National Association of Consumer Bankruptcy Attorneys, at www.nacba.org. Membership in this organization is a good sign that the bankruptcy lawyer is tuned in to the nuances of bankruptcy, both generally and how it can be used to save your house or keep you in it longer. Also, because foreclosure and bankruptcy are so closely related these days, a bankruptcy lawyer will also likely be knowledgeable about foreclosures.

Choosing a Lawyer

No matter how you find a lawyer, these suggestions will help you make sure you have the best possible working relationship.

Keep in mind that you're hiring the lawyer to perform a service for you. So fight any urge you have to surrender to or be intimidated by the lawyer. You should be the one who decides what you feel comfortable doing about your legal and financial affairs.

Second, make sure you have good chemistry with any lawyer you hire. When making an appointment, ask to talk directly to the lawyer. If you don't get through, this may give you a hint as to how accessible the lawyer is.

If you are able to talk to the lawyer, ask some specific questions. Do you get clear, concise answers? Is the lawyer making an effort to teach you about your overall situation? If not, look for someone else. Also, pay attention to how the lawyer responds to your knowledge. If you've read this book, you're already better informed than the average client. Does the lawyer appreciate your efforts to educate yourself?

Your main goal at the initial conference is to find out what the lawyer recommends in your case and how much it will cost. Go home and think about the lawyer's suggestions. If they don't make sense or you have other reservations, call someone else.

When shopping for a lawyer, it's common to hire the first one you talk to, unless the lawyer's fees are way out of your league or you really don't get along with the lawyer. You would be best served by visiting a few people before making your final decision. But how do you bring yourself to say, "Thanks for the information. I'll think about it and give you a call"? I suggest you repeat this to yourself 100 times before you make your first contact. After you walk away the first time, the rest will come naturally.

High-Volume Bankruptcy Law Firms

Some lawyers handle a high volume of cases for fees that are significantly less than the average charged by other local bankruptcy lawyers. These firms depend heavily on paralegals to get the work done, and the lawyer appears only briefly at the beginning of the case and at your creditors' meeting (the one personal appearance you will likely make in a Chapter 7 bankruptcy). If you choose a lawyer by price (which is understandable given the standard fees), you will likely be trading hands-on legal representation for a cookie-cutter approach to your case that might not be in your best interest.

How Much Will a Lawyer Charge?

With a few happy exceptions, plenty! It's not a stretch to generalize that if you need an attorney to help you with your foreclosure, you will have difficulty raising the money to pay for it.

Chapter 13 Bankruptcies

Chapter 13 attorneys commonly charge $3,000 to $4,000 a case, depending on the attorney and where you live. If your case appears unusually complex from the beginning, the fee you are quoted may run even higher. If the fees are below a certain amount set by each court (called no-look fees), the court won't examine them; above that amount and the attorney will have to convince the court that they are justified.

If you can come up with a portion of these fees up front, the rest of the fee can be paid over time through your Chapter 13 plan. How large a portion up front? In routine cases, roughly $1,500 and up.

Chapter 7 Bankruptcies

Attorneys' fees for a routine Chapter 7 bankruptcy case run from $1,200 to $2,000, depending on the lawyer and the locality. Most attorneys require you to pay the full fee before you file the bankruptcy, because bankruptcy legally discharges (cancels) whatever fees are unpaid as of the filing date.

Lawyers can get permission from the court to charge you for work done after you file, but they would rather not be your creditor after they have worked to get you out of debt. So, their up-front charges take into account the work they might have to do after you file.

Filing for Chapter 7 Bankruptcy: How Much Will It Cost?	
Filing fee (unless a waiver is granted)	$306
Mandatory credit counseling (before filing) and budget counseling (after)	$100
If you fill out and file your own bankruptcy papers with the help of *How to File for Chapter 7 Bankruptcy* (Nolo), or	about $40
If you hire a nonlawyer bankruptcy petition preparer to do the paperwork, or	about $150
If you hire a lawyer to represent you	about $1,500 to $2,000
Total	$450 to $2,400

> **TIP**
>
> **Filing for Chapter 7 bankruptcy without an attorney.** You may be able to file for a simple Chapter 7 bankruptcy on your own, with the aid of a good self-help guide (see Books below for recommendations). For a Chapter 13 bankruptcy, however, you'll most likely need a lawyer.

Fighting a Foreclosure in Court

If you want to fight a foreclosure in a judicial foreclosure proceeding or in a separate court action in a nonjudicial foreclosure proceeding, plan on paying an up-front retainer of several thousand dollars, whether you use a bankruptcy or a real estate attorney.

Other Tasks

One way to get help from a lawyer—and pay less—is to pay only for specific tasks. Some lawyers will agree to perform certain limited tasks for you instead of taking responsibility for the whole matter. This is called offering unbundled services. For example, if you file for bankruptcy without a lawyer's help, and then your lender asks the court to let it proceed with a foreclosure, you might be able to hire a lawyer just to oppose the lender's request.

The fee will vary depending on the complexity of the task and the lawyer's enthusiasm for providing unbundled services. An attorney might charge only a few hundred dollars to help you negotiate with your lender. And if you want an attorney to represent you in a judicial foreclosure case where you have no serious challenge to the foreclosure but just want to delay the inevitable, the fee will likely be hundreds of dollars instead of thousands.

As a general rule, you should hire an attorney for an unbundled service whenever the amount of the dispute justifies the fee. If a creditor objects to the discharge of a $500 debt, and it will cost you $400 to hire an attorney, you may be better off trying to handle the matter yourself, even though this increases the risk that the creditor will win. But if the dispute is worth $1,000 and the attorney will cost you $400, hiring the attorney makes better sense.

Unfortunately, many bankruptcy attorneys do not like to work on a piecemeal basis. They worry that by doing a little work for you, they might be on the hook if something goes wrong in another part of your case—that is, if they are in for a penny, they are in for a pound. Also, the bar associations of many states discourage lawyers from providing unbundled services. On the other hand, some state bar associations are encouraging attorneys to offer unbundled services simply because so many people can't afford full representation.

You May Be Able to Afford a Lawyer if You're Not Paying Your Mortgage

A lawyer can often be retained for the equivalent of one or two mortgage payments. Because a lawyer may help you gain many extra months of foreclosure delay and living in your home payment free, hiring a lawyer can be very cost effective.

Foreclosure Websites

If you are facing foreclosure, or worry that you might be facing foreclosure soon, you'll find easy-to understand information about foreclosure and your options at these websites:

- **Nolo's Foreclosure Law Section** (www.nolo.com/legal-encyclopedia/foreclosure). Learn everything you need to know about foreclosure, including how it works, how to avoid it, and your options if you are in danger of losing your home.
- **Federal Reserve System** (www.federalreserve.gov/consumerinfo/foreclosure.htm). The Federal Reserve System has established regional Foreclosure Resource Centers throughout the country to address local concerns about the foreclosure crisis. Click your region to get consumer information and foreclosure resources in your area.
- **Federal Trade Commission (FTC)** (www.ftc.gov/articles/0100-mortgage-relief-scams). The FTC publishes fact sheets for consumers on foreclosure scams.

- **Homeownership Preservation Foundation** (www.995hope.org). The Homeownership Preservation Foundation is a nonprofit that offers free foreclosure counseling. The website also provides links to federal and some state government websites offering foreclosure information.
- **MakingHomeAffordable.gov** (www.makinghomeaffordable.gov). This government website provides comprehensive information about the 2009 federal Making Home Affordable program. You can check eligibility requirements for the loan modification, refinancing, or second lien programs and obtain the forms needed to apply for a modification. You can also find program FAQs and calculators to help determine which program might work for you. The site provides information about foreclosure alternatives and a link to a U.S. Department of Housing and Urban Development (HUD)-approved housing counselor directory.
- **National Consumer Law Center (NCLC)** (www.nclc.org/issues/foreclosures-and-mortgages.html). The consumer section of NCLC's website has helpful information and links on foreclosure, predatory lending, and foreclosure scams.
- **National Foundation for Credit Counseling (NFCC)** (www.nfcc.org). The NFCC website has a national directory of local member agencies—nonprofit credit counseling agencies staffed by NFCC-trained, and certified counselors. NFCC housing counselors can provide assistance with foreclosure and other homeowner issues.
- **U.S. Department of Housing and Urban Development (HUD)** (www.hud.gov). The HUD website has a section on foreclosure that includes tips on avoiding foreclosure, information about various government loan modification and refinancing programs, links to government-assisted rental programs, links to local and state resources, and a national directory of HUD-approved housing counselors who provide assistance free of charge.
- **ForeclosureLaw.org** (www.foreclosurelaw.org). Click a state to get a summary of that state's foreclosure laws. The site also has a handy glossary of common foreclosure terms.

- **Nolo's Bankruptcy Section** (www.nolo.com/legal-encyclopedia/bankruptcy). One-stop shopping when it comes to coping with financial trouble. The website includes comprehensive information on surviving foreclosure, filing for bankruptcy, dealing with debt and credit problems, handling collection agencies, dealing with student loan debt, repairing credit, and more.
- **ForeclosureHamlet.org** (www.foreclosurehamlet.org). A social-network website for people facing foreclosure. The website also includes updates on foreclosure-related cases, blogs, and articles (especially of Florida origin).
- **Foreclosure-Fight.com** (www.foreclosure-fight.com). A website focusing on foreclosure defense in Ohio. The information is relevant to other states where judicial foreclosures are the norm.

Books

As the foreclosure crisis spreads, a number of foreclosure-related books are hitting the bookshelves. I encourage you to read every one you can put your hands on. You probably will not have to pay more than $100 for the lot of them—not a bad deal considering what's at stake.

Every book will have something different to offer. Each author will be giving you the benefit of personal experiences, favorite tips on strategy and tactics, and opinions on the best approach to dealing with foreclosure. While every book is sure to contradict every other one in some particular, that should not worry you. A little confusion can be very helpful if it makes you think. There is no one truth to these matters, and sooner or later you will sort things out.

That said, in addition to the books referenced in previous chapters, I recommend the following books:

- *How to File for Chapter 7 Bankruptcy,* by Stephen Elias, and Albin Renauer (Nolo). As the title says, this book explains everything you need to know about filing for Chapter 7 bankruptcy.

- *Chapter 13 Bankruptcy: Keep Your Property & Repay Debts Over Time,* by Stephen Elias and Kathleen Michon (Nolo). This is a guide to the whole Chapter 13 process.
- *The New Bankruptcy: Will It Work for You?* by Stephen Elias and Leon Bayer (Nolo). If you're not sure whether or not bankruptcy is the right way to go for you and your family, this book will highlight the pros and cons and help you evaluate your situation.
- *Credit Repair,* by Margaret Reiter and Robin Leonard (Nolo). If your credit is in the tank and you want to take steps to make it better, this is the book for you. It provides all the steps that have traditionally been necessary to raise your credit score.
- *Foreclosures: Mortgage Servicing, Mortgage Modifications, and Foreclosure Defense.* Authored by the staff of the National Consumer Law Center, this is the best book out there for in-depth legal research on the subject of foreclosure. It covers many of the areas I've addressed—and some I have not—in considerably more detail, including:
  - how to negotiate preforeclosure workout agreements, and current workout options with Fannie Mae, Freddie Mac, HUD, VA, and RHS
  - the best discussion anywhere on how to challenge mortgage servicer abuses
  - foreclosure litigation, including power of sale, due on sale, and substantive and procedural defenses
  - raising loan broker and loan originator-related claims against the mortgage holder
  - special rights to stop foreclosure of FHA, VA, and RHS mortgages
  - mobile home foreclosures, and
  - tax liens and tax foreclosures.

It comes with access to a companion website that contains a lot of the forms, foreclosure laws, and other materials you will need if you want to fight a foreclosure or do your own workout with your lender. You can buy a copy for around $200, or perhaps find a copy in your local law or general-purpose library. For more information, visit www.nclc.org.

- *Foreclosure Prevention Counseling: Preserving the American Dream.* This excellent and less expensive product (around $60), also published by NCLC, provides a nuts-and-bolts approach to the various modifications offered by different banks and government agencies. It has an excellent appendix detailing state foreclosure and property tax abatement laws.

- *Foreclosure Defenses: Non-Bankruptcy & Bankruptcy Defenses,* by Craig Triance. Published by The King Bankruptcy Practice Series, this book provides valuable information and forms that will assist you in fighting your foreclosure in state and federal courts. Although the book is pricey (about $150), it costs much less than a typical real estate or bankruptcy lawyer will charge for an hour of work. It is especially invaluable if you want to drill deeper into the foreclosure defenses briefly discussed in Ch. 7. Although the book is primarily written for lawyers, the author fortunately writes in plain English. You can order the book online at www.bankruptcybooks.com/triance_foreclosure_defens.htm.

Looking Up Foreclosure Statutes

Your state's page in the appendix lists references to the laws governing foreclosures in your state. These references are termed citations, and the laws are known as statutes. By using the citation, you can find and read for yourself your state's laws on such matters as:

- how much notice you are entitled to before your home is sold in a foreclosure
- how much notice you are entitled to before you are evicted after a foreclosure sale
- how much time you have to reinstate or redeem your mortgage after a default

- whether your lender can sue you for a deficiency judgment and if so, under what conditions, and
- what special protections you are entitled to if you have a high-cost mortgage (one with a much higher interest rate than normal).

You can easily locate statutes online or in most states at a law library or even at a public library.

There are two fundamental ways to find your state statutes on foreclosure:

- Once you find a collection of the statutes, you can browse through various levels of subject headings (usually organized hierarchically by numbered title, article, chapter, and section).
- You can go to the state law collection at www.justia.com and search for the keywords you're interested in.

RESOURCE

More information on legal research. Legal research is its own subject; if you want to delve into it more deeply, see *Legal Research: How to Find & Understand the Law,* by Stephen Elias and the editors of Nolo (Nolo). My goal in this chapter is just to show you how to look up statutes listed on the state pages in the appendix.

Browsing

Here is an example of the steps you could use to find the Vermont foreclosure statutes by browsing. If you go online and follow along, you'll pretty much know how to find the same law for your state.

Start by finding the statute's citation on the Vermont page in the appendix. The law is called Vermont's Strict Foreclosure Law, and the citation is Vermont Stat. Ann., Title 12, Section 4526.

Step 1: Go to www.justia.com.

Step 2: Scroll down to "Laws: Cases & Codes."

Step 3: Click on "Vermont Law."

Step 4: You'll see three Vermont Codes—one for 2005, one for 2009, and one for 2011. For this example, click the link to "2011 Vermont Codes." If you find two or more sets of codes for your state, follow the steps in this example for all of them.

Step 5: Find and click on the relevant title. (For this statute, it's "Title 12.") This opens up a list of chapters.

Step 6: Scroll down until you reach the chapter that contains "Section 4526," the section of Vermont's strict foreclosure statute. It's "Chapter 163 (Chancery Proceedings)."

Step 7: Click on "Chapter 163."

Step 8: Scroll down to "Section 4526, Foreclosure of real or personal property." You're there!

Most other states arrange their statutes in a similar manner: by title, chapter, and section. Use the same method to find the statutes referenced on your state's page.

Some states arrange their statutes in a slightly different manner. For example, if you were looking for Section 2323.07 of the Ohio Revised Code, you would use the first two numbers to find the correct title ("Title 23"). Click on that title, and then find the statute numbered "2323.07."

In New York, the citation to the foreclosure laws reads: N.Y. Real Prop. Acts. Law, Sections 1301 to 1391. You would find these statutes by first browsing the list of legal topics until you found "Real Property Actions and Proceedings." Click on that topic and then browse until you find the article that contains "Sections 1301 to 1391 (Action to Foreclose a Mortgage)."

Your state may use a slightly different model from any of these. You may have to use a little ingenuity to get to the right statutes. As a general rule, the number at the left of the citation will be the number you use to start your search, whether it is the title, article, or chapter number. If for some reason the citation number doesn't work, look for a subject heading dealing with foreclosure, real estate, or real property, or if you are in a judicial foreclosure state, civil procedure.

Foreclosure Statutes Can Be Hard to Read

Especially in Eastern states, foreclosure statutes come from English law adopted here in the 18th century. The language is very different from modern English (even modern legal English), and can be hard to understand.

Also, for reasons that escape me, they aren't organized very well. Sometimes one relevant statute will be found in one section of the law while a closely related one will appear elsewhere. For example, some foreclosure laws are found in the code dealing with court procedure, while other laws are found in the part of the code dealing with real estate. So, be prepared to look in several different parts of the code.

Searching Online

If you aren't able to find your state's foreclosure statutes by using the method described just above, try Google. For instance, by doing an online search for "Vermont's foreclosure statutes," you'll find in your list of results a link to the "Vermont Statutes Online" on the Vermont State Legislature's website. Clicking on that link will take you to a page listing all of the relevant Vermont foreclosure statutes.

Beware of this method of searching. Quite possibly, you will turn up only one statute at a time. Bankruptcy and foreclosure statutes come in swarms, and you need to be able to see the entire array (called the statutory scheme) to fully understand what you are looking at. For example, if you are looking for statutes dealing with restitution or notice before the foreclosure sale, you may find only one of these statutes and not be aware of the others.

Glossary

Acceleration. Requiring a borrower to immediately pay off the balance of a loan. Under a provision commonly found in promissory notes, if the borrower misses some payments, the lender can demand that the total balance of the loan be paid immediately. The loan must be accelerated before the lender can foreclose. In many states, the borrower gets a chance to reinstate the loan (and cancel the acceleration) by paying the arrears, plus costs and interest.

Adjustable-rate mortgage (ARM). A mortgage or deed of trust providing that the interest rate on the underlying promissory note can be adjusted up or down at specified intervals tracking the movement of a federal interest rate or another index.

Administrative expenses. In a Chapter 13 bankruptcy repayment plan, the trustee's fee, the debtor's attorneys fees, and other costs that a debtor must pay in full. Administrative costs are typically 10% of total payments under the plan.

Amortization. Paying off a loan with regular payments over a set period. Part of each payment is applied to principal and to interest.

Amount financed. The amount of money you are getting in a loan, calculated under rules required by the federal law. This is the amount of money you are borrowing after certain financing costs and fees are deducted. The amount financed is far less than the total amount you pay back, because the total amount of the loan includes the interest on the amount financed.

Annual percentage rate (APR). The interest rate on a loan expressed under rules required by federal law. To determine the true cost of a loan, it is more accurate to look at the APR than the stated interest rate.

Appraisal. An expert's evaluation of what a particular item of property is worth in the marketplace. Colloquially, the term is used to describe any opinion about the value of property. For instance, real estate agents and brokers often informally appraise property, even though they aren't expert appraisers.

Arrears. Overdue payments on a loan. With a mortgage, this may include any missed payments, interest on the missed payments, and the costs incurred by the lender in trying to collect the debt.

Assignee liability. Liability of an assignee (an entity that has been assigned ownership of a mortgage or deed of trust) for unlawful or abusive acts of the original lender or mortgage originator. Assignee liability can be important in lawsuits against a foreclosing party for violations of federal or state laws prohibiting predatory lending practices. In most cases, assignees are off the hook for those practices if they conducted a reasonable investigation into the history of the loan.

Assignment. A document showing that ownership of a mortgage or deed of trust (and the underlying promissory note) has been transferred (assigned) from the original owner to a new owner (assignee). In recent times, mortgages have been the subject of many assignments as they have been "securitized" and sold as investments worldwide. In some cases, the assignments have been made electronically, without anything on paper. When it comes time to enforce the mortgage or deed of trust in a foreclosure, the absence of documentation can sometimes defeat the foreclosure, because there is no documentary proof of current ownership.

Attachment. A legal process that allows a creditor to attach a lien to property that you own because of a contract you signed (a car note, for example), a money judgment you owe, or a special statute that authorizes the lien, as in the case of a tax lien. If the lien is on your house, it can be enforced by foreclosure.

Automatic stay. An injunction automatically issued by the bankruptcy court when someone files for bankruptcy. The automatic stay prohibits most creditor collection activities, such as filing or continuing lawsuits, making written requests for payment, or notifying credit reporting bureaus of an unpaid debt.

Balloon payment. A large lump-sum payment due as the last payment on a loan. For instance, if you borrow $10,000, your note might require you to pay $5,000 of the loan over a three-year period, plus one balloon payment for the rest at the end of that period.

Bankruptcy code. The federal law that governs the operation of the bankruptcy courts and establishes bankruptcy procedures. It's in Title 11 of the United States Code.

Bankruptcy petition preparer. Any nonlawyer who helps someone with bankruptcy. Bankruptcy petition preparers (BPPs) are regulated by the U.S. Trustee. Because they are not lawyers, BPPs can't represent anyone in bankruptcy court or provide legal advice.

Capitalization. Treating items owed on a loan as part of a new principal balance. For example, when missed payments on a mortgage are added to the mortgage principal, to be paid off over time, they are capitalized. If missed payments are capitalized and the loan is reamortized, the lender will recalculate the monthly payment using the existing interest rate and new principal balance.

Chapter 7 bankruptcy. A liquidation bankruptcy, in which the trustee sells the debtor's nonexempt property and distributes the proceeds to the debtor's creditors. At the end of the case, the debtor receives a discharge of all remaining debts, except those that cannot legally be discharged.

Chapter 12 bankruptcy. A type of bankruptcy designed to help small farmers reorganize their debts.

Chapter 13 bankruptcy. A type of consumer bankruptcy designed to help individuals reorganize their debts and pay all or a portion of them over three to five years.

Chapter 13 plan. A document filed in a Chapter 13 bankruptcy that shows how all of the debtor's projected disposable income will be used over a three- to five-year period to pay all mandatory debts—for example, back child support, taxes, and mortgage arrearages—as well as a percentage of unsecured, nonpriority debts, such as medical and credit card bills.

Closed-end loan. Any loan that must be paid off within a certain period of time. The federal Home Ownership and Equity Protection Act (HOEPA) currently applies only to closed-end loans. Loans that don't have to be paid off within any particular time—for example, credit card debt—are open-ended.

Collateral. Property pledged by a borrower as security for a loan. If a creditor accepts property as collateral for a loan under a security agreement, and the agreement is properly recorded, the creditor has a lien on the collateral and can repossess it if the conditions of the security agreement (typically, making monthly payments on the loan) aren't met.

Complaint. A formal document that initiates a lawsuit.

Confirmation hearing. A court hearing conducted by a bankruptcy judge at which the judge decides whether or not a debtor's proposed Chapter 13 plan is feasible and meets all legal requirements.

Conforming loan. A mortgage loan that is small enough to be bought by Fannie Mae or guaranteed by the Federal Housing Administration. Currently, a conforming loan for a single-family home is any loan for less than $417,000, except in designated areas with a high cost of living, where the limit is $625,500, down from the previous high-balance limit of $729,750. (The amounts for a confirming loan in Hawaii and Alaska are higher to reflect the higher costs of living in those states.) See "Jumbo loan."

Conventional loan. A mortgage loan issued to a borrower with an excellent or very good credit rating. Conventional loans do not include those insured by the federal government or subprime loans.

Cramdown. In a Chapter 13 bankruptcy, the act of reducing a secured debt to the replacement value of the collateral securing the debt.

Credit and debt counseling. Counseling that explores the possibility of repaying debts outside of bankruptcy and covers credit, budgeting, and financial management. Consumers must go through credit counseling with an approved provider before filing for bankruptcy.

Credit bureau. Another name for a consumer reporting or credit reporting agency. These companies sell information about a consumer's credit history to certain categories of people or organizations. Individuals are entitled to one free credit report per year, not including the person's credit score.

Credit report. Also called a consumer report or a credit record, this documents the credit history and current status of a borrower's monthly payment obligations and contains public information such as bankruptcies, court judgments, and tax liens. Chapter 7 bankruptcies remain on a credit report for 10 years, Chapter 13 bankruptcies and other negative information for seven years.

Credit score. Also called a FICO score, this is a number that supposedly summarizes your credit history. The score is based on a number of factors, including your debt payment history, how much debt you currently have, how long you've had credit, and how recently your major credit transactions occurred. There are several rating agencies, all of which use their own secret formulas, which means that you never know just how a particular score was arrived at. Lenders use credit scores to decide whether to grant a loan and at what interest rate. Scores range from about 350 to 900; a score of 660 or more generally gets you the best loans at the best rates.

Creditor. A person or an institution to whom money is owed.

Creditors' meeting. A meeting that someone filing for bankruptcy must attend, at which the trustee and creditors may question the debtor about property, court documents, and debts.

Curing a default. See "Reinstating a mortgage."

Current market value. The price that property could be sold for.

Current monthly income. As defined by bankruptcy law, a bankruptcy filer's total gross income (whether taxable or not), averaged over the six-month period immediately preceding the month in which the bankruptcy is filed. The current monthly income is used to determine whether or not the debtor can file for Chapter 7 bankruptcy, among other things.

Debt consolidation. Refinancing debt into a new loan. Homeowners sometimes convert relatively short-term unsecured debt into debt secured by the home—putting the house at greater risk if there is a default in payments on the consolidated debt.

Debtor. Someone who owes money to another person or business. Also, the generic term used to refer to anyone who files for bankruptcy.

Declaration of homestead. See "Homestead declaration."

Deed in lieu of foreclosure. An arrangement under which a homeowner can get out from under a mortgage and prevent a foreclosure, by signing the deed to the home over to the lender in exchange for the lender's agreement not to foreclose. Typically, the lender agrees to not hold the homeowner liable for the remaining amount of the mortgage.

Deed of trust. In about half the states, a loan that is secured by real estate is termed a deed of trust. Deeds of trust are like mortgages (which also are loans secured by real estate). However, unlike mortgages, deeds of trust typically have a power of sale clause that lets the lender have the property sold at a public auction if the homeowner defaults on the payments. Foreclosures under deeds of trust are typically referred to as nonjudicial foreclosures because they take place without court supervision.

Default rate. An interest rate that replaces a contractual interest rate if a borrower defaults on a loan. If the default rate is set out in the mortgage loan agreement, it will typically be considerably higher than the contract rate.

Default. Failing to meet the requirements of an agreement. Defaults that lead to foreclosure typically involve the failure to make mortgage payments, but other types of defaults are possible, such as the failure to maintain necessary insurance or to keep the property in proper condition.

Deficiency. The amount a homeowner owes the lender after a house is sold at a foreclosure or short sale for less than the actual debt. In most states, the lender can file a separate lawsuit to recover a deficiency owed by the borrower. However, state laws typically require that the deficiency be measured by the difference between the property's fair market value and the amount of the loan rather than by the sale amount. For example, if a home sells for $300,000 at a foreclosure auction, the fair market value of the home is actually $400,000 and the borrower owes $500,000, the deficiency in most states will be $100,000, not $200,000.

Discharge. A court order, issued at the conclusion of a Chapter 7 or Chapter 13 bankruptcy case, which legally relieves the debtor of personal liability for debts that can be discharged in that type of bankruptcy.

Dischargeable debt. A debt that is wiped out at the conclusion of a bankruptcy case, unless the judge decides that it should not be.

Disposable income. In a Chapter 13 bankruptcy, the difference between a debtor's current monthly income and allowable expenses. This is the amount that the bankruptcy law deems available for a repayment plan.

Equity stripping. The practice of giving high-cost second mortgages to homeowners, reducing the borrower's equity. Some of these loans violate federal or state truth-in-lending laws, and homeowners may be able to cancel (rescind) the loans later or sue the lender. See "Home Ownership and Equity Protection Act (HOEPA)."

Equity. The amount of cash you would pocket if you sold your house and paid off all the liens (for example, mortgages, property taxes, money judgments, mechanic's liens, and tax liens). For example, if you owe $300,000 on your house on first and second mortgages, the IRS has a tax lien on the house for $50,000, you sell your home for $390,000, and costs of sale are $20,000, you will pocket $20,000. That's your equity.

Exempt property. Property described by state and federal laws (exemptions) that a debtor is entitled to keep in a Chapter 7 bankruptcy. Exempt property cannot be taken and sold by the trustee for the benefit of the debtor's unsecured creditors.

Exemptions. State and federal laws specifying the types of property that creditors are not entitled to take to satisfy a debt and the bankruptcy trustee is not entitled to sell for the benefit of the debtor's unsecured creditors.

Fannie Mae (Federal National Mortgage Association). A government-chartered corporation set up to buy mortgages from original lenders and repackage them for private investors. Congress authorized Fannie Mae to stimulate the growth of the housing market by making capital available for new loans. Investors and lenders that deal with Fannie Mae must follow various guidelines regarding mortgage servicing and foreclosure practices.

Federal exemptions. A list of exempt property in the federal Bankruptcy Code. Some states give debtors the option of using the federal rather than the state exemptions.

Federal Home Mortgage Corporation. See "Freddie Mac."

Federal Housing Administration (FHA). A federal agency that insures first mortgage lenders against loss when a loan is made following FHA regulations. The FHA does not lend money; it only insures the loan. The FHA also certifies nonprofit housing counselors.

Federal National Mortgage Association. See "Fannie Mae."

Filing date. The date a bankruptcy petition in a particular case is filed. With few exceptions, debts incurred after the filing date are not discharged.

Forbearance. A lender's willingness to let you skip all or a portion of your monthly payments for a brief period, usually three to six months. You'll have to catch up later, probably with increases in monthly payments. But the lender might be willing to extend the loan so that missed payments can be added to the end of the loan rather than be paid off on top of the regular monthly payment.

Foreclosure "rescue" scams. Scams on people who are facing foreclosure. The scam artist learns about impending foreclosures from public filings, advertisements, and postings and contacts homeowners with promises of help that typically result in the homeowner's losing the house and any remaining equity.

Foreclosure. The legal process by which a creditor with a claim (lien) on real estate forces a sale of the property in order to collect on the lien. Foreclosure typically occurs when a homeowner defaults on a mortgage. See "Judicial foreclosure" and "Nonjudicial foreclosure."

Forgiven debt. Debt that is written off as uncollectable by the creditor. In the foreclosure context, a mortgage owner forgives debt when a foreclosure occurs and the property is sold for less than is owed on the mortgage. Forgiven debt—the amount you don't have to pay back—is taxable as income, and the creditor is required to send you (and the IRS) a Form 1099C stating the amount. Three major exceptions: You won't have to pay tax if you are insolvent when the debt is written off, the debt is discharged in bankruptcy, or you used the money you borrowed to buy or improve the property.

Freddie Mac (Federal Home Mortgage Corporation). Like Fannie Mae, a government-chartered company set up to buy mortgages from original lenders and repackage (securitize) them for private investors.

Ginnie Mae (Government National Mortgage Corporation). A quasi-governmental agency that guarantees pools of FHA- and VA-insured loans that have been packaged into securities for investment purposes.

Good faith. In a Chapter 13 bankruptcy case, when a debtor files with the sincere purpose of paying off debts over the period of time required by law rather than for manipulative purposes—such as to prevent a foreclosure that by all rights should be allowed to proceed.

Government mortgage guarantors. Special government programs that provide mortgage insurance or guarantees to lenders who make purchase-money mortgage loans to certain homebuyers. These programs are offered through the federal government (the Federal Housing Administration, the Rural Housing Service, and the Veterans Administration), or by a state housing finance agency. In addition to being insured, these loans come with rules regarding transactions with homeowners, including a requirement that the lender cooperate with homeowners who are attempting to cure defaults (reinstate mortgages).

Home equity loan. A loan made to a homeowner on the basis of the equity in the house and secured by the house in the same manner as a first mortgage.

Home Ownership and Equity Protection Act (HOEPA). A federal law that provides special protection to homeowners who obtain home mortgage loans at high interest rates or with exceptionally high fees. The protection includes fines and penalties recoverable in a lawsuit against the lender and sometimes a defense to foreclosure in state or federal court.

Homestead declaration. A form filed with the county recorder's office to put on record your right to a homestead exemption. Only a few states require recording. In most states, the homestead exemption is automatic—you are not required to record a homestead declaration in order to claim the homestead exemption.

Homestead. In bankruptcy, a state or federal exemption applicable to property where the debtor lives—usually including boats and mobile homes.

Injunction. A court order prohibiting a person or an entity from taking specified actions—for example, bankruptcy's automatic stay (in reality an automatic injunction), which prevents most creditors from trying to collect their debts.

Interest. The cost of borrowing money over time. Interest on a loan is always described as percentage of the loan payable over a period of time, as in 7% per year. In agreements for the purchase of homes and cars, the interest is computed and amortized over the period of the loan, which makes the amount owed on the secured debt a lot higher than the base loan itself. For instance, if you buy a car for $20,000 and borrow the money over seven years, the amount payable on the note is $20,000 plus the amount of interest that you'll pay over the seven years.

Interest-only loan. A type of mortgage loan, made popular during the 2004–2006 housing boom, where the borrower makes payments only on the loan's interest or part of the interest for a limited period of time. The mortgage payments are much lower than they would be if the payments were applied to the loan as a whole, but the overall amount of the loan may increase (negative amortization). When the amount of the loan reaches a certain level (set out in the loan document), the borrower must begin making much higher payments to make up for the increase. It is the sudden increase in required mortgage payments that pushes so many homeowners into foreclosure.

Insolvent. When a person's or business's assets are worth less than their debts.

Joint debtors. Married people who file for bankruptcy together and pay a single filing fee.

Judgment proof. Description of a person whose income and property are such that a creditor can't (or won't) seize them to enforce a money judgment—for example, a dwelling protected by a homestead exemption or a bank account containing only a few dollars.

Judicial foreclosure. A type of foreclosure, used in about half the states, in which the foreclosing party files a lawsuit in the county where the property is located, seeking a judgment that the property can be sold in a foreclosure sale because the homeowner has defaulted on mortgage payments. A few states use what are called strict foreclosures, which allow the judge to order title to the property transferred to the foreclosing party without the need for a sale. A few other states have hybrid processes, in which the foreclosure proceeds under a power of sale clause but is subject to some court supervision.

Judicial lien. A lien created by recording a court money judgment against the debtor's property—usually real estate.

Jumbo loan. A loan for an amount that exceeds the conforming loan limit (the limit at which the loan will be guaranteed by the Federal Housing Administration) and which usually costs a point or two higher in interest rates as a result. See "Conforming loan."

Lease and buy-back. A scheme in which you deed your home to a third party and then lease it back, paying rent to build up your credit score so you can buy back the loan. Although there might be some legitimate reasons for doing this, most often it's a scam—the third party pockets your mortgage payments and borrows against the property, and the house ends up in foreclosure.

Lien avoidance. A bankruptcy procedure in which certain types of liens can be removed from certain types of property. Liens that are not avoided survive the bankruptcy even though the underlying debt may be canceled—for instance, a lien remains on a car even if the debt evidenced by the car note is discharged in the bankruptcy.

Lien. A legal claim against property that must be paid before title to the property can be transferred. Liens on real estate can also often be collected through foreclosure, depending on the type of lien. Examples of liens include mortgages, tax liens, and mechanics' liens.

Lifting the stay. When a bankruptcy court allows a creditor to continue with debt collection or other activities that are otherwise banned by the automatic stay. For instance, the court might allow a landlord to proceed with an eviction or a lender to repossess a car because the debtor has defaulted on the note.

Loan term. The loan term is the period during which the loan is due to be repaid in full. Most mortgage loans have 15- or 30-year terms. Many predatory consumer loans (payday loans, car title loans, and refund anticipation loans) have very short terms, which increases the annual percentage rate charged by the lender. Mortgage foreclosure rescue scams also frequently employ short-term loans with outrageous interest payments.

Market value. The highest price one would pay and the lowest price the seller would accept on a property on the open market. Market value is used to determine the amount of equity a homeowner has in the property, which can determine whether it makes sense to fight foreclosure or to file for bankruptcy. Market value also is often crucial in determining whether a mortgage holder can recover a deficiency after a foreclosure sale. For example, assume a property sells for $250,000, the former homeowner owes $350,000, and a court later determines that the property's market value was actually $300,000 (which could have been realized if the minimum bid at the foreclosure auction had been set higher). In that event, if the state's laws use the property's actual market value to limit deficiency awards, the court will issue a deficiency judgment for $50,000.

Materialmen's and mechanics' liens. Liens imposed by statute on real estate when suppliers of materials, labor, and contracting services used to improve the real estate are not properly compensated.

Means test. A formula that uses predefined income and expense categories to determine whether a debtor whose income is more than the state median family income should be allowed to file for Chapter 7 bankruptcy.

Median family income. The figure at which there are as many families with incomes below it as there are above it. The U.S. Census Bureau publishes median family income figures for each state and for different household sizes. In bankruptcy, the median family income is used as a basis for determining whether a debtor must pass the means test to file for Chapter 7 bankruptcy, and whether a debtor filing for Chapter 13 bankruptcy must commit all projected disposable income to a five-year repayment plan.

Meeting of creditors. See "Creditors' meeting."

MERS. MERS stands for "Mortgage Electronic Registration Systems," an entity listed as the mortgagee of record for about half the mortgages in America. MERS operates a database of mortgage transactions conducted by its members, supposedly obviating the need to use county real property recording systems.

Modification. Altering one or more terms of a mortgage, such as reducing the interest rate, reducing the principal due (sometimes all the way down to the property's market value), or increasing the term of the loan to account for missed payments. Negotiating a modification is more likely when the borrower can demonstrate a hardship that is likely to last or an error in the mortgage documents or foreclosure process.

Mortgage broker. An individual, usually licensed by the state, who arranges financing for a potential home purchaser by seeking the mortgage products for that particular person.

Mortgage holder. A person or company who currently has the right, under the terms of the mortgage, to enforce it through foreclosure.

Mortgage servicer. A type of business that large mortgage owners hire to administer their mortgage portfolios. The mortgage servicer typically accepts and records mortgage payments, negotiates a workout in case of a default, and even supervises the foreclosure process if attempts at a workout fail. Mortgage owners usually prefer that their homeowners stay current on their loans and stay out of foreclosure, but servicers often have a conflicting economic incentive because when customers default on their mortgages, the servicers get to keep the fees and costs that typically accompany a mortgage default and foreclosure.

Mortgage. A contract in which a loan to buy real estate is secured by the real estate as collateral. If the borrower defaults on loan payments, the lender can foreclose on the property.

Mortgage-backed security. A type of investment backed by mortgage loans that have been packaged into pools or trusts, with payments on the underlying mortgages generating the return for investors. By selling original mortgages to Fannie Mae and Freddie Mac (and other players in the secondary mortgage market, where the packaging occurs) lenders generate more funds for future lending.

Mortgagee. The mortgagee is the lender or other entity that owns the rights and responsibilities granted in a mortgage by the borrower (mortgagor). Typically, the mortgagee is the party who is authorized by state law to bring a foreclosure action.

Mortgagor. Someone who borrows money and signs a mortgage.

Motion to lift stay. A formal request in which a creditor asks the bankruptcy court for permission to continue a court action or collection activities in spite of the automatic stay.

Negative amortization. Negative amortization occurs when payments do not cover the amount of interest due for a loan period. For example, if you have a $150,000 loan at 9% interest for 15 years and make monthly payments of $1,200, your payments won't cover the interest that's accruing each month, and the loan will negatively amortize. At the end of 15 years, even if you make all of your payments, you will still owe more than $50,000. Accordingly, a mortgage that has built-in negative amortization terms often requires a balloon payment at the end of the loan period. Interest-only mortgages also use negative amortization to keep the initial payments low, and then require a dramatic increase in the payments after several years (rather than a balloon payment) to make up the difference.

Negative equity. Negative equity is when a property's market value is less than the total owed on all the liens recorded against it. The popular term for negative equity is "upside down." In the bankruptcy context, negative equity can be very helpful in that you can get rid of liens that are no longer secured by equity even though they were secured when you obtained the loans. For example, say you have a first mortgage of $200,000, a second mortgage of $100,000 and a third mortgage of $50,000. Also assume that your home sank from a value of $400,000 to $175,000. In this case you have a negative equity of $175,000 (the difference between your home's value ($175,000) and the amount of the liens created by all three mortgages, or $350,000). Your first mortgage of $200,000 is partially covered by your home's value of $175,000, but you have no equity to secure the second and third mortgages. In this situation, Chapter 13 bankruptcy can remove the second and third mortgage liens from your house's title.

Nonbankruptcy federal exemptions. Federal laws that allow a debtor who has not filed for bankruptcy to keep creditors away from certain property. The debtor can also use these exemptions in bankruptcy if the debtor is using a state exemption system.

Nondischargeable debt. Debt that survives bankruptcy, such as back child support and most student loans.

Nonexempt property. In bankruptcy, property that is unprotected by the exemption system available to the debtor. In a Chapter 7 bankruptcy, the trustee may sell nonexempt property for the benefit of the debtor's unsecured creditors. In a Chapter 13 bankruptcy, debtors must propose a plan that pays their unsecured creditors at least the value of their unsecured property.

Nonjudicial foreclosure. A foreclosure that proceeds outside of court under a power of sale clause included in a deed of trust (a type of mortgage).

Nonpriority debt. A type of debt that is not entitled to be paid first in Chapter 7 bankruptcy and does not have to be paid in full in a Chapter 13 bankruptcy.

Non-purchase-money security interest. In the foreclosure context, a loan that uses your home as collateral for any purpose other than to buy it—for example, a home equity loan that is used to improve the home or pay for a vacation, college tuition, or medical emergency.

Notice to quit. A formal written notice, given to the occupant of real estate, to leave the premises within a specified period of time or face a judicial proceeding (often called an unlawful detainer, or forcible entry and detainer proceedings) in which a judge can order the sheriff to physically evict the occupant. In many states, a homeowner who continues to occupy the home after a foreclosure must be given a notice to quit before eviction proceedings may go forward.

Open-ended loan. A loan without a definite term or end date. Authorized charges on credit cards are open-ended loans. As a general rule, there are no limits on interest rates charged on open-ended loans but some states cap interest rates on closed-end loans.

Origination fee. A fee paid to a lender for processing a loan application. This fee is commonly called points and is charged as a percentage of the loan amount.

Originator. The entity the loan documents identify as the party making the loan, typically a bank or credit union.

Partially secured debt. A debt secured by collateral that is worth less than the debt itself—for instance, when a person owes $15,000 on a car that is worth only $10,000.

Personal financial responsibility counseling. A two-hour class intended to teach good budget management. Every consumer bankruptcy filer must attend such a class in order to get a Chapter 7 or Chapter 13 bankruptcy discharge.

Personal property. All property not classified as real property, including tangible items, such as cars and jewelry, and intangible property, such as stocks and pensions.

Predatory lending. In the foreclosure context, lending money under terms that are likely to cause a default in payments because of the expense of the loan compared to the borrower's income, or due to hidden fees and costs that are not properly disclosed. Certain categories of predatory loans are prohibited by federal and state law, and homeowners can sometimes use a violation of those laws to defend against a foreclosure or sue for fines and penalties.

Prepetition counseling. Mandatory debt and credit counseling that occurs before the bankruptcy petition is filed. Compare personal financial management counseling, which occurs after the petition is filed.

Priority debt. In Chapter 7 bankruptcy, a type of debt that is paid first if the debtor has any assets available to pay creditors. Priority debts include alimony and child support, fees owed to the trustee and attorneys in the case, and wages owed to employees. With one exception (back child support obligations assigned to government entities), priority claims must be paid in full in a Chapter 13 bankruptcy.

Projected disposable income. In bankruptcy, the amount of income a debtor will have left over each month, after deducting allowable expenses, payments on mandatory debts, and administrative expenses from his or her current monthly income. This is the amount the debtor must pay toward unsecured nonpriority debts in a Chapter 13 plan.

Proof of service. A document signed under penalty of perjury by the person serving a document showing how the service was made, who made it, and when.

Property inspection fee. A charge imposed by a mortgage servicer for a cursory inspection (often just a drive-by) to determine the physical condition or occupancy status of mortgaged property. This fee is often unreasonably high and an unreasonable number of inspections are often made, especially if the homeowner has defaulted on mortgage payments. To get current on a mortgage or propose a Chapter 13 repayment plan, the homeowner must pay these fees as well as the missed payments.

Real Estate Settlement Procedures Act (RESPA). A federal law designed to protect consumers from unnecessarily high settlement charges and certain abusive practices in the residential real estate market. RESPA provides a way for a borrower to challenge a stated loan balance provided by the servicer and to get information about how the loan has been processed. It also requires that certain disclosures be made to borrowers.

Real property. Real estate (land and buildings on the land, usually including mobile homes attached to a foundation).

Reamortization. Recalculating loan payments on different terms. For example, if you have paid for ten years on a 15-year loan, your lender might extend the loan for another ten years at a lower interest rate, lowering your monthly payments. Similarly, lenders sometimes add missed payments to the principal loan (that is, capitalize the missed payments). This reamortization may cause the monthly payments to increase because of the increase in the principal and the interest on it.

Redemption right. In foreclosure, the former homeowner's right to buy back the house after a foreclosure sale by reimbursing the new owner the amount of the purchase price, or, if the property was bought by the lender, paying the lender the full value of the mortgage. In many states, even after a foreclosure sale, the new owner can't take possession until the redemption period has passed. For example, if the state's law gives the former owner up to six months to redeem the mortgage, the new owner can't take possession until that time has passed and no redemption has been made.

Refinance. Using a new loan to pay off the current loan to get a better interest rate and perhaps pull some of your equity out of the house. Refinancing is hard to get if you are more than three payments behind or have troubled credit. But a homeowner who is facing a mortgage interest reset, is still current on the mortgage, and has some equity in the property from a down payment or many years of mortgage payments might be able to refinance at a more affordable fixed rate.

Reinstating a mortgage. Getting current on your mortgage by making up missed payments, paying the lender interest on the missed payments, and reimbursing the lender for various costs and fees incurred during the time you were in default. This is sometimes referred to as curing the default.

Repayment plan. An informal plan to repay creditors most or all of what they are owed outside of bankruptcy. The typical repayment plan provides for amortizing missed payments (and associated interest, costs, and fees) over a period of time by increasing the monthly mortgage payment to include the extra payments. Also refers to the plan proposed by a debtor in a Chapter 13 bankruptcy.

Rescission. The act of canceling a loan agreement and asking a court to restore borrower and lender to the positions they were in before it was signed. Federal and state laws allow a borrower to rescind a mortgage loan transaction within three business days after signing the papers. This period can sometimes be extended for years if the lender violated certain federal laws. The right of rescission may sometimes be used as a defense to a foreclosure.

Reverse mortgage. A type of loan designed for people who are 62 or older and have considerable equity in their homes. The reverse mortgage lender provides the borrower with a set monthly payment based on the amount of the equity in the home. Once a triggering event occurs, such as the borrowers' death, the lender will typically foreclose, sell the house, and recoup what it is owed on the loan. Reverse mortgages are heavily regulated by the Federal Trade Commission.

Second mortgage or deed of trust. A mortgage on property that is already mortgaged or subject to a deed of trust. It comes after any prior mortgages in priority of payment.

Secondary market. The process by which original mortgage lenders sell their loans to buyers (often Fannie Mae and Freddie Mac), who, in turn, package the loans into securities with different risk ratings and resell them to individual and corporate investors with the help of Wall Street brokerages and bond-rating firms.

Secured creditor. The owner of a secured claim.

Secured debt. A debt secured by collateral.

Secured interest. A claim to property used as collateral. For instance, a lender on a car note retains legal title to the car until the loan is paid off.

Secured property. Property that is collateral for a secured debt.

Securitization. The process of converting a mortgage lender's ownership interest in an original mortgage into an investment vehicle that can be handily sold on Wall Street as another type of security.

Serial bankruptcy filing. The practice of filing and dismissing one bankruptcy after another to obtain the protection of the automatic stay, even though the bankruptcies themselves offer no debt relief—for instance, when a debtor files successive Chapter 13 cases to prevent foreclosure even though there are no debts to repay. Courts will ban the debtor from further filings.

Short sale. A sale of a house in which the sale price is less than the mortgage secured by the house. The homeowner must get the lender's approval for a short sale.

State exemptions. State laws that specify the types of property creditors are not entitled to take to satisfy a debt, and the bankruptcy trustee is not entitled to take and sell for the benefit of the debtor's unsecured creditors.

Statutory lien. A lien imposed on property by law, such as tax liens and mechanics' liens, as opposed to voluntary liens (such as mortgages) and liens arising from court judgments (judicial liens).

Stay. See "Automatic stay."

Strict foreclosure. A type of judicial foreclosure used in several states in which the court not only orders that the foreclosure take place, but also transfers title to the foreclosing party without requiring the property to be put up for sale at an auction.

Strip down of lien. In a Chapter 13 bankruptcy, when the amount of a lien on collateral is reduced to the collateral's replacement value. See "Cramdown."

Subprime mortgage loan. A loan that carries a higher interest rate than a comparable loan, generally because of the borrower's low credit rating or other factors, such as the property's location.

Summons and complaint. Legal documents that are served on a homeowner to initiate a lawsuit—for example, a judicial foreclosure or an eviction. The summons tells the homeowner how and when to respond to the lawsuit. The complaint sets out the reasons why the court should, for example, issue a foreclosure judgment or evict a former owner after the sale.

Tax lien. A statutory lien imposed on property to secure payment of back taxes—typically income and property taxes.

Trustee. An official appointed by the bankruptcy court to carry out the administrative tasks associated with a bankruptcy and to collect and sell nonexempt property for the benefit of the debtor's unsecured creditors.

Truth in Lending Act (TILA). A federal law that requires most lenders to give borrowers standard disclosures of the cost and payment terms of the loan. The Home Ownership and Equity Protection Act (HOEPA) is part of the Truth in Lending Act. If the lender violates TILA or HOEPA, the homeowner may be able to stop foreclosure by rescinding the loan, depending on its type and whether it qualifies for protection under these federal laws.

Undersecured debt. A debt secured by collateral that is worth less than the debt.

State Information

The information here summarizes some of the important features of each state's law on foreclosures. When you use it, please keep in mind the following point.

This is only a summary of your state's laws and does not tell the entire story. It is intended for owners of single-family residences and doesn't address special laws for agricultural land or the rights of tenants in foreclosed homes owned by their landlords.

RESOURCE

More state-specific foreclosure information. The Foreclosure Center on Nolo.com has lots of state-specific foreclosure articles, and we are adding to the collection every day. You can find detailed articles on state foreclosure procedures, state foreclosure prevention mediation programs, state protections for homeowners in foreclosure, and other developments in state law.

This discusses only the most common method of foreclosure in your state. For example, it provides information about nonjudicial foreclosures for the states where they are the most common procedure, even though judicial foreclosures are allowed in those nonjudicial states in some circumstances.

Laws change. Foreclosure laws and procedures are complex and subject to change by legislatures and to interpretation by courts. For these reasons, you should use the information in this book as a starting point for additional research using the resources described in Ch. 10. Citations to each state's statutes are included so you can look up the laws themselves.

You can cross-check the information in this appendix with the summaries at www.foreclosure.com/foreclosure_laws.html and the summaries of state law in *Foreclosure Prevention Counseling* by the National Consumer Law Center (see Ch. 10). Also check for updates on this book's "Online Companion Page" using the link in Your Foreclosure Companion.

For bills pending in your state's legislature or recently signed into law by your state's governor, visit www.ncsl.org and click "Issues & Research," "Banking, Insurance & Financial Services," and then "Mortgages & Loans." Remember, a bill does not become law until it is signed by your state's governor. Most proposed laws will never make it to your governor's pen.

Finally, you can also read posts on Nolo's "Bankruptcy, Debt and Foreclosure" blog at http://blog.nolo.com/bankruptcy, which discusses important changes in foreclosure and bankruptcy law that may affect you.

Alabama

Foreclosure laws change! Check for updates at www.nolo.com/legal-updates.

Topic	State Rule
Most common type of foreclosure process	Nonjudicial under a power of sale in a deed of trust
Time to respond	Foreclosing party must publish notice in a newspaper of general circulation at least 30 days before sale and for three consecutive weeks; no requirement that the homeowner be served by mail.
Reinstatement of loan before sale	Not available
Redemption after sale	Available for one year after foreclosure if the property is surrendered to the buyer within ten days after a written demand is made.
Special protections for foreclosures involving high-cost mortgages	None
Special state protections for service members	Ala. Code §§ 31-12-1 to 31-12-10
Deficiency judgments	May be obtained by filing a lawsuit.
Cash exempted in bankruptcy	$300
Notice to leave after house is sold	Entitled to a written ten-day notice to leave before eviction proceedings may be brought.
Foreclosure statutes	Ala. Code §§ 35-10-1 to 35-10-30, 6-5-247 to 6-5-256

Alaska

Foreclosure laws change! Check for updates at www.nolo.com/legal-updates.

Topic	State Rule
Most common type of foreclosure process	Nonjudicial under a power of sale in a deed of trust
Time to respond	Notice of default and sale must be sent by certified mail to owner and occupant not less than 30 days after default and not less than 90 days before sale.
Reinstatement of loan before sale	Available any time before sale, but lender can refuse after three notices of default and sale
Redemption after sale	Not available
Special protections for foreclosures involving high-cost mortgages	None
Special state protections for service members	Alaska Stat. § 26.05.135
Deficiency judgments	Not allowed
Cash exempted in bankruptcy	$1,890 for one person, $2,970 for sole wage earner under state exemptions. About $12,725 for one person, $25,450 for a married couple under federal bankruptcy exemptions. (A 9th Circuit Court of Appeal opinion ruled that Alaska residents can choose the federal bankruptcy exemptions.)
Notice to leave after house is sold	New owner must give former owner a notice to quit (leave); new owner may bring special civil lawsuit to gain possession. Alaska Stat. § 09.45.630
Foreclosure statutes	Alaska Stat. § 34.20.070 et seq.

Arizona

Foreclosure laws change! Check for updates at www.nolo.com/legal-updates.

Topic	State Rule
Most common types of foreclosure process	Nonjudicial under power of sale in deed of trust
Time to respond	Foreclosing party must record a notice of sale at least 90 days before sale and must mail it by certified mail to homeowner within five business days after recording. The notice of sale must also be published for four consecutive weeks and posted on the property at least 20 days before sale.
Reinstatement of loan before sale	Available until day before date of sale
Redemption after sale	Not available
Special protections for foreclosures involving high-cost mortgages	None
Special state protections for service members	Ariz. Rev. Stat. Ann. § 6-1260(L)
Deficiency judgments	Not allowed for property up to 2½ acres or single- or two-family residence. For other properties, allowed if lawsuit is filed within 90 days of foreclosure sale.
Cash exempted in bankruptcy	$150
Notice to leave after house is sold	New owner must demand that former owner leave. The law does not specify a time for former owner to leave. If former owner doesn't leave, new owner may go to court for a writ of possession.
Foreclosure statutes	Ariz. Rev. Stat. §§ 33-721 to 33-749, 33-801 to 33-821, 12-1281 to 12-1283, 12-1566

Arkansas

Foreclosure laws change! Check for updates at www.nolo.com/legal-updates.

Topic	State Rule
Most common type of foreclosure process	Nonjudicial under power of sale in deed of trust
Time to respond	Foreclosing party must give homeowner at least a 30-day notice of default and intent to sell by certified and first-class mail within 30 days of recordation. Notice must also be published consecutively for four weeks prior to sale and posted at the courthouse and on any website where local legal notices are routinely posted.
Reinstatement of loan before sale	Allowed up to the date of sale
Redemption after sale	Not available
Special protections for foreclosures involving high-cost mortgages	Arkansas Home Loan Protection Act is intended as a remedy against abusive lending practices for all loans on a primary residence, other than the first mortgage, that are for $150,000 or less. The act is very technical but offers TILA rescission (see Ch. 7) as a remedy for an intentional violation, as well as monetary damages. Ark. Code Ann. §§ 23-53-101 to 106
Special state protections for service members	Ark. Code Ann. § 12-62-718
Deficiency judgments	Allowed for differences between the lesser of indebtedness minus market value of the property and the indebtedness minus the sales price. Lawsuit must be filed within one year of sale.
Cash exempted in bankruptcy	About $12,725 for one person, $25,450 for a married couple under federal bankruptcy exemptions. $200 if single; $500 if married or head of household under state bankruptcy exemptions.
Notice to leave after house is sold	State law does not specify an amount of notice that must be given before former owner can be evicted. Check with a resource (see Ch. 10) to see what the general practice is where you live.
Foreclosure statutes	Ark. Code Ann. §§ 18-50-101 to 18-50-116

California

Foreclosure laws change! Check for updates at www.nolo.com/legal-updates.

Topic	State Rule
Most common type of foreclosure process	Nonjudicial under power of sale in deed of trust
Time to respond	Lenders must personally contact (or meet the requirements for attempting to contact) homeowners to explore options for avoiding foreclosure 30 days before recording the notice of default. All homeowners get a 90-day notice of default and a 20-day notice of sale.
Reinstatement of loan before sale	Allowed up to five days before date of sale
Redemption after sale	Not available if deficiency judgment is waived or prohibited
Special protections for foreclosures involving high-cost mortgages	Cal. Fin. Code § 4973 makes a number of abusive loan practices unlawful. Section 4978 provides remedies that include authority for a judge to reform the loan to comply with the law. These provisions don't apply to mortgages held by the secondary market (Fannie Mae, Freddie Mac) or to assignees who have no reason to know of the loan origination violations.
Special state protections for service members	Cal. Mil. & Vet. Code §§ 400 to 409.13
Deficiency judgments	Not allowed
Cash exempted in bankruptcy	Up to about $25,340 under California exemption System 2
Notice to leave after the house is sold	New owner must give former homeowner three-day notice to quit (leave) and file an unlawful detainer lawsuit to evict.
Foreclosure statutes	Cal. Civ. Code §§ 2923.5, 2924 to 2924l

Colorado

Foreclosure laws change! Check for updates at www.nolo.com/legal-updates.

Topic	State Rule
Most common type of foreclosure process	Nonjudicial: under power of sale in deed of trust. The foreclosing party must file proof of ownership and the homeowner's default with a public trustee, who oversees the process. The mortgage holder must separately obtain a court order in a Rule 120 hearing authorizing the sale and give the public trustee a copy of the order before the sale date.
Time to respond	Thirty days before recording the Notice of Election and Demand, and at least 30 days after the first default in payments, borrower must be served with information about state hotline and how to contact the foreclosing party's loss-mitigation department. After the Notice of Election and Demand has been recorded, public trustee must mail notice to the homeowner within ten days after recording a notice of sale, and 110 to 125 days before first scheduled sale date. The combined notices mailed by the public trustee must advise the homeowner of the right to reinstate the mortgage.
Reinstatement of loan before sale	Available until noon on the day before the sale, provided that homeowner gives the foreclosing party written notice (no later than 15 days before the sale date) of intent to reinstate the mortgage
Redemption after sale	Available to some lienholders but not to homeowner
Special protections for foreclosures involving high-cost mortgages	None
Special state protections for service members	None
Deficiency judgments	Allowed, but the homeowner can defeat the action for a deficiency judgment if the house was sold for less than its fair market value
Cash exempted in bankruptcy	None
Notice to leave after house is sold	The lender must make a demand for possession. If the borrower does not vacate, then the lender files the lawsuit to evict. The court will issue a summons commanding the borrower to appear before the court at the time and place stated in the summons. The court date will be not less than 7 days and not more than 14 days from the date the summons was issued.
Foreclosure statutes	Colo. Rev. Stat. §§ 38-38-100.3 to 38-38-114

Connecticut

Foreclosure laws change! Check for updates at www.nolo.com/legal-updates.

Topic	State Rule
Most common type of foreclosure process	Judicial; optional strict foreclosure in which court transfers title directly to foreclosing party without ordering a sale.
Time to respond	After the foreclosing party files the foreclosure lawsuit, homeowner has 20 to 30 days to respond. No foreclosure judgment can be entered within 90 days from the return date on the summons and complaint, to allow time for mediation.
Reinstatement of loan before sale	Not available
Redemption after sale	If court orders sale, may also set redemption period
Special protections for foreclosures involving high-cost mortgages	No laws regarding high-cost mortgages. But certain homeowners who are underemployed or unemployed can ask the court for protection from foreclosure and modification of mortgage terms to give relief from paying arrearages.
Special state protections for service members	Conn. Gen. Stat. § 36a-737
Deficiency judgments	May be obtained within 30 days after the redemption period expires.
Cash exempted in bankruptcy	About $12,725 for one person, $25,450 for a married couple under federal bankruptcy exemptions. Any interest of the exemptioner in any property up to $1,000 under state bankruptcy exemptions.
Notice to leave after house is sold	Former owner will be required to move out after the sale under an order of ejectment issued by the court. Check with the marshal to see how much time you have to move out.
Foreclosure statutes	Conn. Gen. Stat. §§ 49-1 to 49-31i

Delaware

Foreclosure laws change! Check for updates at www.nolo.com/legal-updates.

Topic	State Rule
Most common type of foreclosure process	Judicial
Time to respond	Homeowner has 20 days to respond to order to show cause, stating why the foreclosure should not proceed. After court grants a judgment of foreclosure, homeowner gets a ten-day notice of sale. Order to show cause must be posted in ten places, served on homeowner by sheriff, and published two weeks prior to sale.
Reinstatement of loan before sale	Not available
Redemption after sale	Available until court confirms sale
Special protections for foreclosures involving high-cost mortgages	None
Special state protections for service members	None
Deficiency judgments	May be obtained by filing a separate lawsuit after a court has issued a foreclosure judgment
Cash exempted in bankruptcy	$500 if head of family
Notice to leave after house is sold	Five days after sale, new owner can file a summary eviction lawsuit. Former owner has five to 30 days before a hearing on the complaint is held. If former owner loses at the hearing or doesn't appear, court will order the sheriff to remove former owner.
Foreclosure statute	Del. Code Ann. tit. 10, § 5061

District of Columbia

Foreclosure laws change! Check for updates at www.nolo.com/legal-updates.

Topic	State Rule
Most common type of foreclosure process	Nonjudicial under power of sale in deed of trust
Time to respond	Before sale, foreclosing party must send 30-day notice of default to homeowner by registered or certified mail and send a copy of the notice to the mayor. The 30-day period begins when the mayor receives notice. The notice of default must provide information about availability of mediation, and sale of the premises may be delayed until 60 days after period for mediation passes.
Reinstatement of loan before sale	Available up to five days before the sale, once in two consecutive years
Redemption after sale	Not available
Special protections for foreclosures involving high-cost mortgages	None
Special state protections for service members	None
Deficiency judgments	May be obtained by filing a lawsuit
Cash exempted in bankruptcy	About $12,725 for one person, $25,450 for a married couple under federal bankruptcy exemptions; up to $8,925 under the D.C. bankruptcy exemptions
Notice to leave after house is sold	A summons must be served seven days before trial regarding possession.
Foreclosure statute	D.C. Code Ann. §§ 42-815, 42-816

Florida

Foreclosure laws change! Check for updates at www.nolo.com/legal-updates.

Topic	State Rule
Most common type of foreclosure process	Judicial
Time to respond	If foreclosing party asks for an order to show cause why the foreclosure should not proceed, homeowner has 21 days to respond after personal service or 31 days after the date notice is first published. Foreclosing party must publish notice of sale for two consecutive weeks at least five days before sale. Under local rules, courts have power to stay foreclosure proceedings pending mediation.
Reinstatement of loan before sale	Available for high-cost loans. Fla. Stat. Ann. § 494.00794
Redemption after sale	Available until the court clerk files a certificate of sale or as specified in the judgment.
Special protections for foreclosures involving high-cost mortgages	Protections apply to high-cost loans as defined in HOEPA (see Ch. 7). Florida Fair Lending Act, Fla. Stat. Ann. §§ 494.0079, 494.00794
Special state protections for service members	Fla. Stat. Ann. §§ 250.5201 to 250.5205
Deficiency judgments	Allowed if homeowner is personally served in foreclosure lawsuit. Court has flexibility regarding amount of deficiency, regardless of the type of mortgage involved. Foreclosing party may also file a separate lawsuit for breach of contract against homeowner for a deficiency, except that an original lender who ends up with the property at the foreclosure sale can't sue homeowner on a mortgage used to buy the house.
Cash exempted in bankruptcy	Up to $5,000 ($10,000 if married filing jointly) under state bankruptcy exemptions
Notice to leave after house is sold	In Florida, the eviction process is part of the foreclosure action and the right to possession is included in the judgment. It is not usually necessary to file an independent action for possession. After the certificate of title is issued, the lender/servicer files a motion for a writ of possession. When the motion is granted, the clerk of court issues the writ of possession and the sheriff posts the writ to the property. (The writ gives 24 hours to move out.) If the occupant does not vacate, the Sheriff executes the order.
Foreclosure statutes	Fla. Stat. Ann. §§ 701.10, 45.031 and 45.0315

Georgia

Foreclosure laws change! Check for updates at www.nolo.com/legal-updates.

Topic	State Rule
Most common type of foreclosure process	Nonjudicial under power of sale in deed of trust
Time to respond	Foreclosing party must mail notice to homeowner 30 days before sale. Additional notice by publication in a newspaper of general circulation may be required.
Reinstatement of loan before sale	High-cost loans may be reinstated until the sale.
Redemption after sale	Not available
Special protections for foreclosures involving high-cost mortgages	Additional notices required for high-cost loans. Georgia Fair Lending Act, Ga. Code Ann. §§ 7-6A-1 to 7-6A-13
Special state protections for service members	Ga. Code Ann. § 46-5-8
Deficiency judgments	If the foreclosure was nonjudicial, no deficiency judgment until the court confirms that the property was sold at its fair market value
Cash exempted in bankruptcy	$5,600 for one person, $11,200 for a married couple
Notice to leave after house is sold	New owner may demand that former owner leave and may immediately seek an order ousting former owner. Ga. Code Ann. § 44-7-50
Foreclosure statutes	Ga. Code Ann. §§ 44-14-160 to 44-14-191

Hawaii

Foreclosure laws change! Check for updates at www.nolo.com/legal-updates.

Topic	State Rule
Most common type of foreclosure process	Judicial. In the past, most foreclosures in Hawaii were nonjudicial. However, lenders have switched to judicial foreclosures in order to bypass Hawaii's new Mortgage Foreclosure Dispute Resolution (MFDR) program. This could change if the legislature amends the MFDR program.
Time to respond	Homeowner has 20 days to respond after being served with summons and complaint. For judicial foreclosures, the foreclosing party must publish a notice of sale in a newspaper once each week for three consecutive weeks, with the sale taking place no sooner than 14 days after the date of the publication of the third public notice advertisement; or the notice of sale may be published not less than 28 days before the date of the public sale on a state website. (If the public notice is published on a website, the notice must also be published at least once in a newspaper not less than 14 days prior to the public sale.)
Reinstatement of loan before sale	Not available for foreclosures by mortgage holders
Redemption after sale	Not available
Special protections for foreclosures involving high-cost mortgages	None
Special state protections for service members	Haw. Rev. Stat. §§ 657D-1 to 657D-63
Deficiency judgments	Allowed for judicial foreclosures
Cash exempted in bankruptcy	About $12,725 for one person, $25,450 for a married couple under federal bankruptcy exemptions.
Notice to leave after house is sold	Former owner is subject to eviction or ejectment (a common law procedure to "eject" an occupant). Either way, new owner must get a court order to remove former homeowner.
Foreclosure statutes	Haw. Rev. Stat. §§ 667-1 to 667-46, 667-A to 667-AC

Idaho

Foreclosure laws change! Check for updates at www.nolo.com/legal-updates.

Topic	State Rule
Most common type of foreclosure process	Nonjudicial under power of sale in deed of trust
Time to respond	Foreclosing party must give homeowner 120-day notice of default and sale before the date set for sale, make additional attempts to personally serve occupant with notice of sale, post notice of sale on property at least 30 days before the sale, and publish notice of sale over four consecutive weeks at least 30 days before sale. The notice of default and sale must be accompanied by a modification request form. The lender must respond to a request for modification within 45 days and may not proceed to a foreclosure sale until it has responded to the modification request.
Reinstatement of loan before sale	Available within 115 days after notice of default and sale is filed.
Redemption after sale	Not available
Special protections for foreclosures involving high-cost mortgages	None
Special state protections for service members	Idaho Code § 46-409
Deficiency judgments	May be obtained in a lawsuit brought within three months after sale. Amount of deficiency is limited by fair market value at time of sale.
Cash exempted in bankruptcy	None
Notice to leave after house is sold	New owner is entitled to possession of the property on the tenth day following sale but must go to court to evict former owner. An eviction trial must be scheduled within 12 days after the filing of the complaint and service of the summons.
Foreclosure statutes	Idaho Code §§ 45-1502 to 45-1515

Illinois

Foreclosure laws change! Check for updates at www.nolo.com/legal-updates.

Topic	State Rule
Most common type of foreclosure process	Judicial
Time to respond	Homeowner has 20 to 30 days to respond after being served with summons and complaint. After court issues a judgment of foreclosure, notice must be published three times between 45 and seven days before sale. No notice need be mailed to homeowner.
Reinstatement of loan before sale	Available within 90 days after foreclosure complaint is served on homeowner. Under High-Risk Home Loan Act, foreclosing party must serve notice of right to reinstate at least 30 days before starting foreclosure lawsuit.
Redemption after sale	Available for seven months after the complaint is served or three months after foreclosure judgment entered, whichever is later. Property below certain value may be redeemed for 30 days after confirmation of sale by paying sales price plus costs and interest.
Special protections for foreclosures involving high-cost mortgages	Special defenses to foreclosure lawsuit. High-Risk Home Loan Act, 815 Ill. Comp. Stat. §§ 137/1 to 137/175
Special state protections for service members	330 Ill. Comp. Stat. § 60/5.1
Deficiency judgments	May be sought as part of the foreclosure lawsuit
Cash exempted in bankruptcy	$4,000 for one person, $8,000 for a married couple
Notice to leave after house is sold	Court may order homeowner removed 30 days after sale. New owner must file a complaint for forcible entry and detainer to remove any occupant who wasn't personally served in the foreclosure case. 735 Ill. Comp. Stat. §§ 5/9-101, 5/15-1508(g), 5/15-1701
Foreclosure statutes	735 Ill. Comp. Stat §§ 5/15-1501 to 5/15-1512

Indiana

Foreclosure laws change! Check for updates at www.nolo.com/legal-updates.

Topic	State Rule
Most common type of foreclosure process	Judicial
Time to respond	Foreclosing party must give homeowner 30 days' notice before filing foreclosure complaint. The notice must include a copy of the first publication of notice of sale, which must be published at least 30 days before the scheduled sale. Notice of sale must be published once a week for three consecutive weeks. After the complaint is filed, house can't be sold for three months for mortgages signed on or after July 1, 1975 and longer for mortgages signed before July 1, 1975.
Reinstatement of loan before sale	Available for high-cost home loans (defined in Ind. Code § 24-9-2-8) any time before sale
Redemption after sale	Available any time before the final judgment.
Special protections for foreclosures involving high-cost mortgages	If lender violated provisions that apply to high-cost loans, penalties may apply. Violations may also be used to fight foreclosure by rescinding loan under HOEPA (see Ch. 7). Protections not available for loans taken up or guaranteed in secondary market by federal entities (Freddie Mac, Fannie Mae, FHA, VA). Ind. Code §§ 24-9-5-1 to 24-9-5-6
Special state protections for service members	None
Deficiency judgments	Allowed if authorized by loan or written agreement and if homeowner does not waive applicable waiting period (homeowner may agree to waiver in exchange for lender's agreeing not to seek a deficiency judgment)
Cash exempted in bankruptcy	$300 for one person, $600 for a married couple
Notice to leave after house is sold	New owner must ask court for possession of property after giving former owner five-day notice to quit (leave). Ind. Code § 32-30-3-2
Foreclosure statutes	Ind. Code §§ 32-30-10-1 to 32-30-10-14, 32-29-1-1 to 32-29-1-11, 32-29-7-1 to 32-29-7-14

Iowa

Foreclosure laws change! Check for updates at www.nolo.com/legal-updates.

Topic	State Rule
Most common type of foreclosure process	Judicial
Time to respond	Foreclosing party must mail notice of default and right to cure (reinstate) to homeowner at least 30 days before filing suit and must post and publish notice four weeks before date of sale.
Reinstatement of loan before sale	Available within 30 days after homeowner receives notice of default.
Redemption after sale	Available for one year (or, if agreed upon in mortgage document, six months in exchange for a waiver of rights to a deficiency judgment) for judicial foreclosures; not available for alternative voluntary foreclosures
Special protections for foreclosures involving high-cost mortgages	None
Special state protections for service members	Iowa Code § 29A.102
Deficiency judgments	Allowed. If, however, the lender elects to file a foreclosure lawsuit and asks the court to disallow the statutory redemption period, then it also waives its right to sue for a deficiency.
Cash exempted in bankruptcy	$1,000 for one person, $2,000 for a married couple
Notice to leave after house is sold	New owner must file an eviction (forcible entry and detainer) lawsuit. The judge will order a hearing to be held no more than seven days later. Former owner must be personally served with notice not less than three days before the hearing. Iowa Code § 648.5.
Foreclosure statutes	Iowa Code §§ 654.1 to 654.26, 628.26, 628.27

Kansas

Foreclosure laws change! Check for updates at www.nolo.com/legal-updates.

Topic	State Rule
Common type of foreclosure process	Judicial
Time to respond	Homeowner who is personally served with the complaint has 20 days to respond; if notice is only by publication in a local newspaper of general circulation, homeowner has 41 days to respond. After court issues a foreclosure judgment, foreclosing party must publish a notice of sale at least three times; last publication must be between seven and 14 days before sale date.
Reinstatement of loan before sale	Not available
Redemption after sale	Available within 12 months (less if homeowner abandoned premises). Available within three months if homeowner defaulted on mortgage before one-third of original debt was repaid (only homeowner can redeem for first two months; after that, junior lienholders can redeem in place of homeowner). Available within 12 months if all mortgage debt on property totals less than one-third of the house's market value (only homeowner can redeem for first three months). Court may extend three-month redemption period by another three months if homeowner loses his or her job after foreclosure sale.
Special protections for foreclosures involving high-cost mortgages	None
Special state protections for service members	None
Deficiency judgments	Allowed if court confirms that the price paid for property at sale is adequate compared to its fair market value. Sales price that covers foreclosing party's judgment is considered adequate.
Cash exempted in bankruptcy	None
Notice to leave after house is sold	New owner does not have to send former owner a notice to terminate. New owner must file a petition for ejectment, which is a summary process that typically results in a court order evicting former owner within a week or two. Kan. Stat. Ann. §§ 58-2509, 60-1001
Foreclosure statute	Kan. Stat. Ann. § 60-2410

Kentucky

Foreclosure laws change! Check for updates at www.nolo.com/legal-updates.

Topic	State Rule
Most common type of foreclosure process	Judicial
Time to respond	Homeowner has 20 days to respond after being served with the complaint. If court issues a foreclosure judgment, foreclosing party must post notice on courthouse door or publish notice once a week for three weeks at least 15 days before the sale.
Reinstatement of loan before sale	If loan is a high-interest loan (under Ky. Rev. Stat. Ann. § 360.100), foreclosing party must serve notice of right to reinstatement at least 30 days before filing the foreclosure complaint.
Redemption after sale	Available one year after sale, if sale amount is less than two-thirds of property's appraised value. Homeowner must pay full amount of the price paid for property at foreclosure sale, plus 10%.
Special protections for foreclosures involving high-cost mortgages	Laws protect against and provide remedies for abusive lending practices and loan conditions. Ky. Rev. Stat. Ann. § 360.100
Special state protections for service members	Ky. Rev. Stat. Ann. § 38.510
Deficiency judgments	Allowed if homeowner is personally served with the complaint or fails to answer the complaint
Cash exempted in bankruptcy	$1,000 for one person, $2,000 for a married couple under state bankruptcy exemptions. About $12,725 for one person, $25,450 for a married couple under federal bankruptcy exemptions.
Notice to leave after house is sold	Upon ten days' notice, former owner is required to move out under a writ of possession issued by the court.
Foreclosure statutes	Ky. Rev. Stat. Ann. §§ 426.525 to 426.720

Louisiana

Foreclosure laws change! Check for updates at www.nolo.com/legal-updates.

Topic	State Rule
Most common type of foreclosure process	Judicial, but most common process is an "executory" proceeding, which operates like a nonjudicial foreclosure. In the mortgage document, the homeowner will typically have "confessed to judgment" in case of a default. Upon default, the foreclosing party files a foreclosure petition with the mortgage attached, and the court summarily orders the property seized and sold unless the homeowner appeals or brings a lawsuit asking the court to stop (enjoin) the proceeding (see Ch. 7).
Time to respond	Notice of sale is contained in the petition, which is posted on the property. Once court issues writ of seizure, notice of seizure is published at least twice and not less than three days after the debtor has been served with the notice.
Reinstatement of loan before sale	Not available
Redemption after sale	Not available
Special protections for foreclosures involving high-cost mortgages	None
Special state protections for service members	La. Rev. Stat. Ann. § 29:315
Deficiency judgments	Allowed; can be obtained in an ordinary proceeding or in an executory proceeding if the property was properly appraised
Cash exempted in bankruptcy	None
Notice to leave after house is sold	No notice required. Sheriff may seize property after receiving writ of seizure and sale from the court. La. Code Civ. Proc. Ann. Art. 2721
Foreclosure statutes	La. Code Civ. Proc. Ann. Arts. 3721 to 3753, 2631 to 2772

Maine

Foreclosure laws change! Check for updates at www.nolo.com/legal-updates.

Topic	State Rule
Most common type of foreclosure process	Judicial
Time to respond	Homeowner has 20 days to respond after being served with summons and complaint. After the court issues a foreclosure judgment, and within 90 days after the redemption period (see below) ends, foreclosing party must publish notice of public sale for three consecutive weeks. Sale must be held 30 to 45 days after date of first publication. Foreclosing party must also mail a notice of sale at least 30 days before sale date.
Reinstatement of loan before sale	Court can issue a conditional judgment if foreclosing party proves homeowner has defaulted on payments. After judgment is issued, homeowner has two months to reinstate and can get a two-month extension of this right. Also, lender, in its sole discretion, may let homeowner reinstate the loan any time before the sale.
Redemption after sale	Redemption period is 90 days from the date the foreclosure judgment is entered, unless homeowner appeals. Me. Rev. Stat. Ann. tit. 14, § 6322
Special protections for foreclosures involving high-cost mortgages	Law allows for damages and for assignee liability but doesn't appear to provide a defense to foreclosure itself.
Special state protections for service members	Me. Rev. Stat. Ann. tit. 37-B, § 387
Deficiency judgments	Allowed with some limitations
Cash exempted in bankruptcy	$6,400 for one person, $12,800 for a married couple
Notice to leave after house is sold	No special provisions for evictions following foreclosure. New owner will likely have to go to court to get an eviction order. Court-ordered evictions usually take two weeks to a month, depending on whether or not former owner responds to the lawsuit.
Foreclosure statutes	Me. Rev. Stat. Ann. tit. 14, §§ 6101 to 6325

Maryland

Foreclosure laws change! Check for updates at www.nolo.com/legal-updates.

Topic	State Rule
Most common type of foreclosure process	Nonjudicial under power of sale in deed of trust, but a court must ratify the sale for clear title to pass to the new owner
Time to respond	Foreclosing party must serve homeowner with notice of intent to foreclose at least 45 days before filing a foreclosure action in court. The court complaint or order to docket must be personally served on homeowner; if two attempts at personal service fail, the complaint must be mailed by certified mail and posted on the property. The notice of intent to foreclose must be accompanied by an application to invoke the lender's loss mitigation procedures and a notice of the availability of mediation in the event loss mitigation efforts fail. The period allowed for mediation may be as long as 90 days; the sale can take place no sooner than 15 days after the mediation is completed.
Reinstatement of loan before sale	Available until one day before sale date, if homeowner pays foreclosing party the amount due plus costs and fees
Redemption after sale	Not available
Special protections for foreclosures involving high-cost mortgages	None
Special state protections for service members	Md. Code Ann. [Pub. Safety] § 13-705
Deficiency judgments	Foreclosing party may request this of the supervising court within three years after the sale
Cash exempted in bankruptcy	$11,000 for one person, $22,000 for a married couple
Notice to leave after house is sold	No special provisions for evictions following foreclosure. New owner will likely have to go to court to get an eviction order. Court-ordered evictions usually take two weeks to a month, depending on whether or not former owner responds to the lawsuit.
Foreclosure statute	Md. Code Ann. [Real Prop.] §§ 7-105 to 7-105.8

Massachusetts

Foreclosure laws change! Check for updates at www.nolo.com/legal-updates.

Topic	State Rule
Most common type of foreclosure process	Nonjudicial under power of sale in deed of trust
Time to respond	Prior to accelerating the loan and initiating foreclosure proceedings, the foreclosing party must mail to the homeowner by first class mail a 90-day notice of homeowner's right to reinstate the mortgage and that homeowner may be eligible for state agency assistance. After loan is accelerated, the foreclosing party must send by (registered or certified mail) notice to homeowner at least 14 days before the sale date, and publish notice for three consecutive weeks before the sale date.
Reinstatement of loan before sale	90 day right to cure (after service of notice of default) by paying amount due plus portion of late fees.
Redemption after sale	Not available
Special protections for foreclosures involving high-cost mortgages	Homeowner can rescind a high-cost loan and use rescission as a defense to the foreclosure. Assignees of the loan may be sued for lender or loan originator abusive lending activities except for governmental entities, such as Freddie Mac and Fannie Mae. Predatory Home Loan Practices Act, Mass. Gen. Laws Ch. 183C, §§ 1-19.
Special state protections for service members	None
Deficiency judgments	Can be obtained in separate lawsuit if a notice of intent to seek a deficiency is included in notice of sale, and the notice of sale is mailed to homeowner at least 21 days before sale date.
Cash exempted in bankruptcy	About $12,725 for one person, $25,450 for a married couple under the federal bankruptcy exemptions. Up to $6,000 under state exemption system.
Notice to leave after house is sold	If the former owner still resides in the property following the foreclosure sale, then an action for eviction starts with a 3-day or 30-day notice to quit, depending on who else lives in the property
Foreclosure statutes	Mass. Gen. Laws Ch. 244, § 14, 35A

Michigan

Foreclosure laws change! Check for updates at www.nolo.com/legal-updates.

Topic	State Rule
Most common type of foreclosure process	Nonjudicial under power of sale in deed of trust
Time to respond	Foreclosing party must publish notice once a week for four consecutive weeks before sale and post a notice on property within at least 15 days of first publication No notice need be mailed to homeowner.
Reinstatement of loan before sale	Not available
Redemption after sale	If homeowner occupies property and more than two-thirds of the original mortgage is still owed, redemption allowed for six months. If less than two-thirds is owed, the redemption period is one year. If the property is abandoned and at least two-thirds of the mortgage is still owed, redemption period is one to three months. Mich. Comp. Laws § 600.3240
Special protections for foreclosures involving high-cost mortgages	None
Special state protections for service members	Mich. Comp. Laws §§ 32.517, 600.3185, 600.3285
Deficiency judgments	Allowed, if the mortgage holder buys the property at the foreclosure sale.
Cash exempted in bankruptcy	About $12,725 for one person, $25,450 for a married couple under federal bankruptcy exemptions
Notice to leave after house is sold	No special provisions for evictions following a foreclosure. New owner will likely have to go to court to get an eviction order. Court-ordered evictions usually take two weeks to a month, depending on whether or not former owner responds to the lawsuit.
Foreclosure statutes	Mich. Comp. Laws §§ 600.3101 to 600.3180, 600.3201 to 600.3285

Minnesota

Foreclosure laws change! Check for updates at www.nolo.com/legal-updates.

Topic	State Rule
Most common type of foreclosure process	Nonjudicial under power of sale in deed of trust
Time to respond	Foreclosing party must serve notice of sale on homeowner at least four weeks before the sale and must publish the notice six weeks before the sale.
Reinstatement of loan before sale	Available any time before the foreclosure sale
Redemption after sale	For most homeowners, available for six months after the sale. Former owner may stay in the house during this period. Minn. Stat. §§ 581.11, 504B.285
Special protections for foreclosures involving high-cost mortgages	None
Special state protections for service members	Minn. Stat. §§ 72A.20(8)(b),(c)
Deficiency judgments	Not allowed in nonjudicial foreclosure with six-month redemption period (most common type of foreclosure)
Cash exempted in bankruptcy	About $12,725 for one person, $25,450 for a married couple under federal bankruptcy exemptions
Notice to leave after house is sold	New owner must give two month's written notice after redemption period ends before filing an eviction lawsuit. Minn. Stat. § 504B.285
Foreclosure statutes	Minn. Stat. §§ 580.01 to 580.30

Mississippi

Foreclosure laws change! Check for updates at www.nolo.com/legal-updates.

Topic	State Rule
Most common type of foreclosure process	Nonjudicial under power of sale in deed of trust
Time to respond	Foreclosing party must publish notice of sale three consecutive weeks before sale date and post notice on the courthouse door. No notice need be mailed to homeowner.
Reinstatement of loan before sale	Available until date of sale
Redemption after sale	Not available
Special protections for foreclosures involving high-cost mortgages	None
Special State procedures for service members	Miss. Code Ann. § 75-24-5(2)(m)
Deficiency judgments	May be obtained if lawsuit filed within one year of the sale. The deficiency may be denied if lender is also the buyer and the court concludes the house sold for less than its market value.
Cash exempted in bankruptcy	Up to $10,000 ($60,000 for those aged 70 or over) under state bankruptcy exemptions.
Notice to leave after house is sold	No special provisions for evictions following foreclosure. New owner will likely have to go to court to get an eviction order. Court-ordered evictions usually take two weeks to a month, depending on whether or not former owner responds to the lawsuit.
Foreclosure statutes	Miss. Code. Ann. §§ 89-1-55 to 89-1-59

Missouri

Foreclosure laws change! Check for updates at www.nolo.com/legal-updates.

Topic	State Rule
Most common type of foreclosure process	Nonjudicial under power of sale in deed of trust
Time to respond	Foreclosing party must send, by registered and certified mail, 20-day notice to the owner of record.
Reinstatement of loan before sale	Not available
Redemption after sale	Available up to a year after sale, if homeowner gives foreclosing party a notice of intent to redeem ten days before sale and the lender buys the property at foreclosure sale
Special protections for foreclosures involving high-cost mortgages	None
Special state protections for service members	Mo. Ann. Stat. § 41.944
Deficiency judgments	May be obtained in a separate lawsuit, whether or not sales price is the property's fair market value
Cash exempted in bankruptcy	$600; $1,200 if married filing jointly; $1,250 for head of family plus $350 per child.
Notice to leave after house is sold	Former owner must get one month's written notice to vacate premises. Mo. Rev. Stat. § 441.060
Foreclosure statutes	Mo. Rev. Stat. §§ 443.290 to 443.453

Montana

Foreclosure laws change! Check for updates at www.nolo.com/legal-updates.

Topic	State Rule
Most common type of foreclosure process	Nonjudicial under power of sale in deed of trust
Time to respond	Foreclosing party must personally serve occupant and homeowner with a 30-day notice before sale. Notice of sale must also be posted in five conspicuous places 30 days prior to the sale.
Reinstatement of loan before sale	The default can be cured and the loan reinstated at any time prior to sale (so long as the property is not more than 40 acres).
Redemption after sale	Available within one year after sale for judicial foreclosures; no right of redemption for nonjudicial foreclosures
Special protections for foreclosures involving high-cost mortgages	None
Special state protections for service members	Mont. Code. Ann. § 10-1-903
Deficiency judgments	Not allowed
Cash exempted in bankruptcy	None
Notice to leave after house is sold	Former owner may stay during one-year redemption period for judicial foreclosures. There is no right of redemption for nonjudicial foreclosures.
Foreclosure statutes	Mont. Code Ann. §§ 71-1-221 to 71-1-235 and §§ 71-1-301 to 71-1-321

Nebraska

Foreclosure laws change! Check for updates at www.nolo.com/legal-updates.

Topic	State Rule
Most common type of foreclosure process	Nonjudicial under power of sale
Time to respond	Lender must record a notice of default at least 30 days before issuing a notice of sale. Notice of sale must be published once a week for five consecutive weeks; the last publication must be made at least ten days but not more than 30 days prior to the sale. Notice of sale must be sent to any party that files a written request for such notice.
Reinstatement of loan before sale	Homeowner may reinstate by paying amount due within 30 days after recordation of notice of default.
Redemption after sale	Not available
Special protections for foreclosures involving high-cost mortgages	None
Special state protections for service members	None
Deficiency judgments	May be obtained by filing separate lawsuit within three months after foreclosure sale. Judgment cannot exceed the amount by which the indebtedness, costs, and expenses exceed the fair market value, and cannot exceed the difference between the sale price and the indebtedness, costs and expenses.
Cash exempted in bankruptcy	$2,500 for one person, $5,000 for a married couple
Notice to leave after house is sold	Nebraska law does not specify an amount of notice that must be given before former owner can be evicted. Ask a resource about local practice (see Ch. 10).
Foreclosure statutes	Neb. Rev. Stat. §§ 76-1005, 76-1018

Nevada

Foreclosure laws change! Check for updates at www.nolo.com/legal-updates.

Topic	State Rule
Most common type of foreclosure process	Nonjudicial under power of sale in deed of trust
Time to respond	Foreclosing party must give homeowner a three-month notice of default and election to sell (must include notice of right to mediation) and a three-week notice of sale. Nev. Rev. Stat. § 107.085-086
Reinstatement of loan before sale	Homeowner may reinstate within 35 days after notice of default recorded in local land records office
Redemption after sale	Not available
Special protections for foreclosures involving high-cost mortgages	If trust deed was entered into on or after October 1, 2003 and is subject to HOEPA (see Ch. 7), homeowner must be personally served with an additional 60-day notice before date of sale. Violations of high-cost home loan statutes support a defense to foreclosure. Nev. Rev. Stat. §§ 598D.010 to 598D.150
Special state protections for service members	None
Deficiency judgments	Not allowed if first mortgage has not been refinanced and homeowner has resided in home continuously. Otherwise, foreclosing party may obtain deficiency judgment by filing a separate lawsuit within six months of foreclosure sale. Amount of deficiency is limited depending on fair market value, sales price, amount of loan, and other factors.
Cash exempted in bankruptcy	$1,000 under state bankruptcy exemptions
Notice to leave after house is sold	New owner must provide a three-day notice to quit (leave) before filing an eviction lawsuit. Nev. Rev. Stat. § 40.290
Foreclosure statute	Nev. Rev. Stat. § 107.080

New Hampshire

Foreclosure laws change! Check for updates at www.nolo.com/legal-updates.

Topic	State Rule
Most common type of foreclosure process	Nonjudicial under power of sale in deed of trust
Time to respond	Foreclosing party must either personally serve homeowner with notice 25 days before the sale or publish the notice once a week for three consecutive weeks, with the first publication at least 20 days before the sale.
Reinstatement of loan before sale	Not available
Redemption after sale	Not available
Special protections for foreclosures involving high-cost mortgages	None
Special state protections for service members	N.H. Rev. Stat. Ann. § 540:11-a
Deficiency judgments	May be obtained by filing separate lawsuit after the foreclosure sale, provided lender exerts every reasonable effort to obtain a fair and reasonable price at the sale.
Cash exempted in bankruptcy	About $12,725 for one person, $25,450 for a married couple under federal bankruptcy exemptions. Up to $8,000 under state bankruptcy exemptions.
Notice to leave after house is sold	New owner must give former owner a 30-day notice to quit (leave) before bringing an eviction lawsuit. Former owner has seven days to respond after being served by sheriff.
Foreclosure statute	N.H. Rev. Stat. Ann. § 479:25

New Jersey

Foreclosure laws change! Check for updates at www.nolo.com/legal-updates.

Topic	State Rule
Most common type of foreclosure process	Judicial
Time to respond	Foreclosing party must send notice, by registered or certified mail, return receipt requested, to homeowner 30 days before filing a foreclosure lawsuit. Foreclosing party must also post notice on the property four times in four weeks before filing suit or publish notice in two newspapers and mail notice to the homeowner and other parties.
Reinstatement of loan before sale	Available up to date of final judgment of foreclosure. Judgment may be delayed if homeowner needs extra time to reinstate.
Redemption after sale	If mortgage holder obtains a deficiency judgment, homeowner can bring action for redemption within six months after deficiency judgment is entered.
Special protections for foreclosures involving high-cost mortgages	Foreclosure must be filed in court. Six-month forbearance of foreclosure proceeding may be requested in order to pursue mediation. Home Ownership Security Act, N.J. Stat. Ann. §§ 46:10B-22 to 10B-35.
Special state protections for service members	N.J. Stat. Ann. §§ 38:23C-1 to 38:23C-26
Deficiency judgments	May be obtained by filing a separate lawsuit within three months of sale; amount limited to difference between loan and fair market value.
Cash exempted in bankruptcy	About $12,725 for one person, $25,450 for a married couple under federal bankruptcy exemptions. $1,000 under state bankruptcy exemptions
Notice to leave after house is sold	None
Foreclosure statutes	N.J. Stat. Ann. §§ 2A:50-1 to 2A:50-21, 2A:50-56 to 2A:50-58

New Mexico

Foreclosure laws change! Check for updates at www.nolo.com/legal-updates.

Topic	State Rule
Most common type of foreclosure process	Judicial, but nonjudicial foreclosures are on the rise
Time to respond	**Judicial:** Homeowner has 20 to 30 days to respond after being served with summons and complaint. After the court issues a foreclosure judgment, sale may not occur for 30 days. Foreclosing party must publish notice of sale for four consecutive weeks before sale in a newspaper printed in the county (or if there is none, then in the official newspaper for the county) and also post notices in six of the most public places in the county. **Nonjudicial:** 90 days after foreclosing party records notice of sale
Reinstatement of loan before sale	**Judicial:** Homeowner must be given a 30-day opportunity to reinstate before filing of complaint. Homeowner may also reinstate any time before foreclosure sale. **Nonjudicial:** Not available
Redemption after sale	**Judicial:** Available after judgment and before sale. Available for nine months after sale if additional costs and fees are paid plus 10% interest. **Nonjudicial:** Available for nine months after sale unless deed of trust provides for shorter period.
Special protections for foreclosures involving high-cost mortgages	Assignees of high-cost loans may be held responsible for acts of lenders and mortgage originators, and violations may be used to defend against the foreclosure (see Ch. 7). Home Loan Protection Act, N.M. Stat. Ann. §§ 58-21A-1 to 58-21A-14
Special state protections for service members	N.M. Stat. Ann. § 20-4-7.1
Deficiency judgments	**Judicial:** Allowed **Nonjudicial:** May be obtained by filing a separate lawsuit; may not be recovered against a low-income household.
Cash exempted in bankruptcy	About $12,725 for one person, $25,450 for a married couple under federal bankruptcy exemptions. Up to $5,500 under state bankruptcy exemptions.
Notice to leave after house is sold	New owner must give the former owner a three-day notice to quit (leave) before filing an eviction lawsuit, to which former owner has three to ten days to respond.
Foreclosure statutes	N.M. Stat. Ann. §§ 48-7-1 to 48-7-24, 39-5-1 to 39-5-23 (judicial); 48-10-1 to 48-10-21 (nonjudicial)

New York

Foreclosure laws change! Check for updates at www.nolo.com/legal-updates

Topic	State Rule
Most common type of foreclosure process	Judicial
Time to respond	Foreclosing party must provide advisory to homeowner at least 90 days before filing foreclosure complaint. Complaint must be accompanied by notice regarding legal options and explanation of foreclosure procedure. Homeowners have 20 to 30 days to respond to complaints, depending on whether they are served personally or by another method. Notice of sale resulting from judgment in favor of foreclosing party must be served by publication.
Reinstatement of loan before sale	Available any time before final foreclosure judgment (case will be stayed pending payment of arrearages) and any time before sale
Redemption after sale	Not available
Special protections for foreclosures involving high-cost mortgages	Prior to beginning foreclosure action on high-cost loan, subprime loan, or "nontraditional" loan, foreclosing party must send 90-day notice of intent to foreclose and contact information for government-approved housing counselors. N.Y. Real Prop. Acts. Law § 1304. If lender violated provisions that apply to high-cost loans, homeowner may use this as a defense against foreclosure. N.Y. Banking Law § 6-l, N.Y. Real Prop. Acts. Law § 1302; also, Real Property Law § 265-a (Home Equity Theft Prevention Act).
Special state protections for service members	N.Y. Mil. Law § 308
Deficiency judgments	Allowed if homeowner is personally served or appears in the lawsuit. The amount is the amount of the debt less the higher of the fair market value or the sales price.
Cash exempted in bankruptcy	About $12,725 for one person, $25,450 for a married couple under federal bankruptcy exemptions. Up to $11,000 if single; $22,000 if filing jointly under state bankruptcy exemptions.
Notice to leave after house is sold	New owner must give former owner a ten-day notice to quit (leave) and then ask the court for possession. The court petition must be served on former owner five to 12 days before the court hearing on the petition.
Foreclosure statutes	N.Y. Real Prop. Acts. Law §§ 1301 to 1391

North Carolina

Foreclosure laws change! Check for updates at www.nolo.com/legal-updates

Topic	State Rule
Most common type of foreclosure process	Nonjudicial: under power of sale in deed of trust. Property cannot be sold until the court clerk holds a hearing, reviews foreclosing party's paperwork, and certifies sale.
Time to respond	Notice about HUD-approved housing counselors required before notice of default (NOD). 30-day NOD required before notice of hearing. Notice of hearing must be given ten days before the hearing (may be extended for 60 days if loss-mitigation efforts may help). If foreclosure approved at hearing, homeowner must be served with either a 20-day notice of sale (if served by posting and publication) or a 10-day notice of sale (if served by mail).
Reinstatement of loan before sale	Not available
Redemption after sale	Available within ten days after the sale
Special protections for foreclosures involving high-cost mortgages	North Carolina High Cost Mortgage Act applies to loans less than $300,000, secured by a personal residence, and qualify as a mortgage under HOEPA (see Ch. 7). Violations include lack of due diligence regarding borrower's ability to repay the loan and failure to secure a certificate of HUD-certified counseling before signing the loan. Liability is limited to original parties to the loan and borrower can sue only for money; law can't be used to prevent foreclosure. N.C. Gen. Stat. § 24-1.1E
Special state protections for service members	N.C. Gen. Stat. §§ 45-21.12A, 45-21.16
Deficiency judgments	No deficiency judgment in nonjudicial foreclosures for purchase money mortgages. Lender may also be barred from seeking a deficiency judgment if the mortgage is nontraditional (for example, pick-a-payment or option ARM loans) or is a rate spread home loan (where the annual percentage rate exceeds a certain threshold), and the mortgage secures borrower's principal residence.
Cash exempted in bankruptcy	$5,500 for one person, $11,000 for a married couple
Notice to leave after house is sold	New owner must give former owner a 10-day notice to quit (leave) before going to court for eviction.
Foreclosure statutes	N.C. Gen. Stat. §§ 45-21.1 to 45-21.33, 45-100 to 47-107

North Dakota

Foreclosure laws change! Check for updates at www.nolo.com/legal-updates

Topic	State Rule
Most common type of foreclosure process	Judicial
Time to respond	Foreclosing party must serve homeowner with notice of intent to foreclose 30 to 90 days before filing the foreclosure complaint. Homeowner has 20 to 30 days to respond. Notice of sale must be published or posted on courthouse door and five other places. Sale must be set aside if proper notice wasn't given. N.D. Cent. Code § 28-23-04
Reinstatement of loan before sale	Available within 30 days after homeowner is served with notice of intent to foreclose
Redemption after sale	Available within 60 days of foreclosure sale
Special protections for foreclosures involving high-cost mortgages	None
Special state protections for service members	None
Deficiency judgments	Not allowed
Cash exempted in bankruptcy	$7,500 for one person, $15,000 for a married couple
Notice to leave after house is sold	Former owner can stay in the house until redemption period ends; then the sheriff may immediately evict.
Foreclosure statutes	N.D. Cent. Code §§ 32-19-01 to 32-19-41

Ohio

Foreclosure laws change! Check for updates at www.nolo.com/legal-updates

Topic	State Rule
Most common type of foreclosure process	Judicial
Time to respond	After foreclosing party files lawsuit, homeowner has 28 days to respond. After the court issues a foreclosure judgment, foreclosing party files the notice of sale with the court at least seven days prior to the sale and sends a copy to the homeowner. Foreclosing party must publish notice of sale at least three weeks before sale date.
Reinstatement of loan before sale	Not available
Redemption after sale	Available until the court confirms the sale
Special protections for foreclosures involving high-cost mortgages	None
Special state protections for service members	Ohio Rev. Code Ann. §§ 5919.29, 5923.12
Deficiency judgments	Allowed, but judgment is void two years after confirmation of the sale by the court. Property cannot be sold for less than 2/3 of appraised value at the foreclosure sale.
Cash exempted in bankruptcy	Up to $1,575; $3,150 if married filing jointly
Notice to leave after house is sold	No special provisions for evictions following foreclosure. The new owner will likely have to go to court to get an eviction order. Court-ordered evictions usually take two weeks to a month, depending on whether or not former owner responds to the lawsuit.
Foreclosure statutes	Ohio Rev. Code Ann. §§ 2323.07, 2329.26, 5721.38

Oklahoma

Foreclosure laws change! Check for updates at www.nolo.com/legal-updates

Topic	State Rule
Most common type of foreclosure process	Judicial
Time to respond	After foreclosing party files lawsuit, homeowner has 20 to 30 days to respond. After the court issues a foreclosure judgment, foreclosing party must serve a notice of sale on homeowner by mail and publish notice of sale at least 30 days before the sale.
Reinstatement of loan before sale	Not available
Redemption after sale	Allowed until court confirms sale
Special protections for foreclosures involving high-cost mortgages	None
Special state protections for service members	Okla. Stat. tit. 44, § 208.1
Deficiency judgments	Allowed, but amount limited by market value of property. Lender must ask the court for deficiency judgment within 90 days after sale.
Cash exempted in bankruptcy	None
Notice to leave after house is sold	Judge may order immediate possession by purchaser. Failure to move out may be punished as contempt of court.
Foreclosure statutes	Okla. Stat. tit. 12, §§ 686, 764 to 765, 773; Okla. Stat. tit. 46, §§ 41 to 49

Oregon

Foreclosure laws change! Check for updates at www.nolo.com/legal-updates

Topic	State Rule
Most common type of foreclosure process	Probably nonjudicial. In the past, most foreclosures in Oregon were nonjudicial. In 2012, lenders switched to judicial foreclosures for various reasons that are no longer applicable. Lenders will likely revert to nonjudicial foreclosures again. (See "Shift Between Judicial and Nonjudicial Foreclosures in Oregon" in Ch. 2.)
Time to respond	Foreclosing party must record a notice of default and serve it on homeowner by mail. Foreclosing party must also serve a notice of sale on homeowner 120 days before the sale, either by personal service or, if personal service cannot be made, by posting on property.
Reinstatement of loan before sale	Available up to five days before sale. The law limits the amount homeowner can be charged in costs and fees.
Redemption after sale	Not available
Special protections for foreclosures involving high-cost mortgages	None
Special state protections for service members	Or. Rev. Stat. § 105.111
Deficiency judgments	Not allowed after a residential foreclosure
Cash exempted in bankruptcy	$400 ($800 for married couples), plus up to $7,500 of wages deposited into a bank account ($15,000 for married couples)
Notice to leave after house is sold	New owner entitled to possession ten days after the sale; after that, former owner can be evicted without notice. Or. Rev. Stat. § 91.040
Foreclosure statutes	Or. Rev. Stat. §§ 86.735 to 86.795, 88.080 to 88.100

Pennsylvania

Foreclosure laws change! Check for updates at www.nolo.com/legal-updates

Topic	State Rule
Most common type of foreclosure process	Judicial
Time to respond	Before filing a complaint in court, the foreclosing party must serve a 30-day notice of intention to foreclose on homeowner by certified mail. After foreclosing party files foreclosure lawsuit, homeowner has 20 to 30 days to respond. In the Court of Common Pleas of Philadelphia and Allegheny County Court, pilot programs mandate a delay between foreclosure judgment and sheriff's sale to allow for possible conciliation.
Reinstatement of loan before sale	Available until one hour before the bidding at the foreclosure sale, but a maximum of three times in one year.
Redemption after sale	Not available
Special protections for foreclosures involving high-cost mortgages	None
Special state protections for service members	Pa. Stat. Ann. tit. 51, § 4105
Deficiency judgments	Allowed if foreclosing party files separate lawsuit after sale
Cash exempted in bankruptcy	About $12,725 for one person, $25,450 for a married couple under federal bankruptcy exemptions. $300 ($600 if married filing jointly) under state bankruptcy exemptions.
Notice to leave after house is sold	No special provisions for evictions following foreclosure. New owner will likely have to go to court to get an eviction order. Court-ordered evictions usually take two weeks to a month, depending on whether or not former owner responds to the lawsuit.
Foreclosure statutes	Pa. Stat. Ann. tit. 35, §§ 1680.402c to 1680.409c; Pa. Stat. Ann. tit. 41, §§ 403 to 404; Pa. R. Civ. P. 1141-1150

Rhode Island

Foreclosure laws change! Check for updates at www.nolo.com/legal-updates

Topic	State Rule
Most common type of foreclosure process	Nonjudicial under power of sale in deed of trust
Time to respond	Foreclosing party must serve homeowner with a preforeclosure counseling notice at least 45 days before foreclosure is initiated. Notice of sale must be mailed by certified mail to homeowner at least 30 days before sale and published for three consecutive weeks before sale; first publication must be at least 21 days before the date of sale; the third publication must be at least seven days (including the date of publication) before the date of sale and no more than 14 days (excluding the date of publication) before the date of sale. Foreclosing party must serve notice of sale on homeowner by mail at least 30 days before first publication.
Reinstatement of loan before sale	Not available
Redemption after sale	Available up to three years after sale. Former owner must file lawsuit to redeem.
Special protections for foreclosures involving high-cost mortgages	Homeowner can ask court to stop (enjoin) the foreclosure if loan is high-cost or predatory lending practices were used. Rhode Island Home Loan Protection Act, R.I. Gen. Laws §§ 35-25.2-1 to 35-25.2-11
Special state protections for service members	R.I. Gen. Laws § 30-7-10
Deficiency judgments	Allowed if foreclosing party files separate lawsuit after sale.
Cash exempted in bankruptcy	About $12,725 for one person, $25,450 for a married couple under federal bankruptcy exemptions. Up to $5,000 ($10,000 if married filing jointly) under state bankruptcy exemptions.
Notice to leave after house is sold	Former owner has 20 days to respond to a complaint seeking eviction. After that new owner may go to court for a summary eviction procedure that takes two weeks to a month.
Foreclosure statutes	R.I. Gen. Laws §§ 34-27-1 to 34-27-5

South Carolina

Foreclosure laws change! Check for updates at www.nolo.com/legal-updates

Topic	State Rule
Most common type of foreclosure process	Judicial
Time to respond	After foreclosing party files lawsuit, homeowner has 20 to 30 days to respond. After court issues a foreclosure judgment, foreclosing party must publish notice of sale and also post it in three public places three weeks before the sale.
Reinstatement of loan before sale	Not available
Redemption after sale	Not available
Special protections for foreclosures involving high-cost mortgages	Some weak protections, but not likely to provide a defense against foreclosure. South Carolina High-Cost and Consumer Home Loans Act, S.C. Code Ann. §§ 37-23-10 to 37-23-85
Special state protections for service members	None
Deficiency judgments	Allowed as part of the foreclosure lawsuit
Cash exempted in bankruptcy	$5,000 for one person, $10,000 for a married couple
Notice to leave after house is sold	Former owner entitled to ten days' notice of termination. S.C. Code Ann. §§ 27-37-10 to 27-37-160
Foreclosure statutes	S.C. Code Ann. §§ 15-39-610, 29-3-630 to 29-3-790

South Dakota

Foreclosure laws change! Check for updates at www.nolo.com/legal-updates

Topic	State Rule
Most common type of foreclosure process	Nonjudicial under power of sale in deed of trust, but homeowner may choose judicial foreclosure
Time to respond	Before foreclosure, foreclosing party must publish notice once a week for four weeks and must serve homeowner with written notice (including statement telling homeowner of the right to insist on judicial foreclosure) 21 days before sale.
Reinstatement of loan before sale	**Judicial:** Available until court enters foreclosure judgment. S.D. Cod. Laws Ann. § 21-47-8 **Nonjudicial:** Not available
Redemption after sale	**Judicial:** Available for one year after the sale unless mortgage contains language identifying it as a short-term redemption mortgage, which provides a six-month redemption period. S.D. Cod. Laws Ann. § 21-52-11 **Nonjudicial:** Not available
Special protections for foreclosures involving high-cost mortgages	None
Special state protections for service members	S.D. Cod. Laws Ann. § 33-17-15.1
Deficiency judgments	Allowed, but if mortgage holder buys property at foreclosure sale, amount of deficiency is limited to difference between house's actual market value at time of sale and amount owed on mortgage.
Cash exempted in bankruptcy	$5,000 for one person, $7,000 for a married couple
Notice to leave after house is sold	**Judicial:** Judge may order possession given to buyer after redemption period expires. After redemption period ends, new owner must give former owner a three-day notice to quit (leave) and then file an eviction (forcible entry and detainer) lawsuit. **Nonjudicial:** No special provisions for evictions following nonjudicial foreclosure but probably the same as for evictions following a judicial foreclosure.
Foreclosure statutes	S.D. Cod. Laws Ann. §§ 21-48-1 to 21-48-26

Tennessee

Foreclosure laws change! Check for updates at www.nolo.com/legal-updates

Topic	State Rule
Most common type of foreclosure process	Nonjudicial under power of sale in deed of trust
Time to respond	Foreclosing party must send two notices. (1) It must send by registered mail a notice of right to foreclose on or before the first publication of the notice of sale. (2) It must either publish notice of sale 20 days before sale or post notice 30 days before sale.
Reinstatement of loan before sale	Not available
Redemption after sale	Available for up to two years after sale, unless redemption period is waived in mortgage
Special protections for foreclosures involving high-cost mortgages	Tennessee Home Loan Protection Act, Tenn. Code Ann. §§ 45-20-101 to 45-20-111
Special state protections for service members	Tenn. Code Ann. § 26-1-111
Deficiency judgments	Allowed if lawsuit is timely filed after conclusion of the foreclosure proceedings. If the debtor proves that the property sold for less than fair market value, the deficiency judgment will be limited to the amount the debtor owed, plus the costs of foreclosure and sale, minus the fair market value.
Cash exempted in bankruptcy	$10,000 for one person, $20,000 for a married couple
Notice to leave after house is sold	New owner may file forcible entry and detainer lawsuit, which involves serving a warrant on the occupant, trial within six days after service, and a writ of possession ten days from the rendition of the judgment ordering sheriff to evict occupant. Former owner may also be evicted through an ejectment procedure.
Foreclosure statutes	Tenn. Code Ann. §§ 35-5-101 to 35-5-111, 66-8-101 to 66-8-102

Texas

Foreclosure laws change! Check for updates at www.nolo.com/legal-updates

Topic	State Rule
Most common type of foreclosure process	Nonjudicial under power of sale in deed of trust
Time to respond	Foreclosing party must serve notice of default 20 days before serving notice of sale. Notice of sale must be served by mail on homeowner 21 days before sale. Foreclosing party must also post notice of sale on courthouse door (or wherever court commissioners determine is equivalent).
Reinstatement of loan before sale	Available within 20 days after service of notice of default
Redemption after sale	Not available
Special protections for foreclosures involving high-cost mortgages	None
Special state protections for service members	Tex. Civ. Prac. & Rem. Code § 16.022
Deficiency judgments	Allowed if foreclosing party brings separate lawsuit within two years of sale. Amount may be determined by fair market value of the property, if homeowner requests it.
Cash exempted in bankruptcy	About $12,725 for one person, $25,450 for a married couple under federal bankruptcy exemptions
Notice to leave after house is sold	New owner must serve former owner with three-day notice to quit (leave) and then file eviction (forcible detainer) lawsuit. Tex. Prop. Code Ann. §§ 24.002 to 24.005
Foreclosure statute	Tex. Prop. Code Ann. § 51.002

Utah

Foreclosure laws change! Check for updates at www.nolo.com/legal-updates

Topic	State Rule
Most common type of foreclosure process	Nonjudicial under power of sale in deed of trust
Time to respond	Foreclosing party must record notice of default at least three months before the sale and mail it to the homeowner within ten days of recording. At least three months after the recording, the foreclosing party must publish a notice of sale three times; the last date of publication must be at least ten days but not more than 30 days before the sale. The notice of sale must also be posted on the property at least 20 days before the sale.
Reinstatement of loan before sale	Available up to three months after notice of default is recorded. Utah Code Ann. § 57-1-31
Redemption after sale	Not available for nonjudicial foreclosures
Special protections for foreclosures involving high-cost mortgages	None
Special state protections for service members	Utah Code Ann. §§ 39-7-101 to 39-7-119
Deficiency judgments	May be obtained in a separate lawsuit within three months after the sale; the amount is limited by the property's fair market value.
Cash exempted in bankruptcy	None
Notice to leave after house is sold	New owner must give former owner a five-day notice to quit (leave) and then file eviction (unlawful detainer) lawsuit. Utah Code Ann. § 78B-6-802
Foreclosure statutes	Utah Code Ann. §§ 57-1-19, 78B-6-901

Vermont

Foreclosure laws change! Check for updates at www.nolo.com/legal-updates

Topic	State Rule
Most common type of foreclosure process	Judicial (strict foreclosure)
Time to respond	After foreclosing party files lawsuit, homeowner has 20 to 30 days to respond. When the court issues a foreclosure judgment, it may also transfer ownership to foreclosing party (strict foreclosure), if there is no equity in the house after costs of sale are subtracted.
Reinstatement of loan before sale	Available upon agreement before sale
Redemption after sale	Available six months from date of decree unless judge orders or the mortgagor and mortgagee agree on a shorter time.
Special protections for foreclosures involving high-cost mortgages	None
Special state protections for service members	Vt. Stat. Ann. tit. 12, § 553
Deficiency judgments	Must be requested in the foreclosure complaint. If the mortgage holder buys the property, the amount of the deficiency is limited by the property's fair market value.
Cash exempted in bankruptcy	About $12,725 for one person, $25,450 for a married couple under federal bankruptcy exemptions. Up to $8,100 ($16,200 if married filing jointly) under state bankruptcy exemptions.
Notice to leave after house is sold	After foreclosure judgment is issued and redemption period has ended, new owner must serve writ of possession on former owner. Homeowner then has 30 days to leave.
Foreclosure statutes	Vt. Stat. Ann. tit. 12, §§ 4526-4533a

Virginia

Foreclosure laws change! Check for updates at www.nolo.com/legal-updates

Topic	State Rule
Most common type of foreclosure process	Nonjudicial under power of sale in deed of trust
Time to respond	Foreclosing party must serve notice of sale on homeowner by mail or publication. Homeowner has 14 days to respond if service is by mail. If foreclosing party uses publication, generally notice must be published in a local newspaper of general circulation once a week for four consecutive weeks unless deed of trust provides for a different interval. (Rules for publication, or "advertisement," are complicated.) Sale can be held eight to 30 days after last publication.
Reinstatement of loan before sale	Not available
Redemption after sale	Not available
Special protections for foreclosures involving high-cost mortgages	None
Special state protections for service members	Va. Code Ann. § 8.01-15.2
Deficiency judgments	May be obtained in a separate lawsuit after the sale
Cash exempted in bankruptcy	Up to $5,000; up to $10,000 if married filing jointly; additional $10,000 if disabled veteran under state bankruptcy exemptions.
Notice to leave after house is sold	New owner does not have to give former owner notice before filing eviction lawsuit. The officer that will be handling the eviction must serve notice of intent to evict 72 hours prior, and must include the date and time of eviction.
Foreclosure statutes	Va. Code Ann. §§ 55-59 to 55-66.6

Washington

Foreclosure laws change! Check for updates at www.nolo.com/legal-updates

Topic	State Rule
Most common type of foreclosure process	Nonjudicial under power of sale in deed of trust
Time to respond	For mortgages written between January 1, 2003 and December 31, 2008, mortgage holder must personally contact homeowner at least 30 days before serving notice of default. A notice of default must be served on homeowner 30 days before notice of sale is served. The notice of default must be served by both first-class mail and by registered or certified mail, return receipt requested, and by either posting the notice on the premises in a prominent place or by personal service on homeowner. Foreclosing party must serve notice of sale in the same manner as the notice of default at least 90 days before sale date. No sale may occur within 190 days after the first default.
Reinstatement of loan before sale	Available up to 11 days before sale
Redemption after sale	Not available for nonjudicial sales; eight months or one year for judicial sales, depending on circumstances
Special protections for foreclosures involving high-cost mortgages	None
Special state protections for service members	Wash. Rev. Code § 4.16.220
Deficiency judgments	Not allowed for nonjudicial sales; available for judicial sales
Cash exempted in bankruptcy	About $12,725 for one person, $25,450 for a married couple under federal bankruptcy exemptions. $1,500 ($3,000 if married filing jointly) under state bankruptcy exemptions.
Notice to leave after house is sold	New owner entitled to possession 20 days after purchase and may file eviction (unlawful detainer) lawsuit. Summary proceedings may be available.
Foreclosure statutes	Wash. Rev. Code §§ 61.24.020 to 61.24.140

West Virginia

Foreclosure laws change! Check for updates at www.nolo.com/legal-updates

Topic	State Rule
Most common type of foreclosure process	Nonjudicial under power of sale in deed of trust
Time to respond	Foreclosing party must give homeowner notice within a reasonable time before sale (no period of time is specified) by publishing notice and by sending it through registered mail.
Reinstatement of loan before sale	Available for ten days after homeowner is served with notice of right to cure, which can be served five days after homeowner defaults. Not available for defaulting debtor if a notice of right to cure is served three or more times. W. Va. Code § 46A-2-106
Redemption after sale	Not available
Special protections for foreclosures involving high-cost mortgages	Some protections for a home equity line of credit. W. Va. Code § 38-1-14
Special state protections for service members	W. Va. Code § 11-21-61
Deficiency judgments	Allowed
Cash exempted in bankruptcy	Up to $25,800 for individual or married couple
Notice to leave after house is sold	No special provisions for evictions following foreclosure. New owner will likely have to go to court to get an eviction order. Court-ordered evictions usually take two weeks to a month, depending on whether or not former owner responds to the lawsuit.
Foreclosure statutes	W. Va. Code §§ 38-1-3 to 38-1-15

Wisconsin

Foreclosure laws change! Check for updates at www.nolo.com/legal-updates

Topic	State Rule
Most common type of foreclosure process	Judicial
Time to respond	After foreclosing party files lawsuit, homeowner has 20 to 30 days to respond. If foreclosure is granted, court issues judgment and order of sale. Sale can't be held until one year after the judgment is entered or six months after entry of judgment if the foreclosing party waives its right to a deficiency judgment. A notice of sale must either be published over six-week period or posted over a three-week period.
Reinstatement of loan before sale	Available any time before judgment; homeowner may ask court's permission to continue with reinstatement after judgment.
Redemption after sale	Not available. However, the redemption period (ranging from five weeks to one year) occurs prior to the sale. The property can be redeemed at any time during this period.
Special protections for foreclosures involving high-cost mortgages	Wis. Stat. §§ 428.202 to 428.211
Special state protections for service members	Wis. Stat. § 321.62
Deficiency judgments	Must be requested in the foreclosure complaint
Cash exempted in bankruptcy	About $12,725 for one person, $25,450 for a married couple under federal bankruptcy exemptions. $5,000 ($10,000 if married filing jointly) under state bankruptcy exemptions.
Notice to leave after house is sold	Homeowner may remain in possession through the redemption period up until the confirmation of the sale. If the homeowner does not then vacate the residence, the confirmation of the sale usually will entitle the plaintiff to a writ of assistance. The sheriff executes the writ, typically giving 24-72 hours' notice to the occupants.
Foreclosure statutes	Wis. Stat. §§ 846.01 to 846.25

Wyoming

Foreclosure laws change! Check for updates at www.nolo.com/legal-updates

Topic	State Rule
Most common type of foreclosure process	Nonjudicial under power of sale in deed of trust
Time to respond	Foreclosing party must serve notice of intent to foreclose on homeowner ten days before first publication of the notice of sale. Notice of sale must be published at least once a week for four weeks before sale and served on homeowner before date of first publication.
Reinstatement of loan before sale	Not available
Redemption after sale	Available for three months after sale
Special protections for foreclosures involving high-cost mortgages	None
Special state protections for service members	Wyo. Stat. Ann. §§ 19-11-101 to 19-11-124
Deficiency judgments	Allowed
Cash exempted in bankruptcy	None
Notice to leave after house is sold	No special provisions for evictions following foreclosure. New owner will likely have to go to court to get an eviction order. Court-ordered evictions usually take two weeks to a month, depending on whether or not former owner responds to the lawsuit.
Foreclosure statutes	**Judicial:** Wyo. Stat. Ann. §§ 1-18-101 to 1-18-114 **Nonjudicial:** Wyo. Stat. Ann. §§ 34-4-101 to 34-4-113

Index

⚖ NOLO *Online Legal Forms*

Nolo offers a large library of legal solutions and forms, created by Nolo's in-house legal staff. These reliable documents can be prepared in minutes.

Create a Document

- **Incorporation.** Incorporate your business in any state.
- **LLC Formations.** Gain asset protection and pass-through tax status in any state.
- **Wills.** Nolo has helped people make over 2 million wills. Is it time to make or revise yours?
- **Living Trust (avoid probate).** Plan now to save your family the cost, delays, and hassle of probate.
- **Trademark.** Protect the name of your business or product.
- **Provisional Patent.** Preserve your rights under patent law and claim "patent pending" status.

Download a Legal Form

Nolo.com has hundreds of top quality legal forms available for download—bills of sale, promissory notes, nondisclosure agreements, LLC operating agreements, corporate minutes, commercial lease and sublease, motor vehicle bill of sale, consignment agreements and many more.

Review Your Documents

Many lawyers in Nolo's consumer-friendly lawyer directory will review Nolo documents for a very reasonable fee. Check their detailed profiles at **Nolo.com/lawyers**.